EMBODIED

EMBODIED

Victorian Literature and the Senses

William A. Cohen

University of Minnesota Press

Minneapolis • London

The University of Minnesota Press gratefully acknowledges the financial assistance provided for the publication of this book from the Graduate School and the Department of English at the University of Maryland.

Portions of chapter 2 appeared in "Material Interiority in Charlotte Brontë's *The Professor*," *Nineteenth-Century Literature* 57, no. 4 (March 2003): 443–76, and in "Interiors: Sex and the Body in Dickens," *Critical Survey* 17, no. 2 (Summer 2005): 5–19; reprinted with permission of the University of California Press and *Critical Survey*, respectively. Portions of chapter 3 were previously published in "Deep Skin," in *Thinking the Limits of the Body*, ed. Jeffrey Jerome Cohen and Gail Weiss (Albany: State University of New York Press, 2003), 63–82. Portions of chapter 4 appeared in "Faciality and Sensation in Hardy's *The Return of the Native*," *PMLA* 121, no. 2 (March 2006): 437–52; reprinted by permission of the copyright owner, the Modern Language Association of America.

Published by the University of Minnesota Press
111 Third Avenue South, Suite 290
Minneapolis, MN 55401-2520
http://www.upress.umn.edu

Library of Congress Cataloging-in-Publication Data

Cohen, William A.
  Embodied : Victorian literature and the senses / William A. Cohen.
    p.   cm.
  Includes bibliographical references and index.
  ISBN 978-0-8166-5012-5 (hc : alk. paper) — ISBN 978-0-8166-5013-2 (pb : alk. paper)
  1. English literature — 19th century — History and criticism.   2. Senses and
sensation in literature.   3. Self in literature.   4. Subjectivity in literature.   5. Mind
and body in literature.   6. Body, Human, in literature.   7. Body, Human (Philosophy).
8. Psychology and literature — Great Britain — History — 19th century.   I. Title.
  PR468.S43C65   2008
  820.9'008 — dc22   2008032883

Printed in the United States of America on acid-free paper

The University of Minnesota is an equal-opportunity educator and employer.

15 14 13 12 11 10 09   10 9 8 7 6 5 4 3 2 1

For Charlotte and Rachel

Contents

Acknowledgments

The first, last, and best readers of this book as it evolved were Laura M. Green and Elizabeth Young, whose intellectual companionship, friendship, and support over many years have been incomparable. I also feel lucky to have had the engagement and encouragement at crucial stages of Kandice Chuh, Mary Ann O'Farrell, and Catherine Robson, in addition to their enduring friendship and counsel.

For the conversation, advice, and comity that make writing possible, and for reading and discussing parts of this book with me, I thank the following friends and colleagues: Henry Abelove, Jonathan Auerbach, Anston Bosman, Joseph Bristow, Maud Casey, J. Michael Duvall, Robert L. Fenton, Catherine Gallagher, Daniel Hack, Ryan Johnson, Katie King, Susan S. Lanser, Marilee Lindemann, Joseph Litvak, Claire MacDonald, Laura U. Marks, Elizabeth McClure, Karen McCoy, Zita Nunes, Patrick O'Malley, David L. Pike, Sangeeta Ray, Jason Rudy, William H. Sherman, Martha Nell Smith, and Kathryn Bond Stockton. I am thankful to my department chairs, Charles Caramello, Gary Hamilton, and Kent Cartwright; to Eric Berlatsky for research assistance; and to Richard Morrison, whose support as an editor is indispensable. Special thanks to Valerie Hammond for permission to use her artwork on the cover.

The Washington, D.C., interdisciplinary faculty study group on embodiment was the incubator for some of the ideas in this book, as well as a long-standing source of intellectual sustenance. I am grateful to Debra Bergoffen, Carolyn Betensky, Sarah Castro-Klaren, Jeffrey Jerome Cohen, Ellen Feder, Dana Luciano, Robert McRuer, Katharine Ott, Rosemarie Garland Thomson, Gail Weiss, and Stacy Wolf for their contributions.

The love and dedication of friends and family have provided many forms of support; for this I am deeply thankful to Chris Haines, James Gregory, Mark Robbins, Brett Seamans, Eric Cavallero, Astri Kingstone, and Charlotte Cohen and Rachel, Vito, Dante, Lorenzo, and Rosa DeSario.

I am especially grateful to Laurence Schwartz for, among many things, his devoted company in reading and discussing Victorian novels. The loving memory of Helen and Harvey Cohen is everywhere present in this work.

For institutional support, I acknowledge the General Research Board, the Department of English, and the International Travel Committee of the University of Maryland; and the Camargo Foundation in Cassis, France, which provided a residential fellowship during which some of this work was completed.

Introduction

What does it mean to be human? This old-fashioned humanist question received a strikingly antihumanist answer among a range of writers in Victorian Britain. What is human, these writers were excited and frightened to discover, is nothing more or less than the human body itself. Embodied experience was the solution that writers in a variety of styles and genres struck upon in response to contemporary questions about the nature, location, and plasticity of the human essence. This book is about the ways in which Victorian literary writers' conceptions of such embodiment drew from and contributed to materialist theories of human nature. The term *materialist* has many senses; I mean by it the efforts of writers in philosophy, physiology, religion, and evolutionary biology, as well as literature, to locate a unique essence of the human in the physical existence of the body. This essence — whether called by traditional, religiously inflected names such as "soul" or "spirit" or identified with newer, psychologically oriented terms like "mind" and "self" — was almost always imagined as interior to the individual.

In being understood to belong inside each person, this essence generated a number of questions, which were especially acute as problems for literary representation: Is this essence ethereal, or does it have material properties? If it is internal, is it located literally inside the body? How is it reached and altered from the exterior? The conception of this quality of the human has ramifications for the ways in which literary characters are imagined to be embodied, the metaphoric language in which intangible emotions and feelings are represented to readers, and the means through which mind and soul are themselves portrayed. In proposing the body as the source and location of human essence, literary writers established a mode of representation — typified by characterological roundness, depth, and interiority — that has long been regarded as the hallmark of high Victorian literary accomplishment. This book closely analyzes the means by which the effect of such immaterial, psychological depth is produced: surprisingly, through the depiction of physical substance, inter-action, and incorporation. The response of these writers to the problem of interior being was at once demystifying, desacralizing, and desublimating, for it flew in the face of a traditional conception of a distinct, immaterial essence. For many reasons, embodiment came to be the untranscendable horizon of the human.

My gambit is that, far from valorizing the liberal Enlightenment sub-ject identified with the category of the human, many Victorian writers challenged and indeed undermined such concepts, and they did so by grappling tenaciously with the material existence of the human body. This emphasis on the body, in all the messiness and particularity of its fleshly existence, is shared by some twentieth-century theoretical writing, in phenomenological and poststructuralist traditions, that formulates ideas about a world in which the coherence, sanctity, transcendence, and comprehensibility of the human cannot be taken for granted as an essen-tial category. In suggesting the importance of bodily experience, however, the theorists on whom I focus, Georges Bataille, Maurice Merleau-Ponty, and Gilles Deleuze and Félix Guattari — like the Victorian novelists, po-ets, scientists, and journalists I discuss — do not promote a fixed model of physical determinism. Instead, they present a fluid exchange between surface and depth, inside and outside — a type of materialism that under-stands the organs of ingestion, excretion, and sensation not simply to model but to perform the flow of matter and information between sub-ject and world. All of these writers suggest that what makes us human is the matter of our being — not some quality that transcends it — even while considering the various ways in which such being is open to, and partakes of, other materialities.

The chapters in this book focus on key moments, figures, and texts in the nineteenth-century exposition of ideas about bodily materialism; each is exemplary of a particular mode of conceiving of the interior in relation to the exterior and of advancing the primacy of the body in the idea of the human. In every case, the senses play a central role in this process. Although physiological psychology and evolutionary biology are under development throughout this period, their findings are not widely dis-seminated until the 1870s. The literary texts I discuss range from the 1840s to the 1880s, and, at the level of generality at which I argue, the novelists' and poets' formulations sometimes anticipate those of the scientists.

Because my concern is with the convergence of literary and other kinds of writing on a set of ideas about embodiment, rather than a demonstration of how literary writers appropriate scientific models, I have not, in most cases, documented direct routes of influence.

The first chapter provides an overview of the book's argument, placing it in historical, literary, and theoretical contexts. Victorian writers, I suggest, posed the body against or athwart the self, decentering the humanist subject by focusing on its materiality. The chapter first explores some historical and cultural contexts for my investigation and then considers both literary and nonfiction examples, in a range of disciplines and genres from the period, in which material embodiment is salient. I turn next to a discussion of the theoretical works that serve as sources for and incitements to my analysis. The concepts of embodied subjectivity developed by Merleau-Ponty, Deleuze and Guattari, and Bataille both supply some means of understanding the work of nineteenth-century literary writers and are also, in turn, prefigured by them. These theorists' overlapping models present the body as a sensory interface between the interior and the world, as a process of flux and becoming, and as a radical source of both the making and the unmaking of human subjects. The chapter concludes with a discussion of wider critical contexts for the book's argument.

Chapter 2 begins with Charles Dickens, whose consistent representation of human subjectivity as bodily form establishes some of the terms for this book. I discuss Dickens's ideas about material interiority by showing specifically how he imagines gaining access to characters' inner lives through processes of ingestion and incorporation. Examples from *The Old Curiosity Shop* (1840–41) and *David Copperfield* (1849–50) characteristically present interiors as permeable through sensory organs. Dickens finds a concrete figure for such interpenetration in the image of the keyhole, at once a figure *for* the eye and the ear and a channel — *like* the eye and the ear — through which information, emotions, and matter pass from the inside of one character into that of another. While such ideas serve Dickens's comic, sentimental, and moral purposes, they assume a grimmer aspect in the book that is this chapter's main focus, Charlotte Brontë's quasi-autobiographical first novel, *The Professor* (1845–46). By adopting a first-person narrative voice whose masculine gender allows her to imagine being inside a man's body, Brontë is led to defamiliarize — and thus to estrange — the idea of inhabiting any body at all. Relations of desire and conflict between characters are embodied in the flesh and rendered fundamentally material even before they are gendered. The novel represents contact between characters, both amatory and intellectual, as forms of incorporation, and sometimes as violent or sexual penetration. In the figurative language that both Brontë and Dickens employ, embodiment of the interior opens the self to potential sources of pleasure and pain. Brontë's novel in particular anticipates the psychoanalytic theories of masochism propounded by Freud and Deleuze, which conceive of psychical processes in terms of their fleshly enactment.

While chapter 2 explores the external world from the perspective of the interior, chapter 3 charts the movement from the outside in. I interpret Anthony Trollope's serialized story "The Banks of the Jordan" (1861), a tale of tourism and gender disguise in the Holy Land, through a simultaneously historical and theoretical consideration of skin. This chapter brings together discussions of racial and gender identity with psychological and phenomenological accounts of the skin both as a permeable, sensory surface and as a socially coded marker of identity. I put two psychoanalytic models in dialogue with Trollope's story: Didier Anzieu's discussion of the "skin ego" and Frantz Fanon's analysis of the psychological experience of race. Through its portrayal of abrasions to the corporeal surface, the story dramatizes the physical embodiment of racial, sexual, and spiritual identities. I contextualize this embodiment in the issues of racial characterization and urban sanitation revealed by the original magazine publication of Trollope's tale in the *London Review*. By considering the work in the context of other journalism, I suggest that Trollope's story — whose overt subject is female cross-dressing and illicit romance — raises concerns about the relation of the body's surface to its interior that were played out in the Great Stink of London in 1858 (when the river Thames's pollution reached intolerable levels) and in the simultaneous sepoy uprising in India. Dirt on the bodily surface at once metaphorizes racial distinctions and profoundly unsettles the possibility of interior being.

The subject of chapter 4, Thomas Hardy's *The Return of the Native* (1878), also meditates on the sensory interaction between human interiors and the exterior world, although Hardy's interest is in natural, rather than built, environments. Moving beyond Dickens's and Brontë's descriptions of bodily interiors as metaphorically substantial, Hardy presents human inwardness as materially *contiguous* with the external surface of the earth. Collaterally, when he describes heath, moor, or bog, he provides less a pictorial image of a particular place than an account of the perceptual impressions such a location make on an observer. The landscape in this novel is famously perceived as a face, while the faces in it are often read as landscapes; I bring to bear Deleuze and Guattari's conception of faciality from *A Thousand Plateaus* on this discussion, a proposal that faces are peculiarly external to psychological subjectivity, inhuman, and screenlike. I show how, for Hardy, sensory perception radically undermines distinctions between the human and the nonhuman, casting them not as antagonistic but as dynamically interrelated. Body and landscape are mutually evocative, like two sides of a single, porous membrane, through which sensation passes. Hardy's extended focus on perception presents both impaired vision and acute hearing through a proximate model of touch.

The final chapter interprets the poetry and other writings of Gerard Manley Hopkins, who offers a literary conception of human interiors at once more transcendent and more debased than those so far considered. Like Hardy, Hopkins posits a fundamental continuity between the external form of natural objects and their effects on human subjects' sensory, affective, and spiritual interiors. Hopkins lends to this continuity a theological account of the soul, as well as a quasi-mystical poetic theory to which he gives the names "inscape" and "instress." Reading Hopkins's poetry in tandem with his letters, journals, and devotional writings, I show how the bodily interior is the register for perceptions of the natural world that is itself linked to divine perfection and, at the same time, the debased matter that threatens to befoul the spiritual apotheosis. While both Hopkins's spiritual ends and his poetic medium are quite distinct from those of the other writers I discuss, his questions — about what constitutes the inside and how the senses serve as vehicles for reaching from outside in — are surprisingly cohesive with theirs. And while poetry (especially Hopkins's poetry) intensifies attention to the materiality of language, it exemplifies a more distilled version of the functions I attribute to literary language in general, in rendering human subjectivity substantial. This chapter also shows how Hopkins's descriptions of sensory encounters with the perceptible world resonate strikingly with those of Merleau-Ponty and Bataille, and so ultimately returns me to the first chapter's discussions of the body and the senses.

Finally, the conclusion considers some further critical resonances of the argument, discussing briefly its relation to developments in queer theory and disability studies, especially in their phenomenologically oriented modes. Ideas about embodiment, I propose, from both Victorian literature and twentieth-century French philosophy, speak to the experiential as well as the political dimensions of identity and subjectivity. The non-alignment between body and subject suggests that the body has the capacity to *unmake* the human, rather than to secure its coherence and integrity, and opens possibilities for mutable ways of being in the world, both materially and politically. The embodied subject on which this book dwells is not ethereal, transcendent, or fixed, in either form or identity, but rather palpable, porous, and motile. A fundamental aspect of the human turns out to be the strangeness to itself of the fleshly matter that composes it.

1

Subject

Embodiment and the Senses

Why should Victorian writers have felt questions about a human essence to be so pressing? In this period, political, economic, and social forces put pressure on ideas about the self or soul in relation to the human body. Mass industrialism and urbanization provided new locations, such as factories, metropolises, and imperial colonies, in which conflicts over the relation between the body and its interior arose; mechanized labor produced one new kind of body, while conceptions of race and ethnicity as embodied states, indexed by science, generated others. Discoveries in evolutionary biology and geology challenged the notion of a soul that transcends the material realm: the advent of evolutionary theory generated a pervasive concern with the material existence and development of the human species through discussion of the changes and adaptations of the body. Widespread religious controversies and doctrinal disputes — even conflicts over mortuary practices and the disposition of human remains — testify to the urgency of spiritual concern with the materiality of human existence.[1]

The relation of inner essence to outer substance — of soul to body, or mind to body — has been a major interest of philosophers and scientists since at least Greek antiquity. Descartes thought he had solved the mystery in one way with a dualistic model that separated mental reason from physical sensation, while Hobbes, Locke, Hume, and other Enlightenment philosophers proposed solutions with varying degrees of emphasis on rational agency or, alternatively, on bodily mechanisms as the source of intangible entities such as consciousness, will, and selfhood. While Enlightenment rationalism is often understood to have posited a means of knowing that transcends embodiment, even Cartesian dualism, Drew

Leder has shown, relies on some form of bodily materialism from its origin.[2] As Roy Porter argues in his conjoined history of philosophy and medicine, Enlightenment efforts to scrutinize and explain the nature of man shifted from an intangible motive force or transcendent soul to the concrete mechanisms of physical form.[3] This is a complex and contentious history, which did not evolve in a linear fashion, for no given position has ever been without its detractors. While the general trend among scientists and intellectuals in the nineteenth century was toward greater materialism, the pendulum has continued to swing back and forth between the extremes, down to the present: under psychoanalysis, in the first half of the twentieth century, for example, it swung toward the model of an immaterial unconscious as the prime motive force; more recently, it has moved back toward material and mechanical explanations, with the advent of the cognitive neuroscience associated with Antonio Damasio and the so-called meme theory of Richard Dawkins.

In the familiar narrative of post-Enlightenment modernity, debates over a religious idea of the soul gave way, in the face of scientific developments, to new definitions and valuations of life based on physiology, evolutionary biology, and political economy.[4] In particular, an emergent mental science — the precursor to the discipline of psychology — explicitly attempted to localize the self within bodily organs and processes until it came to seem like common sense to describe the mind as a substantial entity.[5] At the same time, this approach actively repudiated both theological and metaphysical concepts of a spiritual or rational agency that transcends the flesh.[6] It found powerful support in the idea, predominantly associated with Darwin, that human existence originates in bodily adaptation to the environment rather than in divine creation. Evolutionary biology and affiliated nineteenth-century sciences promoted the notion that consciousness developed out of the body rather than being implanted in it. The proponents of the new mental science argued vigorously against both philosophical and religious ideas of a self or a soul that could act independently of its corporeal inhabitation. For example, the psychiatrist Henry Maudsley writes in *Body and Mind* (1870):

> The habit of viewing mind as an intangible entity or incorporeal essence, which science inherited from theology, prevented men from subjecting its phenomena to the same method of investigation as other natural phenomena.... We shall make no progress toward a mental science if we begin by depreciating the body: not by dis-

daining it, as metaphysicians, religious ascetics, and maniacs have
done, but by laboring in an earnest and inquiring spirit to understand it, shall we make any step forward.[7]

Such biological determinism was offensive to many different kinds of
thinkers, particularly Christian believers, for whom the term "materialist" principally meant atheist. The feminist social campaigner Frances
Power Cobbe, for example, argued forcefully for "the entire *separability*
of the conscious self from its thinking organ, the physical brain," and
she expressed disgust at the idea of human beings as automata driven
wholly by their physical needs and impulses.[8] Over the course of the
nineteenth century, a number of strong voices, with widely varied political, intellectual, and religious affiliations, arose to contest the emerging
evidence for the physical basis of mind. A persistent religious orthodoxy,
a philosophically based metaphysics of transcendence, and a recrudes-
cent faculty psychology (which was largely immaterial in orientation) all
contributed to these lively debates, which were carried out in the periodical press and were, as Rick Rylance has demonstrated, a rich and ongoing
source of intellectual ferment.[9] Yet the dominant trend was toward materialism, and in support of the new approaches, preeminent Victorian
scientists, physicians, and proto-psychologists such as Alexander Bain,
William B. Carpenter, and George Henry Lewes sought to correlate intangible human qualities like consciousness and selfhood with somatic
conditions. In *Mind and Body: The Theories of Their Relation* (1873), Bain, a
Scottish philosopher and scientist, demonstrates the inextricability of mental entities from the substance of the body. In a final chapter, titled "History of the Theories of the Soul," in which Bain refutes philosophical and
religious traditions that deny the materiality of both mind and soul, he,
like Maudsley, argues for the mind as a material entity, concluding that
there is "one substance, with two sets of properties, two sides, the physical and the mental — a *double-faced unity.*"[10]

One key figure in the effort to establish a somatic basis for the mind,
and to demonstrate the materiality of any notion of the interior, is the
Victorian polymath Herbert Spencer, who wrote influential volumes on
philosophy, evolutionary biology, psychology, sociology, and ethics. In his
evolutionary (largely Lamarckian) *Principles of Biology* (1864), Spencer ini-
tially argues that "the broadest and most complete definition of Life will
be — *The continuous adjustment of internal relations to external relations*";[11]

with respect specifically to physiology, he establishes that there is a basic evolutionary distinction between the "outer and inner tissues" of both plants and animals, a distinction that serves as an organizing principle of his work. Beginning with the most primitive life-forms, Spencer writes, "The first definite contrast of parts that arises is that between outside and inside" (2:282). Primitive evolution establishes this distinction, although it is never absolute: inner tissues brought to the surface acquire the characteristics of external material, and vice versa. The inner and the outer are mutable, the surfaces themselves fungible and adaptable. The inside for Spencer is always a physical entity: what lies beneath the skin or the flesh is matter of a different kind, but matter nonetheless, in both physiological and psychological terms.

Spencer highlights certain structures — notably the organs of sensation, the skin, and the alimentary canal — that he terms morphologically "transitional," for they have evolved from exterior surfaces into vehicles for "alien" matter to enter the organism's interior (2:307). His discussion is particularly interesting when it takes up the evolution of sensory organs, those channels between inner being and surface that lie at the border of the distinction (2:302). Explaining how the sense organs derive from superficies, Spencer expresses amazement that the eyes themselves — so crucial to notions of spiritual depth and mental penetration — have evolved from the outer layers of skin: "That eyes are essentially dermal structures seems scarcely conceivable. Yet an examination of their rudimentary types, and of their genesis in creatures that have them well developed, shows us that they really arise by successive modifications of the double layer composing the integument" (2:303). Presented here in an evolutionary context, Spencer's proposal that eye and skin are fundamentally contiguous shares with the literary texts I examine the idea that seeing can have the characteristics of direct, tactile contact. In both evolutionary and phenomenological terms, an object makes an impression in and on the body of the subject through direct contact with the sense organs, not least the eyes.[12]

While Spencer's differentiation of the inside from the exterior of the body is relatively straightforward in lower animals, in human beings it gets rewritten as a distinction between different *kinds* of insides, the material and the mental; or rather, the mental becomes another form of interior entity, different from the viscera but no less substantial. In *Principles of Psychology* (1855), Spencer considers objections to the materialist position in chapters titled "The Substance of Mind" and "The Composition of Mind." While he acknowledges the untranslatability of "Spirit" and "Matter" in this work, Spencer finally proposes that material terms are the only ones available for analyzing the mind and defies his readers to do any better.[13] Much of Victorian mental science focuses on differentiating interior from exterior states and on the links between physical and immaterial components of human psychology. Spencer's essay "The Physiology of Laughter" (1860), for example, portrays the relation of internal mental and emotional states to their bodily container. Spencer assumes that inner psychological and physiological entities are directly connected in a state of dynamic equilibrium. According to his account of laughter, mental, emotional, or intellectual agitation, when it reaches a pitch of excitement, spills over into physical symptoms, which discharge and relieve it, while physical excitement likewise has invisible affective consequences.[14] The dynamic interchange between inner and outer, material and immaterial, states of being makes mental science one of the crucial locations in which ideas of human embodiment were being worked out in mid-Victorian culture.

Spencer is representative of Victorian practice in placing the organs of sensation and ingestion midway between inner and outer aspects of being, both physical and mental. Considering the terms in which Victorian writers imagine and portray the space of the interior brings me to focus on the means by which they think it communicates with the outside world. For many writers — literary, philosophical, and scientific — the primary routes of ingress, egress, and interaction are the bodily orifices, particularly the sense organs. Like the tradition of considering the inside in material terms, the proposition that the senses reveal the dynamics and dimensions of the interior goes back a long way in the history of philosophy. One influential view is that of the seventeenth-century rationalists following Descartes, who, as D. W. Hamlyn suggests, tend toward idealism: if perception is part of the mind, they argue, then the body is an effect of the mind, whose independent existence cannot be verified.[15] In various ways, later Enlightenment philosophers, including Locke, Berkeley, Hume, and Condillac, place perception at the center of their concerns, adapting and challenging Descartes's dualism, which sought rigorously to distinguish mind from body. Yet Daniel Cottom has proposed that "the artifact known as the Enlightenment was defined from the beginning through an obsession with guts and disgust as much as through the mind and reason."[16] Like all dreams, the dream of reason emerges from a body.

For Victorian writers, attending to sense perception serves several purposes. In physiological terms, it provides a mechanism for showing how the world of objects — including other bodies — enters the body of the subject and remakes its interior entities. In psychological terms, because "feelings" lie in a gray zone between physical sensations and emotional responses, somatic and affective experiences can switch, blend, or substitute one for another. In a phenomenological sense, attending to sense perception enables embodied subjects to experience themselves as objects, and objects reciprocally to function as subjects, so as to permit a mutual perviousness between self and world. And in a particularly literary register, sensation affords writers a means of concretely representing emotions, desires, and impulses that tend — at least in nineteenth-century literary idioms — to be otherwise unrepresentably abstract or ethereal. Giving palpable form to affects by representing them in terms of bodily sensation addresses a basic problem of representation, especially as encountered in realist and lyric modes: namely, how to convey and evoke states of being in the metaphorical terms of feeling.[17] Particularly relevant for my purposes are the proximate senses of smell, taste, and touch, which bring the external world into or onto the body; equally so are the distance senses (hearing and vision) when they are felt to involve tangible contact between subject and object.

While scientific descriptions may seem far afield from literary representations of the human body in relation to its contents, they suggest how pervasive such thinking was in the nineteenth century, and how widely influential this strain of bodily materialism.[18] In turning now to literary writing in several genres, I outline some themes that subsequent chapters take up in greater detail: the depiction of self, soul, and mind as substantial; the access provided to these interior entities by the senses; and the relation between inner being and the surface of the body, especially the skin.

By dint of the exigencies of representation, literary writing gives voice to ideas about the correspondence between an interior self and outer form. Autobiography, by its nature, describes the internal experience of the self, and we can accordingly begin with two such works, which illustrate different ends of the spectrum of embodied selfhood. John Stuart Mill's *Autobiography* (1873) can stand for the impossibility of transcending physical existence, even for one so identified with the proposition that abstract, logical reason would solve social, political, philosophical, and economic problems. Ambivalent though he is about his own embodied state, Mill nonetheless, in a famous section of his memoir, presents "a crisis in [his] mental history" that has both its symptoms and its cure realized in physical form. While Mill's portrait of his childhood shows him laboring intellectually under his father's rigid tutelage in the classics, the sense of bodily confinement is palpable: "I was always too much in awe of him to be otherwise than extremely subdued and quiet in his presence.... I could do no feats of skill or physical strength, and knew none of the ordinary bodily exercises."[19] The constraint imposed on the body by the hypertrophy of the mind is burst by a catastrophe of emotion — which seems to fall between them — in the form of severe melancholy that he experiences when he is twenty. Mill's secular life story recapitulates an Augustinian narrative of fall and redemption, although in this case the crisis is over faith in Utilitarianism rather than in God. Yet unlike the classic spiritual trajectory, in which purification of the soul redeems the sins of the body, here the fall is mental and the redemption at least partly corporeal: Mill passes beyond the nadir of reason-induced torpor with a bodily collapse manifest in his being "moved to tears" by literary reading, immediately after which his "burthen grew lighter" (145). As he progresses through stages of recovery, he discovers the importance of balancing his highly developed "intellectual culture" and an abstract "power and practice of analysis" with "other kinds of cultivation," namely, "the cultivation of the feelings" (147). He aims to foster these emotions through physical sensations, as the auditory balm of music and poetry enlarges his perceptual and sympathetic capacities. An overemphasis on the mind, he suggests, is a pathological condition remedied by recourse to the body; the cultivation of feelings, a marginally embodied experience, is a physic necessitated by the insufficiency of reason. This episode is often read as a judicious tempering of arid Benthamite Utilitarianism with an infusion of Romantic sentiment and feeling. In the context of the new mental science that Mill vigorously endorsed,[20] we can also understand it as an acknowledgment that even so ruthless a commitment as Mill had to ratiocination rests on the ground of embodied experience.

This life story makes an instructive contrast with that of another political theorist, Harriet Martineau, whose *Autobiography* (1877), while contemporaneous with Mill's, focuses intensively on the body's possibilities and incapacities.[21] Whereas Mill's childhood is almost exclusively devoted to developing his intellect, Martineau's is filled with terrors, complaints, and physical deficiencies; while it takes a psychological crisis to drive Mill to cultivate the self he conceives of as inconveniently inhabiting his body, for Martineau selfhood is consistently rendered as experience of and through the body. This distinction might be attributed to gender, for in a society with such highly articulated distinctions on the basis of sex, both the interior essence and the external form of the body were inevitably differentiated by gender. Being inside a body was always understood as inhabiting a sex, and the presumption that women's interiors were more disorganized than men's was common to literary and medical representation.[22] Literary convention, moreover, represented embodiment itself in terms that contrasted a feminine body with a masculine soul.[23] Nonetheless, this dichotomy encountered numerous challenges in the period: both women's intellectual abilities and the manifestly embodied condition of men disrupted any equation of femininity with embodiment, while irrepressible evidence of unorthodox sexualities undermined binary conceptions of gender. Even for Martineau — a far-from-conventional Victorian woman, who had a successful career as a professional writer and declared herself unfit for marriage (132–33) — her gender contributes to her feelings of insufficiency and insecurity.

More than most memoirists, both male and female, however, Martineau highlights the dialectical relation of body and self in representing her physical capacities and disabilities, which are far more salient than her gender in her account of her life. The anomaly of her atheism may lead her to emphasize the material conditions of her existence, but she also understands her life story in terms of sheerly physical development.[24] She admits to having perpetually had "bad health and [a] fitful temper" (11): milk causes her "long years of indigestion" (10), she lacks a sense of smell from an early age (13), and she begins to go deaf at fifteen. Her description of childhood psychological pain is equally acute: she is "panic struck at the head of the stairs" (10), is frightened by the height of a tree, and has vivid nightmares (14); even a magic lantern provokes such fear that it "brought on bowel-complaint" (15). Emotional and physical pain reinforce each other, as when she describes her memory of an ear ache at age five: "I laid my aching ear against the cool iron screw of a bedstead, and howled with pain; but nobody came to me" (21). The *Autobiography* consistently traces her moral, religious, and intellectual development as physical processes. Material and immaterial experiences are especially intertwined insofar as her deafness indicates the emotional and social effects of sensory deprivation; her concern is not that she will miss what others are saying but that she will cause them discomfort and herself embarrassment. When she went deaf, she writes, there was "a resolution which I made and never broke, — never to ask what was said.... One's friends may always be trusted, if left unmolested, to tell one whatever is essential, or really worth hearing" (74).

Focusing on a somatic locus and origin of the self makes a subject of the body and, at the same time, makes an object of the self: both are feeling things, but in different senses. Martineau's autobiography illuminates these processes, even before her deafness, although it is hard to know how much retrospection colors her portrait of childhood and to what extent she was, as she suggests, predisposed to disability by her early illnesses and a morbid imagination. She describes her friendship around age eight with another girl, whom she calls "E.," whose lame leg is amputated; E. becomes an object of scorn and pity but also, because of young Martineau's own physical deficiencies, a source of identification, shame, and envy. The encounter with the deformed body of another extends the development of her own imagined inner qualities in physical form: "By this time I had begun to take moral or spiritual charge of myself" (44), Martineau states, a process that acquaintance with E. fosters:

> I was naturally very deeply impressed by the affair [of the amputation]. It turned my imagination far too much on bodily suffering, and on the peculiar glory attending fortitude in that direction. I am sure that my nervous system was seriously injured, and especially that my subsequent deafness was partly occasioned by the exciting and vain-glorious dreams that I indulged in for many years after my friend E. lost her leg. All manner of deaths at the stake and on the scaffold, I went through in imagination, in the low sense in which St. Theresa craved martyrdom; and night after night, I lay bathed in cold perspiration till I sank into the sleep of exhaustion. All this is detestable to think of now; but it is a duty to relate the truth.... The power of bearing quietly a very unusual amount of bodily pain in childhood was the poor recompense I enjoyed for the enormous detriment I suffered from the turn my imagination had taken. (45–46)

Understanding E.'s abjected frame as both an object of pity and a version of her own deformity, Martineau takes the body to be the source of and screen for the suffering of conscience. Like Spencer's account of laughter, Martineau's discussion of conscience assumes alternately moral, emotional, and physical forms, manifestations that mutate into one another.

The continuity among systems allows her dwelling on E.'s amputation to "injure" young Martineau's "nervous system," which in turn produces its own physical symptom (deafness), as well as a sense of moral failure. Both identifying with and abjecting E., Martineau assimilates these mental and emotional responses as somatic experiences; she feels them to be simultaneously painful and pleasurable, which explains the extension of her response into language at once masochistic (sublimated in religious ecstasy) and masturbatory. Martineau envies the attention E. receives, but she feels embarrassed at being seen with her (46) and ashamed of abandoning her (47). Experiencing deformities of outward shape as lessons about self and soul, Martineau feels herself improved through bodily identification with E. ("we seemed to be brought nearer together by our companionship in infirmity" [48]).

In discussing her deafness, Martineau elaborates this paradigm of exterior privations giving form to interior qualities, for going deaf impedes her reception of external information while making her inner life all the more accessible — and expressible, through writing — to her. That her inner life (her "character") and her bodily morphology are mutually reflective is vividly illustrated in the testimony of one who made her acquaintance: Nathaniel Hawthorne, who recorded the following impressions of her in his journal after a visit in 1854.

> She is a large, robust (one might almost say bouncing) elderly woman, very coarse of aspect, and plainly dressed; but withal, so kind, cheerful, and intelligent a face, that she is pleasanter to look at than most beauties. Her hair is of a decided gray; and she does not shrink from calling herself an old woman. She is the most continual talker I ever heard; it is really like the babbling of a brook; and very lively and sensible too; — and all the while she talks, she moves the bowl of her ear-trumpet from one auditor to another, so that it becomes quite an organ of intelligence and sympathy between her and yourself. The ear-trumpet seems like a sensitive part of her, like the feelers of some insects. If you have any little remark to make, you drop it in; and she helps you to make remarks by this delicate little appeal of the trumpet, as she slightly directs it towards you; and if you have nothing to say, the appeal is not strong enough to embarrass you. . . . This woman is an Atheist, and thinks, I believe, that the principle of life will become extinct, when her great, fat, well-to-do body is laid in the grave. I will not think so, were it only for her sake; — only a few weeds to spring out of her fat mortality, instead of her intellect and sympathies flowering and fruiting forever![25]

This portrait of Martineau makes outsize and explicit the ordinarily over-looked materiality of oral communication: words, as sounds, do "drop in" to the ear, but without one's feeling them so tangibly. Martineau, like some benevolent pachyderm in Hawthorne's description, makes listening a propulsive activity rather than a passive or receptive one. As if he has assimilated the very ideas of hers about the material boundedness of human existence from which he dissents, he dwells on a fantasy of her corpulence decomposing in the grave, leaving no trace but the material impressions her words have made on the ears of others. The conditions of Martineau's embodiment supply an unusual means to a model Victorian end — moral improvement: "Yet here am I now, on the borders of the grave, at the end of a busy life, confident that this same deafness is about the best thing that ever happened to me; — the best, in a selfish view, as the grandest impulse to self-mastery; and the best in a higher view, as my most peculiar opportunity of helping others" (78). Her deafness reorders her relation to the external world, which also entails remaking herself internally.

Like these memoirs, Victorian fiction frequently recurs to the body's materiality in representing interior being. The self or soul consequently assumes the form of a tangible entity, while the body is insecurely bounded. In *Wuthering Heights* (1847), for example, Emily Brontë stages an ongoing contest between material and immaterial claims for the possibility of intersubjective contact. Through both of the novel's primary drives — desire and death — this contest is violently manifest in conflicts over the disposition of the soul in relation to the body. In an effort to explain why she is unable to marry Heathcliff, Catherine indicates that their bodies need not merge (in life, at any rate) because they are already united spiritually: "He's more myself than I am," she states. "Whatever our souls are made of, his and mine are the same."[26] Such spiritual identity is at once deeper than, and an impediment to, physical union in life; yet the idea that souls are "made of" something suggests they have a substantial reality. Amplifying Leo Bersani's suggestion that, in *Wuthering Heights*, personality exceeds individual characters, we might say more specifically that what Brontë calls the soul exceeds individual human bodies.[27] Heathcliff shares the idea of a common soul with Catherine, yet he understands that the only access he has to it is through the body, even when they are both dead. His fixation on mingling his remains with Catherine's is a way of returning to an imagined state of undifferentiation, for he assumes that would put their souls in touch as well. Nelly questions him about disturbing Catherine's grave, asking: "And if she had been dissolved into earth, or worse, what would you have dreamt of then?" He replies: "Of dissolving with her, and being more happy still" (229).

If ashes, merely material remains, preserve a trace of the spirit in this novel, spirits themselves have a substantial presence. At the moment Heathcliff seeks contact with Catherine's embodied form by disinterring her corpse, for example, she returns to him in the ambiguously ethereal form of a ghost. He reports: "I fell to work with my hands; the [coffin's] wood commenced cracking about the screws, I was on the point of attaining my object, when it seemed that I heard a sigh from some one above, close at the edge of the grave.... I knew no living thing in flesh and blood was by; but as certainly as you perceive the approach to some substantial body in the dark, though it cannot be discerned, so certainly I felt that Cathy was there, not under me, but on the earth" (229). The breath of this fleshy ghost displaces the air; when she appears in Lockwood's dream and he scrapes her arm across a broken windowpane, she also bleeds. If ashes contain souls and ghosts can bleed, then the border between material and immaterial existence is thoroughly confounded. Human subjects — here in the form of souls and spirits — are thoroughly porous to one another, as both the commingled ashes and the claims to identity between Heathcliff and Catherine indicate.

Staging debates over the fleshiness of the soul leads writers to meditate on the capability of their own artistic media to convey spiritual contents. While the ongoing embodiment of dead souls concerns Brontë, Robert Browning's "Fra Lippo Lippi" (1855) — the period's most famous poetic rumination on the role of the artist in depicting human essences — takes up the specifically representational question of where the soul is located in relation to the living body. The vital, exuberant visual aesthetic espoused by the dramatic monologue's speaker is often identified with Browning's own poetic doctrine, which aims to convey the spirit of historical characters by vividly portraying their material existence; the painter's realistic representation of physical appearance corresponds to the poet's acute rendering of this fluent, vernacular voice. In the flood of conversation that is the poem, Fra Lippo Lippi recounts the censure of his superior:

> "Your business is not to catch men with show,
> With homage to the perishable clay,
> But lift them over it, ignore it all,
> Make them forget there's such a thing as flesh.

> Your business is to paint the souls of men —
> Man's soul, and it's a fire, smoke ... no, it's not ...
> It's vapour done up like a new-born babe —
> (In that shape when you die it leaves your mouth)
> It's ... well, what matters talking, it's the soul!
> Give us no more of body than shows soul!"

Lippi presents and parodies the inability of his superior to make the very distinction between an immaterial soul and its tangible representation, either as body or as breath, on which he insists. In so doing, Lippi (and likewise Browning) advocates a type of monism whereby the sanctity of the soul is inseparable from the particularity and beauty of any individual body. The speaker even postulates that the soul — at least as represented — might be an *effect* of the body:

> Suppose I've made her eyes all right and blue,
> Can't I take breath and try to add life's flash,
> And then add soul and heighten them three-fold?
> Or say there's beauty with no soul at all —
> (I never saw it — put the case the same —)
> If you get simple beauty and naught else,
> You get about the best thing God invents:
> That's somewhat: and you'll find the soul you have missed,
> Within yourself, when you return him thanks.[28]

Like Tennyson in "The Palace of Art" (1832), Browning worries over the poet's civic function and contribution to the social good. In audacious response, the artist arrogates to himself — or, perhaps more safely, to his spokesman — the function of the deity: he can implant, if not create, the soul. Portray the body vividly enough, he suggests, and there is no discernible difference between a soul deeply held within and its evocation by the illusion of external surface. This is Lippi's argument, which Browning instantiates by means of voice in the monologue that itself gives life to the artist.

While spiritual and aesthetic discussions of the relation between body and soul or body and mind tend to rely, at least implicitly, on the senses, moving perceptual experience into the foreground provides literary writers the opportunity to consider the materiality of the human more minutely. The several meanings of *sensation* pertinent to the fictional subgenre designated by this name make it an especially apt object for inquiry. Wilkie Collins's novel *Poor Miss Finch* (1872) is unusually acute in articulating a relation between an inner self and outer form by emphasizing both the surface elements of the body and the incorporative capacities of sensory perception. Collins's novel tells the story of a blind young woman, Miss Finch, who is terrified of dark things, especially dark people. She falls in love with a man who becomes ill and must then take a medication whose improbable side effect is to turn his skin dark blue. In an increasingly implausible series of events, when surgery temporarily restores Miss Finch's sight, her friends substitute her lover with his wicked — but still white skinned — identical twin brother before her eyes. For all the luridness this novel lends them, the elements of blindness and blueness anatomize the several functions of the skin: it is at once the organ of touch, whose function is salient for the sight-deprived heroine; the porous cover for the body's interior entities, including heart, soul, and mind; and an external signifier, whose appearance, especially color, is freighted with social significance. Blocked from visual means of perception, Miss Finch is shown to be a perceptive reader of people through the sense of touch; like Martineau, her sensory deprivation provides her a degree of moral leverage (and sometimes, as when she listens or feels in the dark, perceptual superiority) over the sighted.[29] While she feels but cannot see, her blue fiancé is the *object* of seeing and feeling: he is loved when touched by her and reviled when seen by others — a horror reinforced by the racial coding of his dark skin.[30] The awkward link Collins establishes between blueness and blindness is Miss Finch's irrational horror of dark things; the novel asserts that this is an ordinary symptom of the blind (223–24), whose fear of visually discernible objects is heightened by being confined to fantasy — by being, in other words, wholly immaterial and interior. By dividing the introjective and expressive functions of the body's surface between the blind character and the blue one, Collins gives narrative form to the ways in which the skin serves as both a physical means of access and an ideational barrier to the apprehension of inner qualities.

Famous gothic tales from late in the century capitalize on both the sensory and the sensational aspects of such fiction. Robert Louis Stevenson's *Dr. Jekyll and Mr. Hyde* (1886) and Oscar Wilde's *The Picture of Dorian Gray* (1890–91) both transpose the interior being onto a distinct material form: in Stevenson's story, the grotesque embodiment of evil, Mr. Hyde, and in Wilde's, the soul-revealing portrait. In both cases, the newly created body, once differentiated from the protagonist's interior, serves as a narratable repository for hidden malevolence. Stevenson's story proposes the compound moral ambiguity of full human existence, which the extrojection of Hyde, as unalloyed evil, disrupts. The generic pastiche of *Dorian Gray* enables Wilde to present characters who are morally one-dimensional while indulging them (and his readers) in purportedly amoral aesthetic and bodily pleasures. Although the gothic plotting didactically insists that the soul repay the sins of the body, the tale blithely revels in bodily sensation through the decadence of its narrative language, imagery, and atmosphere. Wilde's account of the senses provides the link between its otherwise contradictory discourses of gothicism and decadence. In the gothic mode, Lord Henry Wotten's corrupting influence infects Dorian specifically through the ear, in the form of extravagantly playful and seductive language, and the corruption transforms the younger man's interior: "He was dimly conscious that entirely fresh influences were at work within him. . . . The few words that [Lord Henry] had said to him . . . had touched some secret chord that had never been touched before, but that he felt was now vibrating and throbbing to curious pulses."[31] Once internalized, however, this auditory corruption expresses itself visually: cast out from his soul and incarnated in the painting, the sinfulness assumes visible form. Even without the device of the Faustian bargain, the story would rely on the conceit that evil is visibly inscribed on the face of its perpetrator: malevolence is embodied as a look in the eye or a line in the cheek. Although the visual mode is repressed — in the sense that the portrait identified with it is literally locked up — vision ultimately prevails, as Dorian's decrepit face finally comes to record his sins in death.

The moralizing denouement that reveals the painting, however, is out of keeping with the bulk of the novel's celebration of sensual debauchery. The catalogs of jewels, embroideries, musical instruments, perfumes, ecclesiastical vestments, and other objects of sensual luxuriance, while of scant narrative interest, lend the work its pervasive air of aestheticism, expanding the field of sensory experience well beyond the verbal and visual to the senses classically ranked low, and to debasing sensuous indulgences, such as opium consumption and illicit sexuality.[32] Licensed by the closing frame of just punishment, Wilde's novel experiments with extravagant corporeal pleasures through a character magically evacuated of any moral or spiritual interior. Lord Henry gives epigrammatic force to the decadent doctrine: "Nothing can cure the soul but the senses, just as nothing can cure the senses but the soul" (185). Just as Martineau's deafness and Miss Finch's blindness heighten the experience of selfhood as embodiment, so Dorian Gray's hedonistic sensualism suggests that the senses provide the means of access to the soul; it further suggests that this soul might be an effect, rather than the motivating cause, of sensation. Notwithstanding its pious closure, *Dorian Gray* blasphemously implies that inside the body there is only more body. More than a reflexively decadent inversion of the theistic preference for soul over body, this proposition raises the possibility that interior and exterior partake of each other not dualistically but through a series of irreducible interchanges. The conceit, relatively explicit here, is widespread in Victorian literature. While all the works I have discussed stage contests between material and immaterial ways of imagining interior being, the material ultimately prevails, for in being represented as the *form* of interiority, the body also becomes its content.

These literary examples, in a variety of genres from across the Victorian period, argue for the materiality of self and soul, mobilizing the senses to gain access to these entities. Having considered such works, I turn now to some twentieth-century theoretical writing on embodiment. Victorian writers anticipate these formulations, I argue, which reciprocally provide conceptual tools that bring out the theories of embodiment and sensation embedded in the novels and poems. Recent scholarship has tended to regard the human body as the location at which external, objective identity categories — such as race, sexuality, gender, and disability — are inscribed. A focus, by contrast, on the interior, subjective experience of self and sensation can yield an account of the ways in which such politics come to be *felt* internally. This approach arises in the literary works I consider, and it dovetails with certain strains of twentieth-century French philosophy that are consequential for an analysis of embodiment; the ones I find most suggestive are those of Maurice Merleau-Ponty, Gilles Deleuze and Félix Guattari, and Georges Bataille, each of which elucidates a different aspect of embodiment.

Merleau-Ponty supplies phenomenological tools for conceiving of human encounters with the world in perceptual terms and of perception itself as fundamentally corporeal. Arguing against the tradition of Cartesian rationalism, Merleau-Ponty presents human subjectivity, in even its most abstract and ethereal forms, as rooted in the body. Human subjects gain knowledge of external objects through sensory apprehension, a process that incorporates them through organs of perception. Contesting a dualistic framing of the mind/body problem, Merleau-Ponty states: "The perceiving mind is an incarnated body. I have tried . . . to re-establish

the roots of the mind in its body and in its world, going against the doctrines which treat perception as a simple result of the action of external
things on our body as well as against those which insist on the autonomy of consciousness."[33] With this conception of the world outside the
subject as itself contingent on the subject's perception of it, Merleau-Ponty
suggests that the subject mingles with the world through processes of
sensory apprehension, entering into and being entered by it reciprocally.
Elizabeth Grosz explains that "Merleau-Ponty begins with the postulate
that we perceive and receive information of and from the world through
our bodies."[34] Because Merleau-Ponty posits that knowing and feeling
are embodied, physical processes, the corporeal subject itself comes to be
an object. In the influential posthumous essay "The Intertwining — the
Chiasm," Merleau-Ponty is not far from the Victorian physiological psychologists: "We say...that our body is a being of two leaves, from one
side a thing among things and otherwise what sees them and touches
them; we say, because it is evident, that it unites these two properties
within itself, and its double belongingness to the order of the 'object'
and to the order of the 'subject' reveals to us quite unexpected relations
between the two orders."[35] The body acquires a special status, as it did
for Maudsley and Bain, since it can be simultaneously the subject and
object of perception.

Most of Merleau-Ponty's work focuses on visual perception, as vision
is the dominant human sense, the one most richly evoked in language,
and the highest in the classical hierarchy of senses. But in this essay he
presents a model of what has come to be called haptic visuality, of seeing
considered on the model of touch, the sense whose reversible qualities
are most immediately evident.[36] By describing vision as "palpation of
the eye" (133), Merleau-Ponty disrupts the usual associations with sight,
the sense that (along with hearing) allows the greatest distance between
subject and object, to the extent that seeing does not conventionally
implicate the seer (for one can see without being seen but cannot touch
without, at the same time, being touched). Like Spencer and the other
Victorian writers I discuss in subsequent chapters, Merleau-Ponty lends
vision the tactile qualities of proximity and direct contact, turning it from
an objective, distant sense into a corporeally grounded and reciprocal one.
Vision loses its detached, disembodied authority if seeing both brings
the world into the body and puts the subject, as an object-to-be-seen
(what Merleau-Ponty calls "visible"), into the world:

> My hand, while it is felt from within, is also accessible from with-
> out, itself tangible, for my other hand, for example, if it takes its
> place among the things it touches, is in a sense one of them, opens
> finally upon a tangible being of which it is also a part. Through
> this crisscrossing within it of the touching and the tangible, its
> own movements incorporate themselves into the universe they
> interrogate, are recorded on the same map as it.... It is no different
> for the vision — except, it is said, that here the exploration and the
> information it gathers do not belong "to the same sense." (133)

To the simultaneous, mutual constitution of perceiving subjects and perceived objects, Merleau-Ponty gives the name "the flesh." This process is
most readily graspable at moments when perceiving subjects perceive
themselves as perceivable — notably when one hand is felt with the other,
is both touching and being touched. While this model of relations between
subject and object holds that they are reciprocal, it does not collapse them
into each other: in fact, the difference between the two is important, for
subjects can perceive themselves as objects, and can perceive the role of
objects in their own constitution as subjects, only if they remain distinct.[37] Likewise, while touching and being touched have to be thought
of as simultaneous, this simultaneity remains potential in practice: "It is
a reversibility always immanent and never realized in fact" (147).[38] The
model of reversible perception, and the haptic quality this conception
lends in particular to vision, formulate explicitly the qualities of sensory
experience that, I argue, Victorian writers mobilize to represent a substantial interior being coming into contact with the world. In the primacy
it lends sensory experience as constitutive of the self, this model provides
a basis for thinking about the body as the ground of experience, not as its
vehicle or as an impediment to it.[39]

While Deleuze and Guattari are not generally thought of in the phenomenological tradition of Merleau-Ponty, their monumental work *A
Thousand Plateaus* develops themes inchoate in his work and is addition-
ally suggestive for the materialism I identify in Victorian literary writing.
In particular, they elaborate on the ways in which the body fails to align
entirely with the subject, often exceeding and undermining the claims of
interior subjectivity. As Deleuze and Guattari move well beyond the
individual, private self that the metaphysical tradition confines within
the body, they imply that bodies have minds of their own. Emphasizing
dynamic flows and "intensities," whereby human bodies, environments,

animals, and things mutually constitute and materially remake one another, Deleuze and Guattari not only challenge the opposition between
subject and object but also subvert the very logic of cause and effect, self
and other. This decentered subject is formed dialectically with the phenomenal world, into and out of which it flows, changes, and develops, in
their image of the "desiring machine."

Grosz writes that Deleuze and Guattari "provide an altogether different way of understanding the body in its connections with other bodies,
both human and nonhuman, animate and inanimate, linking organs and
biological processes to material objects and social practices while refusing to subordinate the body to a unity or a homogeneity of the kind provided by the body's subordination to consciousness or to biological organization" (164–65). The counterintuitive propositions in Deleuze and
Guattari are suggestive of the dynamic relations among human bodies,
the places they inhabit, and social practices that, as I will argue in subsequent chapters, Victorian writers were already exploiting. The best known
of their formulations, the Body without Organs (BwO), provides a model
for embodiment of the kind that Grosz describes, which partakes of individual consciousness and socially organized identities without being
reducible to any unified formulation. In spite of its name, the Body without Organs is not empty or lacking but overly full;[40] as Deleuze and Guattari state, "the BwO is opposed not to the organs but to that organization
of the organs called the organism."[41] Rather than subjugate bodily sensation to the order of meaning or personhood, Deleuze and Guattari suggest that subjectivity and semiology are effects of the incoherent, fractured — but always connectable — Body without Organs: "The organism
is not at all the body, the BwO; rather, it is a stratum on the BwO, in
other words, a phenomenon of accumulation, coagulation, and sedimen-
tation that, in order to extract useful labor from the BwO, imposes upon
it forms, functions, bonds, dominant and hierarchized organizations,
organized transcendences" (159).

Just as, for Merleau-Ponty, the reciprocity entailed in sensation blurs
the boundaries between subjects and objects, so Deleuze and Guattari's
rejection of transcendence permits flows and exchanges between human
beings and other material objects. They specifically repudiate psychoanalytic theory, which posits a deep, interior being that, though it may be
riven with conflict, defines and drives the "organism." For Deleuze and
Guattari, desire — the driving motor in psychoanalysis — is constituted

not as lack but as possibility and connection. The Body without Organs is a desiring machine; it is profoundly unmotivated and largely without agency, yet it is constantly "plugged into other collective machines" (161). Deleuze and Guattari advance a material notion of human existence whose being, if internal, is located in an irreducibly embodied interior. Yet what lies within is, for them, fully porous to the outside world, functioning more as a process and a site of potential connection than as a homogeneous entity. They do not, however, evacuate subjectivity altogether, maintaining that it can be put to strategic uses: "You have to keep small supplies of signifiance and subjectification, if only to turn them against their own systems when the circumstances demand it" (160).

While Deleuze and Guattari's model of subjectivity is dynamic and generative, it tends to avoid the violence often entailed by imagining entry into the interior in material terms — a violence of particular interest, I will show, to writers such as Charlotte Brontë and Gerard Manley Hopkins. The work of Georges Bataille also aims to annihilate interior depth, but in going into the body, Bataille emphasizes the potential for violence in this process. His writing frequently focuses on the material form of the human, celebrating the products and processes (such as excrement and mutilation) ordinarily considered most debased, finding in them sources for exuberant possibility. Unlike Deleuze and Guattari, Bataille seems practically to abandon the human subject, partly through his persistent focus on the filthiness of the body. Bataille posits an "acephalic" subject — a headless body — in which all the traditional values associated with dominance, hierarchy, and vision are evacuated in favor of the body's lower orders. In part because any sustained engagement with the material existence of the body — and in particular with the influx and outflow through bodily orifices — leads to the contemplation of disgusting or degrading bodily products, Bataille can help address some of the disgust that arises in the face of literary encounters with bodily insides that spill out.

In Bataille's work, a provocative vocabulary of terms and concepts suggests a profoundly, if unsettlingly, material understanding of human existence. From the prewar articles that appeared in the review *Documents* on which I draw, no systematic approach can be distilled that might be applied to other texts, but taken together, these fragments sketch a way of conceiving of the relations among body parts, body products, and external matter. In Bataille's schema, the "pineal eye" — an imagined opening in the head, which corresponds to the gland that Descartes posited as the seat of consciousness — is a privileged locus for access to experiences both supremely exalted and debased: "I imagined the eye at the summit of the skull like a horrible erupting volcano, precisely with the shady and comical character associated with the rear end and its excretions."[42] The pineal eye is connected to the transcendent power of the visible, blinding sun, but it is also directly linked to the anus, to the shit-smeared and sex-focused existence that Bataille (in the mode of primitive anthropologist) always sees subtending human civilization. Bataille reflects on these ideas in the article "The Jesuve," which offers an explanation, in terms of evolutionary anthropology, for civilization's sublimation of the anus and hence his own celebration of it. With Bataille's frequent emphasis on erection, his human being may seem decidedly masculine, but it is also at points crucially invaginating. Perhaps more significant than its gender, however, is its explosiveness: "When I imagined the disconcerting possibility of the pineal eye, I had no intention other than to represent discharges of energy at the top of the head — discharges as violent and as indecent as those that make the anal protuberances of some apes so horrible to see."[43] The connection between pineal eye and anus might look like a simple reversal of what Peter Stallybrass and Allon White trace as the structural and psychological opposition between exaltation and debasement,[44] yet for all his early psychoanalytic affinities, Bataille eschews schematic oppositions, understanding debasement and exaltation to be not simply inversions of each other but explosive forces that upend any possibility of ordered experience.

Merleau-Ponty's account of vision is modeled on the sense of touch, whereby seeing, rather than providing hygienic distance, brings bodies into contact. For Bataille, the ocular organ, usually understood to take the world in without violating the subject, is itself wrenched violently out of the body. He conceives of the eye not only as an organ of touch but also as an object to be touched: a favorite image of his is the enucleated eye, the organ that is pulled out, seen by other eyes, violated, and ingested. This is a chaotic realm of depths, not surfaces — but of emphatically, appallingly *bodily* depths. In Bataille's pseudonymous pornographic novel, *Story of the Eye* (1928), the male narrator and his female lover engage in an orgy of eggs, testicles, and disgorged and invaginated eyes, all easily removed from one body and incorporated into another. As he explains in a postscript, "The entire *Story of the Eye* was woven in my mind out of two ancient and closely associated obsessions, *eggs* and *eyes*. . . . Human or animal balls are egg-shaped and [when removed] look the same as an eyeball."[45] In the novel, eyes, eggs, and balls are cracked open, pulled out, eaten, and adapted for sexual pleasure in a graphic demonstration of how the organ of perceptual subjectivity is sexualized and converted into an object for consumption.

The idea of the body as the source of outflowing, usually repulsive material is frequently the shadowy companion to a notion of it as repository for sensory influx. The overlap between the soul, traditionally imagined as light and airy, and the viscera, held to be dark and disgusting, threatens to degrade the very idea of a human interior: regarded too closely, the inside of the body defiles the human subject identified with it.[46] When Victorian considerations of sensory experience converge with those of bodily filth, they bear surprising affinities with Bataille's perverse avulsion of the body's interior to its surface. Nineteenth-century concerns with filth and attendant disease might be understood not as the obverse of a putative repression but as the active and unembarrassed focus of an emerging collection of discourses.[47] While the culture's fascination with filth has received recent attention, my interest here is in the seepage of such concerns into works that do not overtly thematize them. Bodily interiors assume altogether visceral form in, for example, the metaphors of excrement through which Brontë, in *The Professor,* portrays romance; the penetration of the body's splanchnic interior in Hopkins's poetry and journals; and widespread newspaper coverage of the assault on the nose by the pollution of the Thames in 1858, which, I argue, finds its way into Anthony Trollope's tale of attempted spiritual purification. By approaching such topics from the anthropological-economic perspective that Bataille provides, as well as in the context of the period's social history, we can preserve their basis in the sensory specificity of lived experience.[48]

The three paradigms I have been discussing form a continuum of approaches in relation to the bodily interior, each illuminating a different aspect of Victorian literary materialism. For Merleau-Ponty, interactions between subjects, and between people and objects in the world, are mutually constitutive. Vision in particular operates not as depth perception but as a cutaneous rubbing of surfaces; modeled on the sense of touch, seeing entails a reciprocity between subjects and objects. For Deleuze and Guattari, ordinarily differentiated forms of matter (such as the human and the animal or the inanimate) cannot be strictly distinguished, flowing in and out of each other. The subject is a provisional construction, knowable only in its parts, which carry onto or plug into other things, phenomena, and energies, by which they are constantly remade and remapped. Bataille presents the eye itself as an organ that touches and is touched; he imagines the body's interior exploding outward, and in wrenching the visceral interior to the surface, he gives voice to its violence and horror. All these figures — of seeing as touching, of touching as penetrating, of interacting as a bodily experience — are vividly exploited by the Victorian writers I discuss. While I have elaborated the approaches separately and enunciated differences among them here, I do not apply these theories of bodily materialism systematically to the literary works I consider; rather, I rely on them in combination, as they bear affinities with, help to explicate, or are illuminated by nineteenth-century texts.

Finally, a few words about the contexts and consequences of this argument. First, this work engages with a burgeoning critical interest in the meaning of sensory experience. One might presume that a consideration of the senses in literature would be drawn, first and foremost, to visual and then to auditory sensations. Ordinarily, reading itself is phenomenologically a visual and auditory experience: words enter the reader's body through the eyes or ears; the preponderance of description is visual, and just as the sounds of the words are heard subvocally, so pictures of what is described arise in the mind's eye. Two important studies of nineteenth-century culture illustrate the power of an emphasis on sight, even as they demonstrate the cost to other sensory modalities that an exclusive preoccupation with vision exacts. Nancy Armstrong's book on photographic realism as a literary mode in the Victorian period and Jonathan Crary's work on "suspensions of perception" as a visual phenomenon in the era of photography's birth both place the visual imagination at the center of changing ideas about human subjectivity in the nineteenth century, and both rely on disciplinary notions of visually oriented subjectivity derived from Foucault.[49] Recent work on the history and theory of hearing, deafness, and voice extends cultural and historical criticism to another sensory modality.[50] My interest in the influx from the world into the body through perceptual organs leads me to focus on the proximate senses, and on distance senses when they are rendered proximate. Hans J. Rindisbacher and Janice Carlisle have, in different ways, undertaken systematic efforts to analyze literary representations of olfactory experience.[51] This book, while dwelling on the rendition of sensory experience, is aimed at wider nineteenth-century concepts of how people are imagined to inhabit their bodies.[52]

Somewhat closer to the approach I take here is the model that Steven Connor and Stephen Clucas call "cultural phenomenology," a strategy that adapts phenomenological philosophy for cultural studies. According to Connor, cultural phenomenology tends more to provide rich descriptions of experience — especially embodied experience — than to posit decisive theories about what such experiences mean or to presume to know from the outset what their politics are.[53] While this approach pays close attention to embodied experience, to affects, emotions, and senses, and to bodily transformations across dimensions of time and space, it also understands such experience to be socially, culturally, and historically situated. Connor writes that cultural phenomenology "would take care to steer clear of precomprehended problems, under rubrics such as power, identity, ideology, gender, sexuality, 'race,' ethnicity, the body, or postmodernism, and would do what it could not to consent to the ordering and containing effects of those forms of thought" (5). This is not, however, the arid contextlessness of some phenomenological philosophy, nor is it the deracinated individualism of some psychoanalysis. Attention to the experiential dimension of the body, rather than to its domination by overarching social formations, need not come at the cost of a historical or political account of power differentials; indeed, it specifies the distribution of power by tracing its material effects on, and manifestations in, particular bodies and embodied experiences.[54] The designation of race on the basis of skin pigmentation, for instance, or of gender on the basis of anatomical organs, is as much an experience of the subjective inhabitation of a body as it is of external, objective power structures.[55]

Discussions of the body and power, especially in studies of the nineteenth century, have largely been carried out in the shadow of Foucault's theory of the relation between social institutions and subjectivity in the modern era. In his most influential work on power, Foucault takes the body to be the material site of subjectification; individuals internalize surveillance mechanisms, for instance, by experiencing them through and as their sexuality. The revelatory insight of Foucault's reversal of Enlightenment dualism — condensed in the epigrammatic statement that modernity is signaled by the soul becoming "the prison of the body" — entails a power whose discursive operations always (and instantly) succeed. Subjects thus constituted are resigned to the inescapable conditions of their own embodiment.[56] While this book engages with related issues concerning ideas about human nature in relation to social formations, it proceeds under an analytic rubric that asks questions *other* than whether any particular representation colludes with or aims to undermine power. Foucault's writings themselves argue that power cannot simply be reduced to a question of domination versus subversion. Yet despite his model of complexity (or in some cases self-contradiction), as Eve Kosofsky Sedgwick has suggested, this stark set of alternatives — or, at best, an ambivalent negotiation between them — has wound up as the almost inevitable end point of criticism that starts from a basis of regulation and normalization.[57] An emphasis on interiority and sensation can circumvent a fixation on discipline and surveillance, the guideposts of much Foucault-inspired criticism. Thus rather than considering the eye as the source for a circuit of disciplinary power between the Panoptic tower and the prisoner in his cell, we can, in the context of Victorian materialism, understand it as both an orifice — an opening into the body — and a tactile surface for drawing together the subject and the object of sight. The materialist strain in Victorian writing presents the relation between subject and object-world less in terms of abstract distance than proximate contact: people are not so much cut off from one another as rubbing up against each other, even when they seem to look at or hear each other from afar. The writers I discuss in this book are excited, terrified, or awestruck by the material embodiment of their existence, but this means neither that they are fully in the grip of a power that constitutes them nor that they actively engage in resisting it. They find cause for writerly provocation and explanation in embodiment as they seek to work out the effects not of the soul being the body's prison but of the soul giving up its ghost to the material of the body.

Just as this book both engages with and departs from critical models derived from Foucault, it is also, finally, in implicit dialogue with queer theory. My work puts into question relations between body and subject, and between the self and the world, through its discussion of embodiment, and in this sense it takes seriously the radical proposition of queer theory: not to advance identities organized around object choice but to interrogate sexual subjectivity itself.[58] While a number of the works I discuss evince unorthodox sexual objects and gender arrangements, I am concerned less with the sexually counternormative, sometimes homoerotic themes in particular texts than with the relations these works describe between body and mind, flesh and soul, and the routes for getting from one to the other. Although these processes are often erotic, the sexual can be understood as belonging to a wider series of bodily transformations across surfaces and depths. Accounts of human experience that take the body to be its untranscendable source may, as one of their consequences, disrupt norms of sexual desire, but more fundamentally they challenge the stability and coherence of a subject that claims to be anything more than a body in the first place. As I discuss in the conclusion, we may want to call such phenomena queer not because they fail to abide by an orthodox set of sexual norms but because they mutually remake subjects and objects, bodies and minds, selves and worlds.

2

Self

Material Interiority in Dickens and Brontë

Writing about the body supplies Victorian authors a concrete means of giving form to intangible thoughts and feelings. In embodying subjective interiority, characters in works by Charles Dickens and Charlotte Brontë are open through their senses to incursions from outside. Interaction with other subjects and with the phenomenal world engenders emotional and intellectual changes in them, which are realized in physical form. Conceiving of characters as essentially embodied also has consequences for literary form itself. One of these consequences — often regarded as the great achievement of Victorian realism — is the effect of characterological psychology, consciousness, and inner depth that seem to exceed the representation.[1] This impression, I suggest, is propagated by means of physical embodiment in characterization, as well as in other dimensions of representation, including affect, setting, dialogue, and narration itself. Brontë's novel *The Professor* (1845–46), the particular case that I examine here, is often judged a literary failure precisely because it exaggerates the conditions of embodiment; in so doing, however, it usefully exposes the mechanisms of such representation. Another literary effect of the materialist approach is registered in figural language: a metaphoric object — frequently an architectural element — conveys the experience of a self enclosed in a physical container. As a figure for that which contains, protects, and makes accessible the self within, such a metaphoric object (a house, for instance, or a room or a piece of furniture) itself stands in for the body, that porous, material container of inner human entities.

This conception of profound embodiment is also consequential for the senses, particularly for vision, the sense classically understood as least immediately corporeal and culturally valued most highly. The thematics of insight and blindness, panoptics and myopia, might reasonably be comprehended by critical accounts of visual pleasure and surveillance — in the Victorian novel specifically and in post-Enlightenment European culture more generally. The metaphoric texture of the works I consider here, however, is striking for its obdurate, if sometimes repellent, insistence that perception, interaction, and communication are irreducibly corporeal: the world enters human subjects through bodily orifices, of which the eyes are but two. Seen in this light — or, perhaps, sniffed out in this odor — currents of sensory apprehension that have been disavowed in deference to their being so long discredited (because literally invisible) assume new importance. In appropriating vision to senses that eliminate the distance between subject and object — and which thereby redound as much on their agent as on their object — these novels alert us to the creative potential of bodily sites and senses traditionally cast onto the refuse heap of culture.

While construing the self as a material entity solves certain problems, it inevitably raises concerns about the body's perviousness and its excrescences. Portrayed in concrete terms, the introjection of external material — perceptions, ideas, and feelings as well as things — can be imagined as bodily penetration, and the range of such incorporation's emotional valence is wide: it can be arousing, frightening, disgusting, or exciting. The works I discuss in this chapter figure such introjection as penetration with special vividness, notably in their accounts of relations between characters. While such contact includes the sexual, that is not its exclusive domain; interaction and communication are fully embodied affairs. For both Dickens and Brontë, the erotic is one dimension of bodily contact, but as such it only dramatizes more ordinary procedures for bringing material selves together. Moreover, while these novels employ a gendered eroticism, we will find, in pressing on the metaphors they use to depict selfhood, that gender does not determine the relative permeability or imperviousness of characters' bodies. This is not to evade the gendered dimension of penetration but rather to avoid prejudging the embodied particulars of a self on the basis of that body's sex. Brontë in particular — precisely because she seeks to de-emphasize the perceived deficiencies of her sex — makes the physical inhabitation of the interior more salient than any given body's gender.

Although the figural techniques these authors employ for portraying the embodiment of subjectivity are similar, Dickens uses a material conception of the interior as a means of comically, often exuberantly, opening the self to the world — particularly to other embodied selves, in relations of desire and antipathy. Brontë has a sharply bounded, highly defended conception of the self, one lodged deep within an edifice that both is and stands for the body; through its emphasis on pain, her work is more unsettling than Dickens's in exploring the consequences of material subjectivity. Both authors represent subjects who derive a certain satisfaction from experiences, often painful, of themselves as embodied. Such representations conform to a model of masochistic pleasure, a concept I find useful in approaching their work as well as comprehended by it.

In Dickens generally, and especially in his depiction of children, the soul or the heart is often reached through the mouth, so that perception is rendered as ingestion. Through the many grotesque, deformed, exaggerated, and diminished characters who inhabit his work, Dickens frequently exploits the body as the site at which external world and internal self partake of each other. To focus the dauntingly large subject of bodies in Dickens, I discuss the relation between the interior and the exterior as Dickens gives it especially vivid form in one specific manifestation: the keyhole. In English fiction, the keyhole is typically the mechanical opening through which spying or surveillance takes place — a kind of optical device that frames a scene and distances it from an unseen, observing eye — and in this sense it might be assimilated to a model of disciplinary surveillance derived from Foucault. But the keyhole is also a figure *for* the eye, a bounded embrasure on one side of which is the viewing subject's body, on the other the witnessed scene. The keyhole, moreover, is just as frequently the channel through which one character listens in on another, and one of its useful properties is that it works just as well as a figure for the ear as for the eye; indeed, while the hole itself might look like an ocular aperture, its corrugated tumblers set within a channel are reminiscent of auricular whorls.

There is hardly a Dickens novel that does not contain a scene in which one character puts an eye or an ear to a keyhole, spying on another within. By comparison, not a single instance of such spying occurs in the work of George Eliot. It is rare in Anthony Trollope and Henry James; it is comparatively more frequent in William Makepeace Thackeray and Wilkie Collins, for they, like Dickens, have closer ties to the eighteenth-century novel, where looking through and listening at keyholes are routine.[2] It is striking that in most cases the person outside the door is a servant, usually female, and the one on the inside someone who employs servants. This pattern may simply reflect a sociological fact about who is situated where in the bourgeois home of the nineteenth century (the usual setting for domestic fiction), and it relies on stereotypes of gossiping, mendacious working-class women. But it is also a relation rich with literary possibility, a way of tracking how servants literally view, frame, and gain secret knowledge of their masters. The comments made by a character in *Nicholas Nickleby* (1838–39) about his maid presume the convention of the servant who lurks about keyholes: "She's very frugal, and she's very deaf; her living costs me next to nothing, and it's no use her listening at keyholes for she can't hear. She's a charming woman — for the purpose; a most discreet old housekeeper, and worth her weight in — copper."[3] Dickens takes for granted the class attributes of keyholes, but Trollope characteristically explains them, providing a sardonic little essay on the subject in *Barchester Towers* (1857):

> It would be a calumny on Mrs. Proudie to suggest that she was sitting in her bedroom with her ear at the keyhole during this interview. She had within her a spirit of decorum which prevented her from descending to such baseness. To put her ear to a keyhole, or to listen at a chink, was a trick for a housemaid.
>
> Mrs. Proudie knew this and therefore did not do it, but she stationed herself as near to the door as she well could, that she might, if possible, get the advantage which the housemaid would have had without descending to the housemaid's artifice.[4]

Trollope explicitly announces that listening at keyholes is déclassé; he shows how Mrs. Proudie's vulgar desires combine hypocritically with her overweening sense of bourgeois propriety, which prescribes a certain distance between her ear and the keyhole. The use of the word "chink" here is a reminder of the literary genealogy of the keyhole, which goes back to *A Midsummer Night's Dream* (which in turn carries it over from Ovid's *Metamorphoses*), with the comedy surrounding the play-within-the-play turning on the embodied performance of the wall and its hole. Ovid and Shakespeare establish the conventions whereby a wall is a barrier that separates people, but that separation is knowable only by the chink, the place in the wall that defeats its function and, at the same time, confirms it, providing deliciously partial contact between star-crossed lovers. The keyhole is an updated, mechanical form of the chink, but where the comedy in Shakespeare comes from a player representing a wall, and in particular from embodying its hole, in Dickens these relations are reversed: the chink, formalized in the keyhole, is itself a figure for certain openings in the body. Unlike his contemporaries, Dickens does not wholly restrict looking through or listening at keyholes to the activity of servants. In describing the experience of witnessing the eye or the ear of another in the act of eavesdropping on oneself, Dickens is also unusual in tending to identify with the object rather than the subject of keyhole spying. Most scenes of looking through or listening at keyholes in Dickens are followed by doors opening and bodies passing through them, just as the voice does. Making tangible the speech, breath, and other matter that passes through the keyhole, rather than limiting the hole to a one-way channel of observation, Dickens transforms the device: not simply a mechanism that shields one character in the social hierarchy from another, more powerful one (or that temporarily reverses such power relations), the keyhole becomes a virtual bodily orifice.

Why should Dickens find the keyhole so appealing, both as a plot device and as a literary figure, while his contemporaries mostly shun it? One answer to this question has to do with narrative form: for all his interest in omniscience, Dickens tends to prefer showing observation in action to imagining it. In works by the other authors I have named, the figure of a postulated, rather than an actual, onlooker appears in inverse proportion to keyhole spying. With a frequency impossible to catalog, fiction by Eliot, James, and Trollope contains phrases like "some unknown observer looking on this scene would have thought x and y"; in *Middlemarch* (1872), for example, a line of this type arises in almost every chapter. Such phrases occur relatively rarely in Dickens, not because he does not conjure up onlookers but because they tend to look on from within rather than from without a narrated scene — because they tend to be substantial rather than hypothetical. This difference in narrational device has consequences for how a reader identifies with point of view — whether it is routed through an abstract third party or through the idiosyncratic perspective of an embodied character.[5]

Traditional scenes of keyhole spying, in which readers witness one character spying on another, also represent and intensify the inherently novelistic activities of eavesdropping on and telling about other people's private lives. Such spying has been read as a figure for narrating and consuming fictive lives, either as a convenient way of conveying narrative information — by routing it through a particular character — or as a reflexive surrogate for the narrator or author.[6] While it is tempting to comprehend such acts of spying as allegories of narration, and particularly of omniscient narration — with all the disciplinary apparatus of surveillance such an allegory would entail — I wish to forestall this reading and to suggest what might be gained by reintroducing the physicality of perception to such a scene. Embodied acts of looking and listening in Dickens, especially as they are focused and localized by keyholes, are not remote, controlling, and transcendent but rather proximate, intersubjective, and material; they have as much impact on the observer as on the observed, for the keyhole has openings in both directions.

While striking keyhole scenes appear in *Martin Chuzzlewit* (1843–44), *Barnaby Rudge* (1841), *Our Mutual Friend* (1864–65), and elsewhere in the Dickens corpus, I focus on *The Old Curiosity Shop* (1840–41) — the keyhole seeker's paradise — and *David Copperfield* (1849–50), which develops and extends notions of embodied interiority established in the keyhole. When asked at one point how he has materialized in a room, *The Old Curiosity Shop*'s dwarfish villain, Quilp, replies, "Through the door. . . . I'm not quite small enough to get through keyholes. I wish I was."[7] The fantasy that the whole person might squeeze bodily through a keyhole is not merely a piece of Quilpish depravity; it permeates Dickens's work. This particular villain often spies on others, terrorizing them with the idea that he knows and sees all, that his flagitious miniature form is sure to follow up looking with slipping through holes at any time. When Quilp discovers his wife and her friends celebrating his presumed death, his ability to materialize out of thin air is lent an almost supernatural dimension:

> The prospect of playing the spy under such delicious circum-
> stances, and of disappointing them all by walking in alive, gave
> more delight to Quilp than the greatest stroke of good fortune
> could possibly have inspired him with. . . .
>   The bedroom-door on the staircase being unlocked, Mr. Quilp
> slipped in, and planted himself behind the door, . . . having a very
> convenient chink (of which he had often availed himself for pur-
> poses of espial, and had indeed enlarged with his pocket-knife),
> [which] enabled him not only to hear, but to see distinctly, what
> was passing.
>   Applying his eye to this convenient place, he descried Mr.
> Brass seated at the table with . . . all things fitting; from which
> choice materials, Sampson . . . had compounded a mighty glass of
> punch reeking hot. (369–70)

The party partakes of his food and drink until the outraged monster bursts in, scatters them violently, and swallows the remains of their festivities. The keyhole (or, in this case, spy hole) is a figure not only for looking but for consuming as well: it is one version of Quilp's great mouth that strives to bite, chew, and swallow all that it encounters, including, most especially, Little Nell — the figure spied on, persecuted, and possessed by almost every man in the book.[8]

The other character consistently associated with keyholes is the servant whom Dick Swiveller dubs the Marchioness. One of the many deformed, stunted, and suffering bodies that populate the novel, the Marchioness is little, like both Nell and Quilp, and the victim of extraordinary physical and emotional violence, like almost everyone else in it. The whole plot of the Marchioness revolves around keys and keyholes. Because she is kept starving in a kitchen where food is locked up, she is always on the lookout for the keys to the larder. These she does not find, but she eventually discovers the key to her kitchen prison, and she makes use of it to free herself and wander through the house at night, picking up scraps of food and taking, as Dick says, "a limited view of society through the keyholes of doors" (435). By means of such spying, she both befriends Dick and lays bare the conspiracy between the Brasses and Quilp to frame Kit Nubbles, a discovery that precipitates the downfall of the melodrama's villains and the redemption of its heroes. By looking and listening through keyholes, in other words, the Marchioness finds not the key she was looking for but the key to the story. Here is a classic Dickensian deconstruction: keys are found not in keyholes but through them.

The Marchioness's search for keys and her passage through keyholes are motivated by hunger. She is practically an embodiment of appetite — a characteristic that joins her to Quilp and distinguishes her from her self-abnegating double, that "chubby, rosy, cosy, little Nell" (81), as Quilp calls her, whose craving for food is always subordinated to caring for her crazed grandfather. Dick observes how, hungry though she is for nourishment, the Marchioness stuffs herself instead with information:

> "But, Marchioness," added Richard, . . . "it occurs to me that you must be in the constant habit of airing your eye at keyholes, to know all this."
>
> "I only wanted," replied the trembling Marchioness, "to know where the key of the safe was hid; that was all; and I wouldn't have taken much, if I had found it — only enough to squench my hunger."
>
> "You didn't find it then?" said Dick. "But of course you didn't, or you'd be plumper." (435)

The Marchioness's hunger indicates her habitual relation to the world: taking sights, sounds, and tastes into her body to satisfy needs. Yet while she strives to "squench" that hunger, things flow out of as well as into her body, and this is why her performance at the keyhole is so vital. For when she and Dick finally make contact, it happens through a keyhole:

> Mr. Swiveller began to think that on those evenings when Mr.
> and Miss Brass were out...he heard a kind of snorting or hard-
> breathing sound in the direction of the door, which it occurred to
> him, after some reflection, must proceed from the small servant,
> who always had a cold from damp living. Looking intently that
> way one night, he plainly distinguished an eye gleaming and glis-
> tening at the keyhole; and having now no doubt that his suspi-
> cions were correct, he stole softly to the door, and pounced upon
> her before she was aware of his approach. (429–30)

By contrast with the scenes in which Quilp spies on others — and with
the usual conventions of keyhole spying — this scene is shown from the
viewpoint of the one under scrutiny. Rather than seeing through the eyes
of the Marchioness what Dick does in private, we learn what he perceives
of her, lurking outside his door: her hard breathing and her gleaming
eye. If this is an allegory of narration, then we readers identify with the
character who looks back at the ordinarily unseen observer. This reversal
emphasizes the physical manifestation of observation itself: he hears and
sees her seeing and hearing him. The virtual contact between Dick and
the Marchioness, in the form of her exposed eyeball and her wheezy ex-
halations, is almost immediately actualized: he invites her in, recognizes
in her a prospective partner for his endless cribbage game, and then
stuffs her emaciated frame full of food and drink.

This scene plays on two earlier episodes in which Dick stands outside a door, looking through a keyhole, only to be "pounced upon" by
those he spies. Early in the novel, after Nell and her grandfather have
escaped Quilp's imprisonment of them in the shop by abstracting its key
from him, Quilp looks at the keyhole only to see himself being seen:
"The day-light which had been shining through the keyhole was inter-
cepted on the outside by a human eye" (106). Thinking he sees the eye of
his wife (on whom he frequently spies), Quilp rushes through the door to
attack the observer, which turns out to be Dick — who returns the violence
in kind, then follows Quilp back into the shop. Through the "mystery
of the key," they discover the inmates to have fled, and "Mr. Swiveller
looked, as he was, all open-mouthed astonishment" (109). In a great
comic episode later, another object of keyhole scrutiny — the character
known as the single gentleman — comes bursting out of his room to accost
the observers, in that case Dick again, as well as Sampson Brass, whose
eye is described as "curiously twisted into the keyhole" (269). The single
gentleman castigates Dick for waking him from his heroic slumbers, then

asks him in, serves him a drink, and befriends him over a meal. In all these cases, the direct result of peering through a keyhole is that the door opens, the spy is captured, and then the mouth opens. Architectural and corporeal openings — doors and mouths, keyholes and eyes — frequently correlate, both by standing in for each other and by literally opening onto each other.

The keyhole enacts a continuity between perception and other forms of bodily ingestion. It signifies and enables not distance but connection between two bodies, functioning less as wall and more as chink. That contact is reciprocal: not long after Dick and the Marchioness meet, he falls ill and she turns to caring for him, feeding him assiduously to restore him to health and securing the bond between them. While the matrimony in which this relationship terminates has disappointed readers,[9] it is sustained by a certain erotic energy, oriented around food and eating, which exceeds even the perversity attached to the youth of the Marchioness. (She is only thirteen when Dick sets his sights on her, but the marriage is delayed until she turns nineteen.) One could interpret the routing of their courtship through the keyhole as a type of sexual penetration, but it is more complicated — because it is more full-bodied — than that. It is a penetration, or more precisely an interpenetration, that involves the breath and the mouth and the eye and the ear; it is a commingling, not a passive receiving, brought into focus by passing through a narrow conduit. Getting Dick and the Marchioness inside each other at the end of the novel serves as a comic counterweight to the melodrama of that other perverse pair — Nell and Quilp — whose deaths, though widely separated in space, happen simultaneously.

The bodily connections between Dick and the Marchioness — which include looking, touching, feeding, playing, and, presumably, maritally sanctioned sexual congress as well — are both initiated by and condensed in the figure of the keyhole. *David Copperfield* even more decisively stages an overlapping series of bodily interactions, which bring the surface and the interior into proximate relation. Like other children in Dickens's work, the young David Copperfield encounters the world primarily through his mouth: he kisses his mother, bites his stepfather, and is alternately stuffed and starved by the adults who care for him. By means of oral ingestion and oral aggression, *David Copperfield* charts the interpenetration of external world and interior being and, like *The Old Curiosity Shop*, often depicts perception as incorporation. Early on, for example, the narrator describes his beloved nursemaid, Peggotty, as having "cheeks and arms so hard and red that I wondered the birds didn't peck her in preference to apples. . . . I have an impression . . . of the touch of Peggotty's forefinger as she used to hold it out to me, and of its being roughened by needlework, like a pocket nutmeg-grater."[10] By metaphorically associating Peggotty's body with apples and nutmeg, the narrator identifies a subjective effect — visual, tactile, and gustatory — in the textural "impression" of her objective form;[11] he says, in essence, "her very roughness draws her to me in the same way that comforting foods appeal to my palate." The superficial unattractiveness of Peggotty's tactile hardness and apparent redness conveys sentimental delectability, once allegorized to the realm of taste — which is to say, once imagined as ingested within the narrator's body.[12]

This relatively simple condensation of sensory impressions intensifies when Copperfield elaborates on the complexion of his nurse. "I thought [Peggotty] in a different style from my mother, certainly; but of another school of beauty, I considered her a perfect example. There was a red velvet footstool in the best parlour, on which my mother had painted a nosegay. The ground-work of that stool, and Peggotty's complexion appeared to me to be one and the same thing. The stool was smooth, and Peggotty was rough, but that made no difference" (66). The narrator again apprehends the character through texture — how her surface feels, or appears to feel, to the touch — yet he discounts the very trait (roughness) that distinguishes her. He indicates that she is rough by emphasizing her red color but in the same gesture identifies her with smooth-feeling velvet. That the velvet with which she is compared belongs to a footstool confirms Peggotty's degraded class position (she is, after all, employed by the family), even while his mother's having painted on the stool elegantly redeems its appearance. In visually representing an object with pleasant olfactory associations (the nosegay), the footstool, like the apples, allows him metaphorically to incorporate her surface, through his senses, into the interior of his body. By supporting the feet and, at the same time, visually mitigating whatever unpleasant odor might be imagined to arise from them, the decorated footstool (like flowered wallpaper in a toilet or a decorative sewer grate) synesthetically revalues the servant whom it allegorizes.

David's sensory internalizations of Peggotty's goodness culminate in a keyhole. His punishing stepfather, Murdstone, locks David in his room, and soon Peggotty comes to occupy the usual servant's position on the other side of the door. But rather than spying on him, the nurse uses these means to communicate with him. As she whispers through the keyhole, however, its technology breaks down. "I was obliged to get her to repeat [her message]," David says, "for she spoke it the first time quite down my throat, in consequence of my having forgotten to take my mouth away from the keyhole and put my ear there; and though her words tickled me a good deal, I didn't hear them" (110). As if holding a telephone receiver upside down, Copperfield finds that words go down his throat rather than into his ear. Instead of functioning as audible vibration freighted with meaning, language here becomes the tactile sensation of breath felt inside the body. Displacing it from the eardrum to the throat, Dickens proposes the materiality of a language so palpable it can be swallowed: just as Copperfield earlier likened Peggotty's appearance to comforting food, so he here conceives her words as matter to ingest. In implicitly aligning her expulsions with a kiss dispersed through the oral cavity, moreover, he suggests the fierce, nearly erotic attachment he feels to her, which he goes on to portray:

> We both of us kissed the keyhole with the greatest affection —
> I patted it with my hand, I recollect, as if it had been her honest
> face — and parted. From that night there grew up in my breast a
> feeling for Peggotty which I cannot very well define. She did not
> replace my mother; no one could do that; but she came into a
> vacancy in my heart, which closed upon her, and I felt towards
> her something I have never felt for any other human being. (111)

In "coming into his heart" by coming into his mouth, Peggotty's kind words permeate the young protagonist; he introjects her beneficence, incorporating her treatment of him in the "vacancy" left by the failure of his mother's love. Like some Victorian Pyramus and Thisbe, whose eros is transvalued into the mutual affection of kindly nursemaid and pitiable child, David and Peggotty cling to that osculatory keyhole, which both metaphorizes their mouths and serves as the channel through which their breaths and voices mingle.

While this is the only keyhole scene that appears in *David Copperfield*, its language of absorption and ingestion sets the pattern for Copperfield's future expressions of intense feeling. When he falls in love, he describes himself as soaked through with love for his inamorata: "If I may so express it, I was steeped in Dora. I was not merely over head and ears in love with her, but I was saturated through and through. Enough love might have been wrung out of me, metaphorically speaking, to drown anybody in; and yet there would have remained enough within me, and all over me, to pervade my entire existence" (535). Copperfield gives form to his desiring self by routing it through a series of metaphors, which he mobilizes self-consciously ("If I may so express it... metaphorically speaking"). He is "steeped in Dora," as if she expanded diffusely through him; from this association with wetness, he becomes a sponge, and the love imbues him. His body is the absent but implied link between intangible emotion and concrete image. The comedy comes from imagining his body as a sponge that could be squeezed — a malleable, dynamic body, which is reordered physically by the desires it expresses and contains. Like the routing of perceptions through keyholes, this image gives a palpable form to such emotions, portraying the usually amorphous space of the interior in absurdly material terms.

The phenomenon of Copperfield's embodied love for Dora is not quite presented as *her* getting inside him, but rather as *his desire for her* pervading him: that this love is barely interactive comports both with the narcissistic nature of David's desire and with the conclusion that Dora can never be more to him than an object. Copperfield's even more intense feelings of antipathy for Uriah Heep are a mutual affair, however, for he often experiences Heep as actively seeking to penetrate him. The uncanny effect of Heep's creepiness is indeed that it seems so invasive. When David first sees him, he states: "I caught a glimpse... of Uriah Heep breathing into [a] pony's nostrils, and immediately covering them with his hand, as if he were putting some spell upon him" (275). Heep gets under the skin of others, human and animal alike, and his own integument is positively repulsive when it seems to adhere to David: "Oh, what a clammy hand his was!" David exclaims after shaking his hand; "as ghostly to the touch as to the sight! I rubbed mine afterwards, to warm it, *and to rub his off*" (281; italics in original). If it is disagreeable to gaze on Heep, it is disgusting to be touched by him. The move from looking at Heep to touching him intensifies Copperfield's revulsion, and their ongoing contact haunts the hero as it seeps into him. The infectious surface of Heep's body oozes into David's consciousness in a distinctly tactile way: "Immediately feeling myself attracted towards Uriah Heep, who had a sort of fascination for me... I found [him] reading a great fat book, with such demonstrative attention, that his lank forefinger followed up every line as he read, and made clammy tracks along the page (or so I fully believed) like a snail" (290). Heep's imagined secretions give form to the powerful feelings of "attraction" and "fascination" he inspires, as if the stickiness of his body explained his capacity for clinging to the mind.

This collapse of interior and exterior leads David to fantasize that Heep's subjectivity itself is inverted, his repulsive outer form somehow seized by his menacing soul. He describes Heep as "sitting all awry as if his mean soul griped his body," and this thought makes him seem "to swell and grow before [his] eyes" (441). Wearing his mendacity on the outside, Heep in turn gets inside of Copperfield, pervading his consciousness to the extent of occupying his dreams on two occasions (293, 443). David counters this intrusion by imagining a violent reverse penetration: "I believe I had a delirious idea of seizing the red-hot poker out of the fire, and running him through with it" (441), he confesses when he learns of Uriah's interest in Agnes. The poker gets mixed up in David's dreams of Heep's disgusting form:

> I was so haunted at last by the idea ... that I stole into the next room to look at him. There I saw him, lying on his back, with his legs extending to I don't know where, gurglings taking place in his throat, stoppages in his nose, and his mouth open like a post-office. He was so much worse in reality than in my distempered fancy, that afterwards I was attracted to him in very repulsion, and could not help wandering in and out every half-hour or so, and taking another look at him. (443–44)

In retribution for feeling haunted and invaded by Heep, David fantasizes about skewering him, as though to say that the only way of overcoming the one form of penetration is to respond with another. Both the stabbing fantasy and the atrocious sight of the unconscious Heep assert the intermingling of Uriah's outward form and his appalling mental, spiritual, and moral interiors. That post office of a mouth is itself another kind of keyhole, a passageway between the inside and the outside of Heep's body and, at the same time, a pervious membrane between Heep and Copperfield.

It is tempting to read David's violent fantasies about Uriah in sexual terms, as some critics have done, not least because his anger is motivated by conscious loyalty to (and unconscious love for) Agnes, on whom Heep's interest lights.[13] That Agnes represents an idealized replacement for the inadequate Dora, who herself clearly replicated David's weak mother, only reinforces the Oedipal reading. While David's fantasized attack on Heep may be a form of rape, the psychological allegory should not obscure the somatic terms in which the novel casts these intersubjective relations. Rather than regarding psychoanalytic motives as the underlying explanation of the physical violence, we might read in the opposite direction, understanding the combination of antipathy and eroticism itself to arise from the portrayal of human relations in substantial, embodied form. Dickens imagines characters' insides as fleshy in order to depict them, even at the risk of degrading them; the illusion of psychological interiority arises from the very embodiment that would seem to contradict it.[14]

Charlotte Brontë's works share many of these practices, although their frequently paranoiac first-person narrative voices lend a far darker cast to the material shape of psychological interiority than Dickens's. While for Dickens, embodiment of the interior generally opens the self pleasurably to others, in Brontë's work, sensory incursion on an enclosed interior self is a potential site of pleasure, but only when its means of access is pain. *The Professor,* the first complete novel that Brontë wrote, provides her most dramatic staging of the relation between interior subject and the body. Rejected nine times by publishers and finally discarded by the author herself, the work appeared in print only posthumously, in 1857, and readers have always considered it minor, ill conceived, and uncompelling. Some critics have expressed gratitude for the novel's failure, which spurred Brontë to write the works for which she is renowned: *Jane Eyre* (1847), whose composition followed immediately upon *The Professor* and was intended as an antidote to it; and *Villette* (1853), which reworked much of its thematic material.[15] Yet to approach *The Professor* is not quite the exercise in desperation or antiquarianism that such a reputation might predict. At least one of its attributes merits attention: almost alone among Victorian novels written by women, *The Professor* has a sustained male first-person narrator.

It is tempting to explain this anomaly by way of Brontë's infatuation with Constantin Heger, the schoolmaster under whom she labored for two years in Brussels just before writing the novel. Unable to overtly articulate the passion she felt for her married Belgian *maître,* Brontë, according to this interpretation, sublimated her erotic blockage into fiction making. The tale — of a British man who travels to Brussels to teach English, where he marries a French-speaking student — would then embody the author's fantasy solution to her real-life frustration. Accordingly, Margaret Smith, in her introduction to the Oxford World's Classics edition of the novel, describes its plot as "a transcript of the author's experience rather pathetically brought to a happy conclusion by a piece of wish-fulfilment."[16] Such an explanation might be satisfactory but for the bizarre forms of authorial identification it requires. Under her male pseudonym, Currer Bell, Brontë puts the virtues of mastery, masculinity, and English-ness on the side of the narrator; the female writer seems to identify at once with teacher and student, man and woman, Englishman and for-eigner. The hero of *The Professor*, in this reading, represents a strange alloy of the author and the object of her affections: collapsing desire with identification, Brontë seems to imagine that if she cannot *have* the master, then perhaps she can *be* him.

Inviting though it is to attribute the novel's masculine narrative voice to these psychobiographical circumstances, to do so risks preemp-tively laying to rest its most remarkable feature. For whatever its causes, the work's peculiar narrative situation supplies Brontë the opportunity to imagine being a man, and in particular to speculate about how it feels to inhabit a male body. In pursuing a fantasy of male embodiment in *The Professor*, Brontë, I suggest, dramatizes the strangeness of the idea of *being inside any body* at all. Dwelling on this idea brings Brontë to a mode of representation cognate with Dickens's in its emphasis on the physical embodiment of selfhood. Through the voice of the male narrator as well as through the novel's imagery, Brontë makes peculiarly vivid the taken-for-granted situation of human interiority — the idea that human sub-jects dwell in their bodies and that bodies serve as containers or vehicles for invisible spiritual, psychological, or mental contents. By portraying in palpable terms the human body's enclosure of intangible subjectivity, she exploits the paradox of an immaterial soul, heart, or mind inhabiting the flesh. Pervaded by metaphors of entombment and boundary viola-tion, the novel's language exaggerates and estranges the conditions of embodiment. If adopting a male narrator leads Brontë to contemplate embodiment *tout court*, it also frees her from certain conventions; in con-trast to the stereotype of inflexible Victorian sexual roles, whereby mas-culinity entails dominance and femininity submission, Brontë does not consistently align modes of domination and subjugation with gender. More pertinent to her presentation of bodily invasion than a bifurcated model of gender are psychoanalytic accounts of masochism, some of which have helped to detach dominance status from gender. Yet while theories of masochism illuminate Brontë's work, *The Professor* requires us to modify such formulations, insisting, as it does, on the untranscendably material basis of subjectivity and eros. The novel suggests that a range of intimate human relations — working, loving, fighting, teaching — partake of penetration: subjects resist or submit to the incorporation of variously aversive and attractive objects, and that which is other than the self enters the self through processes that often painfully alter the subject.

The plot of *The Professor* (titled "The Master" until late in its career) parallels that of *Villette*, Brontë's more directly autobiographical final novel, but with the crucial difference of the narrator's gender. In an aggrieved first-person voice, William Crimsworth tells his story, that of an Englishman descended from aristocrats who finds that he must earn a living. At the start of the tale, he seeks out his brother, the owner of an industrial mill, who grudgingly agrees to hire him as clerk. When his employment and his relations soon become intolerable, Crimsworth travels to Brussels, where he is employed as an English teacher in adjoining boys' and girls' schools. As in *Villette*, the protagonist's adventures abroad make up the bulk of the novel, supplying the occasion for him to deride French manners, Belgian nationality, Roman Catholic religion, and Continental schooling. Crimsworth is tempted by a romance with Zoraïde Reuter, the directress (as she is known) of the girls' academy, but when he learns that she is already engaged to the director of the boys' school, he repudiates her. Despite her own engagement, Mlle Reuter grows jealous when soon thereafter Crimsworth meets and falls in love with a young Anglo-Swiss woman, Frances Henri, who is both a fellow teacher and his pupil in English. After some trials in their courtship, William and Frances marry and return to England to find domestic bliss.

At the level of metaphor, *The Professor* presents individual self-sustenance in terms of adamantine self-enclosure. The narrator frequently portrays himself as figuratively encased within armor or confined in a building, a portrayal that renders his psychological interior spatial and morphological: being stuck inside himself is like being lodged within a structure. The missing link between the interior and the structure is his body, which both oppressively and protectively encloses the self. For example, Crimsworth describes receiving from his belligerent brother "blasphemous sarcasms . . . on a buckler of impenetrable indifference" and further notes: "Erelong he tired of wasting his ammunition on a statue — but he did not throw away the shafts — he only kept them quiet in his quiver" (19). Concerned that a soft, pliable inside would be accessible to such barbs, Crimsworth exhibits extraordinary anxiety that others will pierce his armor or get under his skin. Instead of becoming strong and aggressive, however, he consistently makes himself hard and impervious. When he faces his female students for the first time, he recapitulates the imagery: "In less than five minutes they had thus revealed to me their characters and in less than five minutes I had buckled on a breast-plate of steely indifference and let down a visor of impassible austerity" (77). By enclosing the protagonist within metaphorical armor, Brontë alludes to the idea of the human subject inhabiting the material container that is the body. The vulnerability of this carapace, however, disrupts any secure idea of enclosure, and embodiment comes to seem both a limit and a possibility for the self or soul immured within.

The novel's settings, both literal and figurative, evoke a cloistral darkness that enhances the reader's sensation of being lodged in a paranoiac imagination with no possibility of escape.[17] Pervasive architectonic language makes bodies and buildings stand for each other; in addition to girding the protagonist in armor, the narrative extends such images to the edifices that enclose him. When he finds it impossible to stay at his teaching post in Brussels because of romantic tensions between himself and his employers, for instance, Crimsworth portrays himself as shut within rigid confines: "I seemed like one sealed in a subterranean vault, who gazes at utter blackness; at blackness ensured by yard-thick stone walls around and by piles of building above, expecting light to penetrate through granite and through cement firm as granite" (181). This profoundly dark conception of interior enclosure lies at the core of Brontë's notion of personhood, evoking through an objective metaphor the idea of the body as container of the self. When the narrative thematizes breaks into and out of an edifice, moreover, it describes these ruptures as physically degrading. When Crimsworth reaches the threshold of tolerance for his brother's insults, for example, he presents this convoluted figure: "The Antipathy, which had sprung up between myself and my Employer, striking deeper root and spreading denser shade daily, excluded me from every glimpse of the sunshine of life; and I began to feel like a plant growing in humid darkness out of the slimy walls of a well" (25). The image of vegetal infection is itself strangely infectious: the negative faculty ("Antipathy") is the foliage that shades Crimsworth from light, but he too becomes a plant — not thriving (like the emotion, which absorbs the light and nutrients) but sickly, a plant that suffers for its unfortunate placement. Contained within himself, the narrator imagines himself entombed in a well; because he also regards such enclosure as an effective resistance to infiltration, however, it becomes a miraculous resource for him. Having traveled so far down, he can go only up — a sentiment epitomized in the novel's epigraph: "He that is low need fear no fall" (2).[18]

Through these metaphors of structural confinement, Brontë affiliates psychological enclosure with physical entombment, showing both to be debasing. When early in the story William arrives at the factory town owned by his brother, the place itself is a nauseous landscape pulsating with industrial offal: "The Mill was before us, vomiting soot from its long chimney and quivering through its thick brick walls with the commotion of its iron bowels" (14). This excremental external landscape corresponds so closely with the narrator's internal one as to make it seem the dirt of the body's interior projected outward.[19] Throughout the novel, there is a fearful danger that the container will fail to keep the insides from spilling out or the outside from pressing in. The threat to interior integrity is especially worrisome when the protagonist encounters others; describing his resistance to his brother's abuses, for example, William states: "I had an instinctive feeling that it would be folly to let one's temper effervesce often with such a man as Edward. I said to myself, 'I will place my cup under this continual dropping — it shall stand there still and steady; when full it will run over of itself — meantime — patience'" (16). Taking the term *understanding* literally, by imagining himself as standing under his brother's steady drip, William recognizes — well in advance of his professorial vocation — that intellectual comprehension entails being permeated: it is the infusion of one mental presence by another, which effects changes in both. The process is both liberating and dirtying.

In light of recent historical scholarship, these densely planted, sometimes suffocating metaphors for mental faculties might be attributed to extraliterary sources. In her important book *Charlotte Brontë and Victorian Psychology*, Sally Shuttleworth aligns the plot of *The Professor* with shifts in Victorian social relations, illuminating the ideological content (especially in class and gender terms) of the phrenological, psychological, and social-science discourse that runs through Brontë's prose. Through a discussion of social power that explicitly invokes Foucault and an account of character evolution that implicitly relies on Freud, Shuttleworth charts a series of parallel developments: the protagonist moves from effeminacy to masculinity, from being an obsolete aristocrat to a productive bourgeois, from living in paranoid isolation to achieving socially integrated disciplinary subjectivity, and from conceiving of femininity as degraded to seeing it as chaste. In this model, the line of influence runs from psychological science to the literary work: Shuttleworth shows how, by way of both Zeitgeist and a glancing familiarity with medical sources, Brontë absorbed and reproduced ideas that originated elsewhere.[20] As an alternative, I propose that Brontë, with her uniquely literary tools, imagined the inside of the person as physically inhabiting the inside of the body in a way that resonates with other aspects of Victorian culture but is not necessarily determined by them. Most dramatically in *The Professor*, Brontë's practice of precariously piling up objective metaphors gives vivid form to the idea of embodied human subjectivity, of an interior with the properties of a material entity.

An example can suggest what might be gained by extending an analysis of the interior beyond a historicist assessment of ideology. Early in the novel, Crimsworth, while working for his brother, is assigned to translate some letters; following his usual practice, he guards his inner resources by shielding himself vigilantly against his brother's imagined examination: "I thought he was trying to read my character but I felt as secure against his scrutiny as if I had had on a casque with the visor down — or rather I shewed him my countenance with the confidence that one would shew an unlearned man a letter written in Greek — he might see lines, and trace characters, but he could make nothing of them — my nature was not his nature, and its signs were to him like the words of an unknown tongue" (17). Shuttleworth argues that the description in this passage refers to particular psychological methods of reading inner qualities from the surface: the scene "draws specifically on the discursive framework of phrenology which operated to legitimate the rising middle classes' claims to social power. The semiotic system in play is not that of physiognomy where signs were open for all to read, but the more competitive system of phrenology: bodily form still articulates inner qualities, but the signs hold meaning only for the initiated, schooled in the rules of translation."[21]

Shuttleworth's placement of the scene within nineteenth-century scientific contexts is illuminating, but the historical alignments of her reading obscure the peculiar ways in which the literary imagery renders material an enclosed interior. Brontë metaphorizes the speaker's self, at first by portraying him as ensconced within a helmet, which contains his "character" and so stands in for his body; but then the image shifts ("or

rather...."), and the body absented by the armor reappears to show its
face. This "countenance" is itself immediately metaphorized, however, and
becomes incomprehensible written language, which makes it as obscure
as his invisible "character." In portraying himself as an illegible character — both a person and a letter — Crimsworth thus condenses in himself
the very work of translation that he performs: the scribal drudgery at
which he labors becomes his body, both texts made obscure and difficult in
order to keep them secure and inviolate. The passage alludes to a system
of thought in which external features both dissemble and express interior
reality, but its overt mode of so doing is as much linguistic translation as
phrenology. William's supervisor (literally, the one who overlooks his
imagined visor) inspires his aggression because he is a reader — perhaps
a reader of skulls, but more demonstrably a reader of texts. As he goes
on to admit at the end of the passage, his brother is hardly illiterate and
can "read both French and German" (17); the narrator's hostility is thus
all the more surprising for its frank unfairness. Instead of either contract-
ing the scene to an instance of phrenological allusion or expanding it to
an ideologically laden allegory, we can preserve its psychological and
phenomenological complexity by observing how Brontë lends material
form to selfhood and, at the same time, folds it back into specifically tex-
tual terms. Brontë here grapples with the very question of how flat,
printed characters on a page generate an illusion of subjective depth, at
once indicating profundity and denying access to it.

In this example, the metaphor of the obscure text supplements the
narrative's usual depiction of human interiors as structurally enclosed;
the danger remains that someone else will reach inside and touch the
immured subject. Having considered how in the novel's first phase Brontë
depicts interiority, both in isolation and in conflict, I turn now to the
next, where she expands it to include romance. This shift coincides with
the protagonist's move abroad (appropriately enough, to "the Low Countries" [92]), where he opens himself to others; instead of dissolving, however, the conception of an enclosed interior intensifies. When Crimsworth
assumes the post of English master in a Brussels school, he soon finds himself threatened again, but this time the danger emanates from a woman:
the aggression of Zoraïde Reuter, directress of the neighboring girls'
academy, is an overt erotic enticement for Crimsworth. His employer at
the boys' school, M. Pelet, drives a probing question at the hero on the
subject of her penetration:

"Did she find out your weak point?"

"What is my weak point?"

"Why the sentimental. Any woman, sinking her shaft deep enough, will at last reach a fathomless spring of sensibility in thy breast, Crimsworth."

I felt the blood stir about my heart and rise warm to my cheek. (84)

The narrative contravenes even the pretense of ordinary romance in this courtship game manqué: gender distinctions are thrown over in favor of the more salient order of penetration, which positions Mlle Reuter and Crimsworth in respective roles of dominance and submission.

Penetration, as this passage suggests, is a capacious concept. For while it entails comprehension and sentiment, penetration also persistently retains the force of its physical meaning in the narrative's metaphorical tissue. Crimsworth develops the image in his description of Mlle Reuter's seductive tactics: "I watched her as keenly as she watched me; I perceived soon that she was feeling after my real character, she was searching for salient points and weak points and eccentric points; she was applying now this test, now that, hoping in the end to find some chink, some niche where she could put in her little firm foot and stand up on my neck" (80). The speaker again construes the psyche in architectural terms: the mind is a wall that his antagonist scales with her ingenuity. In allowing him to fantasize the directress pushing on the fleshy embodiment that encloses him, the distancing set of images lends material form to his subjectivity.[22] Pressing on us the morphology of a body ordinarily taken to be merely expressive of, or epiphenomenal to, a deep, invisible essence, this language gives form to that which is usually construed *as* the form.

In preserving both meanings of "penetration," Brontë's rhetoric solidifies the usually amorphous corporeality of intellectual and emotional phenomena. The metaphors reach a climax in this abortive flirtation when Zoraïde Reuter finally overcomes Crimsworth's resistance:

Me, she still watched, still tried by the most ingenious tests, she roved round me, baffled yet persevering; I believe she thought I was like a smooth and bare precipice which offered neither jutting stone nor tree-root, nor tuft of grass to aid the climber.... I found it at once pleasant and easy to evade all these efforts; it was sweet, when she thought me nearly won — to turn round and to smile in her very eyes, half scornfully, and then to witness her

> scarcely-veiled though mute mortification. Still she persevered and
> at last — I am bound to confess it, her finger, essaying, proving
> every atom of the casket — touched its secret spring and for a mo-
> ment — the lid sprung open, she laid her hand on the jewel within;
> whether she stole and broke it, or whether the lid shut again with
> a snap on her fingers — read on — and you shall know. (95–96)

The image of a person as a cliff to be surmounted, while unusual, is not entirely unaccountable. But Brontë imagines that cliff as smooth and barren of footholds — which, if one still holds the person in mind as the tenor of the metaphor, generates (negated) images of a character with ledges and tufts in him. This hyperbole has comic effects that are realized at the end of the passage, when Mlle Reuter moves from climbing the narrator to probing him: in either case, she prospects for secret information, and the surprise is that she ultimately finds it within the morphologically ambiguous "casket." When Mlle Reuter reaches her hand into Crimsworth's boxlike being, within which lies the "jewel" of his selfhood, one wonders what exactly she is doing. If she is metaphorically touching his heart, then why should the images be so concrete? Aim to read more anatomically than metaphysically and they become implausibly erotic or disgusting. If, in this erotically charged moment, that box is an opening low in the body, then the contours of the tightly guarded jewel it contains would, in physiological terms, have to be a point of stimulation hidden within flesh, such as a clitoris or a prostate. When the external form is penetrated to reach an internal being, the body cannot be fixed in terms of either gender or sexual position: in being opened, it displays features both female and male, anterior and posterior.[23]

Within the plot, this scene violates the protagonist's typical technique of protecting himself with impermeability. Yet its staging more than sufficiently enacts that strategy for the reader, as the narrative mimetically predicates revelation on an aggressive withholding. In a gesture familiar to readers of *Villette*, the paragraph deflects the mistress's hostility onto the protagonist, and from there it ricochets out onto the reader: he taunts us with his "wait and see." Like the professor's students, readers are made to suffer his punitory tutelage elsewhere in the novel. Sometimes there is a mimetic justification: "I turned; at my elbow stood a tall man . . . though just now, as I am not disposed to paint his portrait in detail, the reader must be content with the silhouette I have just thrown off; it was all I myself saw of him for the moment" (20). At other points, his withholding is more overtly capricious: "Now, reader, during the last two pages

I have been giving you honey fresh from flowers, but you must not live entirely on food so luscious; taste then a little gall — just a drop, by way of change" (210).

While bodily penetration is Brontë's dominant metaphor for access to human interiority, an important psychological component of the process is the subject's willing submission. Such submission intensifies the pleasure in self-enclosure, as when William, in the scene that convinces him to seek his own fortunes outside England, recounts being horsewhipped by his brother: "He flourished his tool — the end of the lash just touched my forehead. A warm excited thrill ran through my veins, my blood seemed to give a bound, and then raced fast and hot along its channels" (37). To a post-Freudian reader, such a passage begs to be understood in terms of masochism, the psychoanalytic concept most attuned to the dynamics of psychic life in its corporeal inhabitation. Masochism theory cannot wholly explain such language, but it usefully addresses the paradox of satisfaction deriving from pain or discomfort. Brontë's work compels us to revise psychoanalytic conceptions of masochism to understand how the material form of subjectivity might be more fundamental to desire than is gender, which both literary criticism and psychoanalytic theory have tended to see as the crucial factor. In Freud's theory, sadism and masochism are complementary and reversible: turning an aggressive impulse onto the ego produces masochism; displacement of a masochistic drive onto an object results in sadism. Equally pertinent to *The Professor* is Gilles Deleuze's account, which insists on the dissociation of masochism and sadism, treating them as two separate, incommensurable systems. For Deleuze, both systems comprise a master and a slave, but the subject positions they posit are radically incompatible. Deleuze presumes a masculine masochistic subject, while the normative masochist for Freud is female — or, to be more precise, for Freud masochism is a constituent of ordinary femininity.

Brontë, by contrast, does not associate masochism with one sex: with masochism, as with penetration, the novel eschews immutable gender positions. While in this respect her work conforms to neither theory, her account shares with Deleuze's the notion of a scene in which dominant and submissive roles are orchestrated by the submissive. At the same time, as in Freud's account, the roles are not fixed but reversible: the submissive figure may transform into the dominant one.[24] That Mlle Reuter subjugates Crimsworth does not, in itself, essentially distinguish Brontë's novel from a conventional order of sexuality, which can accommodate masochistic practices (such as those of Sacher-Masoch himself). Instead, erotic relations in *The Professor* remain dynamic, a fluid positionality that stands against a static conception of gender or dominance status, either in orthodox terms or in simple inversion. As John Kucich has shown, the "reversibility of power [is] a primary condition for sexual love" in Brontë's novels, where "a privileged, eroticized kind of subjectivity...bears no direct relationship to social or sexual identity."[25]

These theories of masochism clarify some of the psychic contortions in *The Professor* and suggest why inhabitation of a material interior should be so abasing as well as so pleasurably penetrable. Like the reversible masochist of Freud, the novel's protagonist, once he is degraded by the object of his affections, turns to gain mastery over her. As he is "on the brink of falling in love" with Mlle Reuter (97), Crimsworth discovers (to the gratification of his appetite for humiliation) that she is betraying him with his employer, M. Pelet (98–101). After eavesdropping on them, the narrator savors the embarrassment of hearing himself abused: "But Zoraïde Reuter? Of course her defection had cut me to the quick? That sting must have gone too deep for any Consolations of Philosophy to be available in curing its smart? Not at all.... Reason was my physician; she began by proving that the prize I had missed was of little value" (103). Despite this disavowal, the painful penetration ("that sting...too deep") cannot so blithely be dismissed. When he determines to repudiate Mlle Reuter, the woman he momentarily imagined he desired, Crimsworth unwittingly stimulates *her* desire both to attract and to rebuff him. To his dismay, he discovers that his tutelage in subjugation (first at his brother's factory, then at her school) has rendered him all too competent a master: like a self-vindicating dictator, he explains that "servility creates despotism." Not quite blaming the victim, he now discovers the masochism in her, which generates in him a corresponding tyrant to tend to her needs. "This slavish homage," he continues, "instead of softening my heart, only pampered whatever was stern and exacting in its mood. The very circumstance of her hovering round me like a fascinated bird, seemed to transform me into a rigid pillar of stone; her flatteries irritated my scorn, her blandishments confirmed my reserve" (118). The stiffness that Crimsworth here exhibits in response to Mlle Reuter's obsequiousness complies with the novel's imagery of enclosure: it is less an amorous erection than the ossification induced by encountering another's assertive desire.

The directress thus comes to represent the type of masochist that interests Deleuze, for she cultivates in her partner the refusing master that her desire requires. Yet Crimsworth is not content to remain a consensual dominator; he soon develops a full-fledged appetite for seeing her vanquished. His is not, however, a conventional form of Sadean domination either, for in repudiating Mlle Reuter in favor of Frances Henri, he displays a mastery that comprehends subjugation so well because of its perfervid identification with the slave:

> Now it was precisely about this time that the Directress, stung by my coldness, bewitched by my scorn, and excited by the preference she suspected me of cherishing for another, had fallen into a snare of her own laying, was herself caught in the meshes of the very passion with which she wished to entangle me. . . . I had ever hated a tyrant, and behold the possession of a slave, self-given, went near to transform me into what I abhorred! There was at once a sort of low gratification in receiving this luscious incense from an attractive and still young worshipper and an irritating sense of degradation in the very experience of the pleasure. When she stole about me with the soft step of a slave — I felt at once barbarous and sensual as a pasha — I endured her homage sometimes, sometimes I rebuked it — my indifference or harshness served equally to increase the evil I desired to check. (169–71)

Crimsworth chafes at finding himself Mlle Reuter's master, yet he is surprised to discover that he enjoys it — not in spite of feeling demeaned by degrading her, but *as a result* of being brought so low. The sense of degradation — by which the master comes to imitate the slave — itself becomes enjoyable ("low gratification"), until there seems to be no top-pleasure at all. Recapitulating this dynamic by projecting it onto a national screen, the narrator imagines himself a "sensual" Oriental despot: exalted by rank and gender, he is at the same time deplored for his "barbarous" nature.

This depiction of erotic pain differs from both the Freudian model, in which a gendered subject moves between masochistic and sadistic phases, and the Deleuzian one, in which masochistic and sadistic scenes prescribe gendered positions of master and slave. With its indeterminate gender and variable position, the debased subject in Brontë's portrayal determines the course of action despite being penetrated. In the Brontean dynamic, neither gender nor the axis of dominance and submission arrests subjects in position, for each participant identifies with the other; power is ceaselessly abdicated in order continually to be reinvented. The erotic itself becomes another site at which to worry over the material status of interiority, for these relations suggest that human subjectivity has a fundamentally corporeal basis, grounded not in anatomical sex (which critics usually regard as the foundation of characters' embodiment in Brontë's works) but in the body's degraded substance. Materiality conceptually precedes and corporeally overwhelms the attributes of gender in this account of reshaping the interior. Erotic attachments between characters are masochistic not simply because they adopt a language of penetration but because, in reaching and affecting the heart or the spirit, such connections occur across a tissue of embodied substance.

Obdurately enclosed inwardness combines with convoluted gender identifications throughout the novel, making it difficult to ascribe to Crimsworth any psychological development toward something like sympathy, either with other characters or with the reader. As the novel advances, however, it pursues the material representation of interiority and expatiates on new and varied forms of debasement, penetration, and masochism. In building on the narrator's relations with his brother and the directress, these dynamics become increasingly interactive, principally in the arenas of romance and pedagogy. An *intersubjective* inwardness develops in Crimsworth's courtship of and marriage to his pupil Frances Henri, for the novel's site of identification, as it progresses, partly shifts to her. The change in the location of abjection is accomplished so smoothly because of the powerful identification between William and Frances: like him, Frances is a teacher, and she assumes his old traits of reserve and self-denial, discipline and weedlike tenacity. By the time he encounters her in his Belgian classroom, William is no longer presented as "a plant growing in humid darkness"; now he is the suave horticulturist who brings her up and out. She in turn takes on the characteristics of his immature self, and as *her* inwardness receives narrative attention, he exfoliates it:

> To speak truth, I watched this change much as a gardener watches the growth of a precious plant and I contributed to it too, even as the said gardener contributes to the development of his favourite. To me it was not difficult to discover how I could best foster my pupil, cherish her starved feelings and induce the outward manifestation of that inward vigour which sunless drought and blighting blast had hitherto forbidden to expand. Constancy of Attention — a kindness as mute as watchful, always standing by her, cloaked in the rough garb of austerity and making its real nature known only by a rare glance of interest, or a cordial and gentle word; real respect masked with seeming imperiousness, directing, urging her actions — yet helping her too and that with devoted care. (137)

Crimsworth portrays his favored pupil in the same language of gardens and nourishment that he had earlier used to describe himself.[26] He is the agent of Frances's blossoming who helps externalize her inner qualities, yet even as he assists her, he keeps up the guard on his own interior: each is veiled to the other and yet visible beneath the veil. The identification between them creates the impression that their relations occur between two phases — one inchoate, the other advanced — of a single subject. That the relationship takes place virtually within a single consciousness contributes to the story's prominent inwardness.[27]

Crimsworth molds Frances into the woman that he wants her to be, and his effort is successful largely because, in so doing, he makes her into the woman he has already been. Evidence for William's immature femininity abounds in the novel's early phases. In describing himself by contrast with his brother (who, as if to secure his own masculinity, is surrounded by "a group of very pretty girls with whom he conversed gaily"), William says: "I looked weary, solitary, kept-down — like some desolate tutor or governess" (19). Such is the prototypical Brontë heroine, and such is Frances Henri too, when she eventually appears. That she has two men's names lends credence to the notion that she, in turn, is an immature male heroine. Brontë makes gender itself seem volitional, practically determined by the exigencies of particular narrative configurations rather than affixed to either anatomical sex or a character's dominance or submission. Like the female author who adopts a masculine pseudonym and a male narrative voice, the characters in the novel at times seem capable of choosing their genders.

With the emergence of the romance between William and Frances, the novel turns to what appear to be standard heterosexual relations, but it does not thereby diminish the threat that contact between them might be perilously penetrating for both parties. When the two lovers reunite after a painful separation, for example, the master, discovering his student rooted in the earth of a cemetery, approaches her unseen from the rear:

> I put on my spectacles and passed softly close behind her.... While bending sullenly earthward beneath the pressure of despondency, while following with my eyes the track of sorrow on the turf of a grave-yard, here was my lost jewel dropped on the tear-fed herbage, nestling in the mossy and mouldy roots of yew-trees!
> ...I loved the tones with which she uttered the words:
> "Mon maître! Mon Maître!"
> I loved the movement with which she confided her hand to my hand; I loved her, as she stood there, pennyless and parentless,

for a sensualist — charmless, for me a treasure...personification
of discretion and forethought, of diligence and perseverance, of
self-denial and self-control. (154–56)

William admires Frances for those qualities of mind — of a well-defended,
carefully shielded mind — that reflect him back to himself. Her value appears in the contrast (or, perhaps, the tantalizing contact) she makes with
the fetid atmosphere surrounding her. He discovers the gemlike Frances
emerging from the graveyard's putrescent matter much as Mlle Reuter had
earlier located a pleasure-giving "jewel" buried within him. Like Frances,
this jewel cannot be reached without the dirt, imagined to surround it, con-
taminating the penetrator. In adapting the penetration imagery to Frances,
William installs in her the same interior depth that marks him as an embodied subject. While the story might here appear to conform to the normative heterosexuality of the marriage plot, this institution is nearly un-
recognizable in the embodied form that Brontë lends it with these objects.

Frances's submission is the goad to William's desire, yet her "self-
control," the sign of her desirability, serves magically to control *him*.
Unlike Mlle Reuter, whose penetration Crimsworth found intolerable
and whose submission he thought repellent, Frances dominates him
through her very self-degradation. Their romantic relations are not organized by traditional alignments between masculinity and dominance,
yet neither do they conform to Sacher-Masoch's scene, wherein a phallic
dominatrix rules over (even as she is ultimately motivated by) her devoted male slave. As Crimsworth indicates, he, the master, is held in
thralldom to his pupil, who in turn derives pleasure from being domi-
nated by him:

> Reproofs suited her best of all: while I scolded she would chip
> away with her pen-knife at a pencil or a pen; fidgetting a little,
> pouting a little, defending herself by monosyllables, and when
> I deprived her of the pen or pencil, fearing it would be all cut away,
> and when I interdicted even the monosyllabic defence, for the
> purpose of working up the subdued excitement a little higher, she
> would at last raise her eyes and give me a certain glance, sweet-
> ened with gaiety, and pointed with defiance, which, to speak
> truth, thrilled me as nothing had ever done; and made me, in a
> fashion (though happily she did not know it), her subject, if not
> her slave. (164)

The mutual infliction of pain — he chides in order to excite her, she defies
so as to captivate him — elaborates the relations between master and

pupil. Frances actually makes the permanent institution of pedagogy a condition for her acceptance of William's proposal. Her insistence that the intercourse of husband and wife replicate that of teacher and student, while it nominally affirms supposedly ordinary, Freudian-style feminine masochism, also functions emphatically to enslave him:

> "Monsieur désire savoir si je consens — si — enfin, si je veux me marier avec lui?"
>
> "Justement."
>
> "Monsieur sera-t-il aussi bon mari qu'il a été bon maître?"
>
> "I will try, Frances."
>
> A pause — then with a new, yet still subdued inflexion of the voice; an inflexion which provoked while it pleased me; accompanied too by a "sourire à la fois fin et timide" in perfect harmony with the tone:
>
> "C'est à dire, Monsieur sera toujours un peu entêté, exigeant, volontaire — ?"
>
> ...My arm, it is true, still detained her, but with a restraint that was gentle enough, so long as no opposition tightened it. (206–7)[28]

Perversely insisting on speaking French (as she does whenever she wishes to irritate — and then to be punished by — William), Frances coerces him so that he will submit to controlling her. "Provoked while it pleased" — this is how a Brontean marriage is sustained. And sustained it is: "Give me a voluntary kiss," he commands paradoxically after she accepts his proposal (209). Ten years later, it continues: "She rarely addressed me in class, when she did — it was with an air of marked deference — it was her pleasure, her joy to make me still the Master in all things" (232). Although such language could be read as exemplifying patriarchal control, it encodes a more flexible dynamic, by virtue of the gender-inverted narration, the unstable power relations in the eroticism depicted, and the persistently material form taken by the intersubjective contact.[29]

Through its plot of a master marrying his student, *The Professor* merges the realms of working, teaching, and loving; as all three activities fundamentally entail relations between self and body, they also overlap in representing ethereal interior qualities by means of material form. We have seen how, in the arena of romance, erotic contact takes invasive metaphors and how mental contact is itself imagined as erotic. In the register of pedagogy, Brontë's language of debasement and penetration is particularly pronounced: peppered with tutorials in ramming a foreign tongue down student throats, *The Professor* suggests that, like the visual, verbal communication pierces the bodily shell. Learning a foreign language — the principal subject of instruction in this classroom drama — has corporeal effects, and characters' nationalities, along with their attendant moral valuations, are correspondingly imprinted on their bodies. Crimsworth records seeing "a band of very vulgar, inferior-looking Flamandes, including two or three examples of that deformity of person and imbecility of intellect whose frequency in the Low Countries would seem to furnish proof that the climate is such as to induce degeneracy of the human mind and body" (92). By contrast, the relative plainness of Crimsworth's British students and the disorder of their toilettes testifies not to slovenliness but to an ingenuous lack of sexual precocity:

> Their characteristics were, clean but careless dress, ill-arranged hair (compared with the tight and trim foreigners) erect carriage, flexible figures, white and taper hands, features more irregular but also more intellectual than those of the Belgians, grave and modest countenances, a general air of native propriety and decency; by this last circumstance alone I could at a glance distinguish the daughter of Albion and nursling of Protestantism from the foster-child of Rome, the protégée of Jesuitry. (94)

Similarly recognizing Frances's quality by discerning her "pure and silvery" English accent (115), Crimsworth recruits her for Britain in what amounts to a simultaneous cultural makeover and national recovery of her. By means of tutorials in English, he reorients his star pupil's cultural identity, producing a shift in allegiance from her French-speaking Swiss father to the hearty stock of her mother, whose "ancestors were all English" (128). The mutual identification between the two characters, which precipitates their romance, prevails in national terms as well.[30] For as long as William feels himself an alien in a barbaric land, he is subject to degrading penetrations by others; once he is transformed into a master, he becomes the confident native while Frances assumes his discarded national insecurity.

If nationality is expressed physically, it stands to reason that the transformation from foreigner to native, which both William and Frances undergo, would also be recorded on the bodily frame. So long enfeebled by inhabiting the lowlands, Frances experiences somatic improvements as a result of "becoming" British.

> [She] did not become pale or feeble in consequence of her sedentary employment [studying English] — perhaps the stimulus it

communicated to her mind counterbalanced the inaction it imposed on her body. She changed indeed, changed obviously and
rapidly — but it was for the better. When I first saw her, her countenance was sunless, her complexion colourless . . . ; now the cloud
had passed from her mien. . . . That look of wan emaciation . . . having vanished from [her face], a clearness of skin, almost bloom —
and a plumpness almost embonpoint softened the decided lines of
her features. Her figure shared in this beneficial change — it became rounder and as the harmony of her form was complete and
her stature of the graceful middle height, one did not regret (or at
least *I* did not regret) the absence of confirmed fulness, in contours, still slight, though compact, elegant, flexible. (136)

William's detailed catalog of his bride's physical attributes demonstrates
the bodily benefits of her linguistic acculturation. Like some early Berlitz
hawker, he seems to promise, "Learn English — you'll look better, too!"
Zoraïde Reuter, who "was quite sufficiently acquainted with English to
understand it when read or spoken in her presence, though she could
neither speak nor write it herself" (138), suffers accordingly. The fate of
her body, by contrast with Frances's, is to wind up miserable and fat: at
the end, Crimsworth learns, the Pelets' "domestic harmony is not the
finest in the world," and "she weighs twelve stones now" (246–47).

Crimsworth develops various pedagogic means to train Frances as
wife, mother, teacher, and citizen, and as she cultivates expertise in the
arts of reading and writing, she becomes a new, less surprising face for
authorial identification. Frances's replication of William's efforts explains
one curious fact about the novel: despite its foregrounding of Crimsworth as narrator and the self-consciousness in his relations with the
reader, it is Frances whom we ultimately see engaged in literary composition. Certainly there are the obligatory scenes of William composing
his life story; toward the conclusion, for example, he states, "It is in the
library of my own home I am now writing" (237; see also 241–47). Yet
William has always known how to write, while the real education in literary accomplishment belongs to Frances, a development concomitant with
her romantic discovery of pleasure in pain and with the recovery of her
national identity. Although these are his *mémoires*, they thus often look
like her *devoirs*. Mlle Reuter's initial objections suggest the social inversion threatened by so elevating Frances: "Her sphere of life is somewhat
beneath [that of the students]. . . . She rather needs keeping down than
bringing forward; and then I think, Monsieur — it appears to me that ambition — *literary* ambition especially, is not a feeling to be cherished in

the mind of a woman" (139; italics in original). If Brontë's composition has proved anything, however, it is the error of Mlle Reuter's proposition: literary accomplishment results not from "bringing forward" those who are low but rather from "keeping [them] down."

Putting aside Mlle Reuter's antifeminism and his own misogyny, William sees his task as being to make an English *littérateur* of Frances: "The young Anglo-Swiss evidently derived both pleasure and profit from the study of her Mother-tongue; in teaching her I did not of course confine myself to the ordinary school-routine; I made instruction in English a channel for instruction in literature" (135). Drilling an emblematic English Channel in this Swiss through which to flush the greasy French out of her, Crimsworth refreshes his student with antiseptic British national literature. And naturally enough, when Frances writes, she composes tales of rising triumphantly up from — or in — degradation. First she writes an essay about a fallen king who, exalted in his debasement, makes an apt persona for the self-abnegating *étudiante* (121). Her second composition is a poem that tells the story of "self-denial and self-control" on the part of a student (156), which enables her ultimately to rise up and unite with her harsh, refusing master: "Obedience was no effort soon, / And labour was no pain" (200). The work sensually elaborates her self-abasement:

> The prize, a laurel-wreath, was bound
>   My throbbing forehead on.
>
> Low at my master's knee I bent,
>   The offered crown to meet;
> Its green leaves through my temples sent
>   A thrill as wild as sweet.
>
> The strong pulse of Ambition struck
>   In every vein I owned;
> At the same instant, bleeding broke
>   A secret, inward wound. (204)

The composition is successfully, even aggressively, performative: it accomplishes Frances's admission of interest in William and immediately precipitates the marriage proposal from him, far more decisively than happens within the poem itself. The "secret, inward wound" of her poem, that is to say, breaks open within *him*, for the resisting hardness of the student's abasement dissolves the master's cold refusal. This poem nested in a fiction condenses the whole structure of Brontë's imaginative enterprise. In her authorial persona, the masterful Currer Bell condescends to "his" character, the masochistic professor, who in turn writes a tale that enables him to achieve the romance at which the author herself failed. Crimsworth inspires his self-effacing student to write a story of her own — a story in which, once again, a student who loves her master overcomes national difference and personal diffidence in order that they can profess their love to each other. Crimsworth translates and transcribes this poem of Frances's, which Brontë herself wrote while resident at the Pensionnat Heger (in English — Frances's French "original" is itself a fiction).[31] Brontë modifies and incorporates the lyric in her next novel, a work in which the student protagonist, who again falls in love with an enticingly abusive master, borrows her name from the poem: "Jane."[32]

The embodiment of pedagogy extends to pupils besides the one whom the hero plans to marry; in portraying the classroom, Brontë makes teaching and learning altogether physical activities.[33] In Crimsworth's description of his male Belgian pupils, for instance, they threaten him with immovable obstructions to the flow of knowledge:

> Their intellectual faculties were generally weak, their animal propensities strong; thus there was at once an impotence and a kind of inert force in their natures; they were dull, but they were also singularly stubborn, heavy as lead and like lead, most difficult to move.... They recoiled with repugnance from any occupation that demanded close study or deep thought; had the abhorred effort been extorted from them by injudicious and arbitrary measures on the part of the professor, they would have resisted as obstinately, as clamorously as desperate swine; and though not brave, singly, they were relentless, acting en masse. (60)

The teacher presents instruction as a process by which he forces intellectual matter against the students' resistant musculature. Like so much else in the novel, it is a filthy interaction, befouling master and pupil alike. Yet having established the repellently obdurate nature of this swinish, subliterate "mass," Crimsworth expounds not on the need for aggressive force to manage them but instead on the value of moderation to pedagogy:

> It was necessary then to exact only the most moderate application from natures so little qualified to apply; to assist, in every practicable way, understandings so opaque and contracted; to be ever gentle, considerate, yielding even, to a certain point, with dispositions so irrationally perverse; — but, having reached that culminating point of indulgence — you must fix your foot, plant it, root it in rock — become immutable as the towers of Ste. Gudule, for a

> step — but half a step further, and you would plunge headlong
> into the gulph of imbecility — there lodged, you would speedily
> receive proofs of Flemish gratitude and magnanimity in showers
> of Brabant saliva and handfuls of Low-Country mud. (60–61)

Through their superfluity of repugnant objective metaphors, these passages portray instruction as a struggle between a master and students who physically resist comprehending him. Confronted by their implacable hardness, the teacher must be harder still: to get learning into their heads is a battle of wills, enacted as one of brute strength. When the metaphor shifts, Crimsworth endures the risk of falling into the putrescent "gulph of imbecility," replete with Flemish ordure. The dialectic continues one turn further, for he fears that in not being understood (penetrated) by the students, he will be materially infected (penetrated) with the foulness of their idiocy. Pedagogy thus amounts to the professor's debasement of himself down to the lowest position he can tolerate, identifying with the students (who are lower even than that) and then asserting his mastery over them. "Having thus taken them down a peg in their self-conceit," he states, "the next step was to raise myself in their estimation" (57).

Try as he might to dominate his charges, Crimsworth turns out to be enslaved by them. The rhetoric of his pedagogical approach to his male pupils resonates strikingly with the language of his female love objects toward him, showing in another register how Brontë subordinates gender to other kinds of distinctions in the novel. The narrator conceives of himself as standing above his students, in a posture echoing the one that the directress assumes with respect to him: with a foot planted on the neck of the inferior, exacting obedience. The connection to Mlle Reuter, along with the fact of Frances herself being a student, ensures not only that romance and pedagogy are always close together but also that, here too, the way to mastery is through degradation. Deleuze's discussion of the relation between pedagogy and masochism is instructive in this context:

> [Masochism] is all persuasion and education. We are no longer [as
> in sadism] in the presence of a torturer seizing upon a victim and
> enjoying her all the more because she is unconsenting and un-
> persuaded. We are dealing instead with a victim in search of a tor-
> turer and [one] who needs to educate, persuade and conclude an
> alliance with the torturer in order to realize the strangest of
> schemes.... [The masochist] is essentially an educator and thus
> runs the risk inherent in educational undertakings.[34]

Contrary to the implications of a language in which *professeur* is synony-
mous with *maître,* Deleuze's masochist is the teacher who instructs a
dominatrix in the lessons of his pain. Yet just as with romance, so too
with pedagogy does Brontë's material imagery make the structural positions (now of teacher and student) reversible. For even if at first glance
Crimsworth looked like a pedant, far from the Deleuzian educator-as-
masochist, the relations between teacher and student make these roles as
fungible as those of master and slave.

When his teaching takes him before a class of female students,
Crimsworth both identifies with and expresses desire for them. His gender identifications and dominance status are so mobile that his approach
to his female pupils, although more erotically charged than with the
boys, again shows mastery and subjugation to be transmutable. In striv-
ing to differentiate his own abasement from that of his female pupils,
Crimsworth points out that he sees more, and worse, of his charges than
others do:

> Know, O incredulous Reader! that a master stands in a somewhat
> different relation towards a pretty, light-headed, probably igno-
> rant girl to that occupied by a partner at a ball or a gallant on the
> promenade.... He finds her in the schoolroom, plainly dressed,
> with books before her; owing to her education or her nature books
> are to her a nuisance and she opens them with aversion, yet her
> teacher must instil into her mind the contents of these books —
> that mind resists the admission of grave information, it recoils, it
> grows restive; sullen tempers are shewn, disfiguring frowns spoil
> the symmetry of the face, sometimes coarse gestures banish grace
> from the deportment while muttered expressions, redolent of
> native and ineradicable vulgarity, desecrate the sweetness of the
> voice.... In short, to the tutor, female youth, female charms are
> like tapestry hangings of which the wrong side is continually
> turned towards him, and even when he sees the smooth, neat,
> external surface, he so well knows what knots, long stitches and
> jagged ends are behind that he has scarce a temptation to admire
> too fondly the seemly forms and bright colours exposed to gen-
> eral view. (109–10)

At once lowering himself beneath his students and lording his superiority over them, Crimsworth distinguishes his interest in the girls from that
of a deluded suitor ("a partner at a ball"), with whom he nonetheless
claims a right to compete. Teaching morphologically approximates love-
making, as the master "must instil" knowledge "into [the student's] mind"
and thereby supply an antidote to external vulgarity and coarseness.

According to the simile of the tapestry, the teacher sees behind or below his charges, confronting regions of neglect ordinarily hidden from sight; the unappealing backside comprises ignorance and bad temper, while the pleasing "external surface" includes fashion, accomplishment, and *politesse*. Like the plants and architectural elements, the tapestry introduces a metaphoric object for the person's fleshly existence, suggesting in its unappetizing connotations the debasement consequent on subjective embodiment itself.

Gazing on such deceptive figures might promise an onlooker some hygienic distance from them, for vision ordinarily offers spatially remote, disembodied authority. And indeed (as more famously in *Villette*), discipline is maintained in the Belgian academy by means of "a building with porous walls, . . . a false ceiling; every room . . . has eye-holes and ear-holes, and what the house is, the inhabitants are, very treacherous" (134). Like Dickens's keyholes, this architecturally embodied model of perception provides an alternative to the association of vision with modern disciplinary power — a link that critics have often made on the basis of Foucault's discussion of Bentham's Panopticon.[35] We might instead consider how Brontë challenges the sensory hegemony of distanced looking by presenting vision as one among many bodily sensations. Visual consumption is no less wholly embodied than other forms of apprehension in the novel — as it is in the works we have considered by Dickens — for while Mlle Reuter's *pensionnat* symbolizes her deceitfulness ("what the house is, the inhabitants are"), Brontë, in describing the academy, reverses the procedure of metaphorizing a character as a building: here she animates the schoolhouse itself, portraying it as a body replete with ocular and auricular organs. Instead of opposing embodied authority, surveillance comes to seem corporeal: the novel begs the question whether the "eye-holes and ear-holes" in "every room" are holes for the eyes and the ears or, rather, the bodily holes that *are* the eyes and the ears. Looking (unseen) and listening (unheard) are less a detached means of control than an elaboration on the dynamics of one person's insides being penetrated bodily by another.

In this imaginative landscape, the human interior can materially be reached through even the most apparently insubstantial contact. In the passage quoted earlier in which Crimsworth describes his professional crisis as making him feel "like one sealed in a subterranean vault, who gazes at utter blackness," he goes on to console himself with the knowledge that "there are chinks, or there may be chinks in the best adjusted masonry; there was a chink in my cavernous cell; for eventually I saw, or seemed to see a ray; pallid indeed, and cold, and doubtful, but still a ray, for it shewed that narrow path which Conscience had promised" (181). If the body that encloses the self is a building, then it is not entirely sealed shut: sight itself is a means of egress and contact. As if to substantiate a mistrust of distance vision, both William and Frances (like the author herself) are nearsighted (29, 177). This myopia impedes the lures of disembodied surveillance; figuratively, these characters, like the blind, read with their hands. Just as the porous schoolhouse bodies forth Mlle Reuter's capacity for spying, so too Crimsworth's short sight (like so much else about his body) finds a vivid architectural inhabitation. Upon learning that a boarded-up window in his bedroom faces the garden of the girls' school, William reports:

> The first thing I did was to scrutinize closely the nailed boards,
> hoping to find some chink or crevice which I might enlarge and so
> get a peep at the consecrated ground; my researches were vain —
> for the boards were well joined and strongly nailed; it is astonish-
> ing how disappointed I felt — I thought it would have been so
> pleasant to have looked out upon a garden... to have studied
> female character in a variety of phases, myself the while, sheltered
> from view by a modest muslin curtain. (58–59)

The blind window gives substantive form to the protagonist's own dimness of vision: his search for a "chink or crevice" in the boards (echoing Mlle Reuter's distinctly haptic probing of him) extends the structural elaboration of his body. His self inhabits a body that is like a building; by analogy, his body inhabits a building that is itself like a body. Modesty moves metaleptically from the person of the narrator (or from the "female characters") to become an attribute of the curtain. Such a displacement serves modestly to indicate that were the master to spy the female students, it would be tantamount to sexually violating them. Probing with the eyes shades into other penetrations, as we learn from the narrative's violently tactile metaphors for sight. Like loving and teaching, this embodied account of looking — another version of Dickens's keyhole — mutually implicates subject and object, because it gets inside both.

My dual interests in this chapter, in the form of the interior and in the sensory channels for reaching it, indicate the critical approaches in relation to which I have situated my argument. On the one hand, my analysis accords with the type of psychoanalytic theory that supplies a basis for conceiving of subjective inwardness in material terms. In using the psycho-analytically derived concept of masochism, I have aimed to apply its insights about psychic arrangements among eroticism, domination, and embodiment while eschewing its prescriptive dimensions, which locate such practices in perceived perversions that emerge from dysfunctional family dynamics (such as a failure to resolve the Oedipal complex). Further, in focusing intensively on the language of particular scenes, I have avoided accounting psychologically for plotlines or character evolution — a usual (and often unarticulated) psychoanalytic approach that essentially retraces a novel's plot to expose its developmental logic.[36] I have instead sought to use psychoanalysis as a tool for exploring the psychic and symbolic dimensions of Brontë's material presentation of the inside.

At the same time, my interest in the embodiment of subjectivity puts into practice some phenomenological methods for attending to depictions of sensory experience and interiority. Merleau-Ponty's theory that subjects and objects are mutually and reversibly constituted through bodily perception, outlined in the previous chapter, supplies a means of approaching the dynamic account of the interior that Dickens and Brontë present. I have resisted assimilating bodily signification into a predetermined set of ideological positions, aiming instead to stay with the verbal particulars for evoking embodied experience, and emphasizing its intersubjective aspects and the fungible quality of identity formations. By dwelling on some of the perplexing weirdness of these representations, we may discover possibilities other than assigning them to a grand narrative of Oedipal anxiety or disciplinary coercion.

In presenting the self as physically inhabiting the body, the novels we have considered by Dickens and Brontë conceive of a human subject actively engaged in palpable, reciprocal exchange with the world, including other embodied subjects. Through the body's sensory channels and orifices, the material world comes into and goes out of the self, altering and affecting mind, soul, and heart. These processes generate a self at once bounded in the body's material substance and open to being changed and reshaped. The interior being is both inextricable from the flesh and mutable; its identifications (masculine or feminine, dominant or submissive, master or student) shift fluidly, while it remains fundamentally embodied. In this literary performance, the senses open the subject to the world, allowing the interior to be imagined as both material and ethereal, physical and metaphysical; the body that encloses the subject is mutually constitutive of its mental, emotional, and spiritual contents.

3

Skin

Surface and Sensation in
Trollope's "The Banks of the Jordan"

This chapter originates in a fundamental question about embodiment: what does the skin cover? Responses to this question are traditionally articulated in two different registers: the physical and the spiritual. The skin is the integument that encloses the visceral interior of the body, yet it is also the membrane within which, mysteriously and ethereally, the human essence is supposed to reside. The outside surface of the body and its first line of defense against the external world, the skin is also the psychically projected shield that contains the self within. Both tactile membrane and enclosure, the skin is a permeable boundary that permits congress between inside and outside, whether that interior is conceived in material or metaphysical terms. The skin thus forms the border not only between bodily interior and exterior but also between psychical and physical conceptions of the self. As a social signifier, moreover, the color, texture, and appearance of the skin have often been presumed to testify to what resides within or beneath it.

By virtue of its peculiar status as both physical embodiment and psychical envelope — both a surface projected from inside and a mask immediately comprehensible from without — the skin has crucial, if sometimes conflicting, psychological, spiritual, and social functions. Most materially, as the exquisitely sensitive seat of tactile perception, capable of fine discriminations on the basis of pressure, density, texture, and temperature, the skin has physiological functions that situate it at the crossover point between the phenomenal world and all that is contained inside: the internal organs, the mind, the emotions, the soul.[1] As the physical embodiment of the imagined boundaries of the self, the skin also gives a morphological dimension to the ego; its external appearance in turn has shaping effects on subject formation and self-perception. The skin is the beginning and end of the body.

The following discussion addresses these issues through three separate but converging lines of inquiry: literary, theoretical, and historical. My analysis focuses on a tale by Anthony Trollope that dramatizes the expressive and impressionable capacities of the skin through the story of a body subject to confusions of gender and race, as well as physical distress. I employ some insights of Didier Anzieu's psychoanalytic discussion of the so-called skin ego to think through Trollope's representations and, in so doing, also use Frantz Fanon's analysis of race to consider how Trollope's work requires revisions of Anzieu's theory. By situating Trollope's story within a contemporary frame of racial characterization and urban sanitation, I demonstrate how historical context shapes the literary, psychological, and spiritual functions of the skin as both enclosure and projection.

Trollope's story "The Banks of the Jordan" supplies an especially incisive staging of the question: how to go beneath the surface of the body and reach profound truths within? The answer, I will suggest, is that, in 1861, one cannot get very far: the narrator of Trollope's tale finds himself perpetually stuck on the surface. When Trollope, like Dickens and Brontë, aims to portray a transcendent, immaterial spirit, he finds himself compelled to write about the body, which presents a profoundly debasing materialism. Trollope's story conspicuously poses the problem of the relation between surface and depth in several different registers: first, through an exotic setting that dramatizes English contact with unfamiliar nationalities and nonwhite races; second, through a plot of cross-gender masquerade; and third, through an evocative depiction of human bodies at odds with a quest for spiritual fulfillment. In each case, the narrative seeks to move from outside to inside, from external form to inner truth, but is blocked: the surface, variously conceived as pigment, clothing, or tactile membrane, is untranscendable, and the confusion induced by passing beneath it only reinforces what was already known from without.

Although not nearly so well known a chronicler of empire as Rudyard Kipling, Joseph Conrad, or H. Rider Haggard, Trollope set many stories in overseas colonies, such as Jamaica, the East Indies, and Australia, places with which he was familiar from his extensive travels. "The Banks of the Jordan" (reprinted under the title "A Ride across Palestine") itself serves as a world tour in miniature, with characters such as Bedouin desert guides, a Catholic French dragoman, Austrian sailors, a Polish hotelier, and a collection of Eastern Christian pilgrims.

> It must be remembered that Eastern worshippers are not like the churchgoers of London, or even of Rome or Cologne. They are wild men of various nations and races — Maronites from Lebanon, Roumelians, Candiotes, Copts from Upper Egypt, Russians from the Crimea, Armenians and Abyssinians. They savour strongly of Oriental life and of Oriental dirt. They are clad in skins or hairy cloaks with huge hoods. Their heads are shaved, and their faces covered with short, grisly, fierce beards. They are silent mostly, looking out of their eyes ferociously, as though murder were in their thoughts, and rapine. But they never slouch, or cringe in their bodies, or shuffle in their gait. Dirty, fierce-looking, uncouth, repellent as they are, there is always about them a something of personal dignity which is not compatible with an Englishman's ordinary hat and pantaloons.[2]

For all its cosmopolitanism, Trollope's story performs the usual imperial work of demonstrating British superiority, pluck, and cultivation, expressed through a brutalizing hierarchy of physical appearances and hygiene. Collapsing race with nationality and religion in dismissing all those around him, the blithely imperious narrator feels confident of his own supremacy. In the context of British colonialism and the long history of Western racism based on pigmentation, the skin and other outward markers are taken as a wholly reliable register of character. The narrator never doubts his instinctive impression of the people and places he witnesses as dirty, disgusting, and alien. Foreignness here lacks the possibility of a deep identification for the Englishman, such as one finds in other British fictions of empire, in which European characters (like Kurtz, Kim, and Holly) "go native" or meaningfully encounter nonwhites.

The importance this analysis will attach to skin consciousness — and particularly skin-color consciousness — in "The Banks of the Jordan" derives in part from the story's historical context. Such attention is ratified by the pages surrounding the fiction in the *London Review,* the periodical in which it originally appeared in three serial parts, on January 5, 12, and 19, 1861. Prominent in the news during those weeks were the early stirrings of the American Civil War. The leading article in the issue containing the third installment of Trollope's story, for instance, discusses the "Missouri slave" case, in which Canadian courts had to determine whether to extradite an escaped slave back to Missouri, where he had

inadvertently killed a white man who was trying to recapture him. The
editorial opines against extradition:

> The law of the British Empire not only does not recognize the sta-
> tus of slavery, but regards it as contrary to human nature.... If a
> negro or man of colour had been pursued in any of the British
> dominions by persons with the avowed intention of restoring him
> to slavery, he would be justified in employing all reasonable
> means to avert the consequences with which he was threatened....
> The occurrence of this discussion at a period when America is agi-
> tated on the question of slavery is most remarkable, and presents
> the materials for deep reflection to the statesman, the lawyer, and
> philanthropist.[3]

This "deep reflection" on slavery, race, and justice might indeed be fur-
thered by turning the page and reading the final part of Trollope's tale, in
which colonial condescension toward ignorant, wily, or invidious races
is, if mocked with dramatic irony, also implicitly endorsed by a comic
smugness indistinguishable from irony.

   Even before arriving at Trollope's story, however, a reader would
encounter another editorial, this one at odds with the liberal sentiments
expressed in the righteous condemnation of American slavery. Here the
editorial gaze shifts to another part of the British Empire and expresses
jingoistic support, in the most baldly racist terms, for the bloody suppression of Maori natives in New Zealand.

> The natives of New Zealand are as warlike as savages usually are,
> but they possess, according to most accounts, a greater degree of
> natural intelligence than the negro or Red Indian races that have
> hitherto come most frequently into collision with the Anglo-Saxon
> and Anglo-Scandinavian races, who are now peopling and sub-
> duing the world.
>   It would, therefore, seem that the task of reconciling them to
> the inevitable necessity of white occupation of the land, would be
> easier than with barbarians of less brain, and that their civilization
> and conversion to Christianity would not be so hopeless as has
> been the case elsewhere. But, from some cause or other, an idea
> has got into the heads of these poor people, that it is possible either
> to expel or extirpate the whole white population, and to re-establish
> a native sovereignty, and consequently a native barbarism. Leav-
> ing all sentiment out of the question, and all merely abstract ideas
> of the rights of the natives to the lands where they were born, and
> to the hunting-grounds where their forefathers prowled like wild

beasts, and with about as much relish for the flesh of man as the lion or the tiger, it is quite clear that the British and other settlers will not allow themselves to be either expelled or exterminated; that they will not submit to a Maori sovereignty; that they will not give up their farms to men of dusky skins, to be reconverted into wilderness; and that as long as such ideas have possession of the native mind, so long will war, overt or covert, be the normal condition of affairs in New Zealand.

The experience of America and other parts of the world is before us, to prove that in all such struggles the white race must and does prevail; that the aboriginal savage must either conform to the new state of things, and consent to be civilized, or disappear altogether from the face of the earth. . . . The civilization and christianization of the savage will follow in due course, if he be capable, as we believe the New Zealander is, of accommodating himself to altered and superior circumstances. But all attempts to pamper him with exalted notions of Maori sovereignty, or lead him astray by exaggerated estimates of his natural right over lands which he nor his predecessors never knew how to turn to account, and which owe their whole value to white energy, capital, and skill, can but lead to future misery and bloodshed, and to the gradual extinction of his race.[4]

In the most explicit form, the editorial gives voice to the bloodthirsty racist ideology that justifies colonial conquest — an ideology that, if in comparatively muted terms, equally motivates the national, racial, and religious taxonomies (based on fine discriminations of perceived hygiene and cultivation) by which Trollope's narrator makes sense of his surroundings. The portrait of the Maoris collapses together savagery, degeneracy, cannibalism, paganism, ignorance, and dark skin, relying on both mythical and anthropological stereotypes to justify the conquest. The "dusky skin," set in contrast to "white energy, capital, and skill," is the register of civilization; plainly at stake is a justification for extending imperialism, no matter if genocidal conquest is required. Yet to discover alongside Trollope's story of epidermally coded conflict a news item that repeats so many of its themes is hardly the fantastic coincidence that might be imagined. Rather, it is the very ordinariness of the ideas that deserves emphasis: skin is presumed to be so reliable an indication of the inside that it gets only casual mention in the racist account of New Zealand; one could expect to find similar language in a newspaper from almost any week in the Victorian period. Trollope's story does, however, give peculiar extension to the theme, amplifying it from the terms of race to those of selfhood, gender, spirituality, and, especially, the superficies of physically embodied experience itself.

"The Banks of the Jordan" is told in the voice of an Englishman who adopts the pseudonym Jones and pretends to be a carefree bachelor. He narrates his travels through Palestine at Easter time, where he meets a mysterious fellow tourist, a young man who likewise identifies himself with an implausibly generic name, John Smith. Together the two visit holy sites, where they encounter Eastern Christian pilgrims as well as non-Christian natives, all described in characteristically Victorian racist terms of disparagement. As part of his tour, the narrator bathes in the river Jordan and the Dead Sea, only to be horrified at the repulsive desiccation of his skin. A surprisingly homoerotic intimacy springs up between the two strangers, although the enigmatic young man, Smith, exhibits a peculiar anxiety and reticence. All is explained at the story's end, when Smith is exposed as a woman in disguise, and the two are discovered by her guardian, who accuses the narrator of seducing the unprotected young lady. The tale concludes when the narrator reveals that he is himself married and so cannot mend matters by wedding her. The outré plot of an impossible love between men is resolved into the almost equally scandalous story of a married man intimately associating with an unmarried young woman. The tale's violations of sexual propriety were immediately condemned, first by *Cornhill*, which declined to publish the story because, as Trollope's biographer N. John Hall notes, it "was filled with sexual resonances that Smith and Thackeray felt too explicit for the magazine"; and after the story's eventual publication in the *London Review,* by readers who protested against its apparent appeal to the "morbid imagination & *a low tone of morals.*"[5]

The tale's most overt theme is deceptive appearances. This is so familiar a convention of literary fiction as to be one of its defining features, however exaggerated it is here by the exotic contexts. "I was taken with John Smith, in spite of his name," Jones states early on. "There was so much about him that was pleasant, both to the eye and to the understanding. One meets constantly with men from contact with whom one revolts without knowing the cause of such dislike.... But, on the other hand, there are men who are attractive, and I must confess that I was attracted by John Smith at first sight" (110). The story proceeds by an almost banal logic of the surface hiding a depth that contradicts it: the young man is in fact a woman, the Holy Land is really a squalid tourist trap, the repulsive outward form of the Eastern pilgrims covers a soul no baser than that of the conceited Englishman. One is eventually made to see the narrator's obtuse blindness, on a range of subjects, as the sign of his foolish arrogance and self-absorption. Indeed, rather than focus on the disguised objects, we are finally meant to recognize how the *subject* of perception has distorted vision — be that subject the narrator or the reader (if one fails to discern Smith's disguise before the denouement). The cross-dressed young woman suggests just such a shift of attention from the object to the perceiver: "Do we not know that our thoughts are formed, and our beliefs modelled, not on the outward signs or intrinsic evidences of things, — as would be the case were we always rational, — but by the inner workings of the mind itself?" (126). One sees from the inside out, such a remark suggests: the mind determines what the eyes perceive.

Although the narrator blunders through the story unaware of the young woman's disguise, the reader is amply supplied with clues to her true sex. "I thoroughly hate an effeminate man," the narrator says at one point, "but in spite of a certain womanly softness about this fellow I could not hate him" (128). Or a little later: "I did love him as though he were a younger brother. I felt a delight in serving him, and though I was almost old enough to be his father I ministered to him, as though he had been an old man, or a woman" (134). Jones is unable to see beneath the surface of his companion's male costume, and his humiliation at the conclusion is proportionate to his obliviousness along the way. The device of the cross-dressed woman permits an intense homoeroticism in the story, yet the revelation that explains it is available only retrospectively. After his bathing, for example, the narrator says, "I found myself lying with my head on his lap. I had slept, but it could have been but for a few minutes, and when I woke I felt his hand upon my brow. As I started up he said that the flies had been annoying me, and that he had not chosen to waken me as I seemed weary" (128). For a reader as taken in as the narrator, the retroactive alibi hardly seems adequate to defuse the force of such contact between two characters who both appear to be men.[6] The story's overt narrative of disguised gender identity in an exotic setting, along with its covert implication of male homoeroticism, seems almost designed for queer and postcolonial reading, a critical effort that Mark Forrester has undertaken in a persuasive interpretation.

Through the cross-dressed romance plot, Trollope ironizes and thus criticizes Jones's inability to recognize the most obvious sort of deceptive surface: clothing, the second skin. The story's conspicuous emphasis on the narrator's bodily experience of his tour allows the skin both to metaphorize and to literalize the more general theme of deceptive appearances — to estrange it, that is to say, by giving it bodily form. The link between clothing and skin is made deliberately in Smith's unwillingness to strip off "his" outfit and bathe, as to do so would expose the female body beneath ("He did not like bathing, and preferred to do his washing in his own room" [122]). As with the cross-gender plot, the narrator is equally egocentric in the realm of nationality: he is unerringly persuaded of his superiority to the ostensibly barbaric foreigners he encounters and of the rightness of his perceptions on the basis of their superficial appearance. While this aspect of the narrator's attitude is also gently mocked, however, it is less clear that Trollope intends us to view it as wholly wrongheaded.

Jones's relentless superficiality becomes still more significant when we recognize that, while the story satirizes the vulgar tourism of consumer culture, it takes the *form* of a sacred religious pilgrimage. The narrator supplies no explanation for his presence in the Holy Land at Easter, but as a Christian traveler there, he might be expected to seek spiritual gratification. His visits to major biblical sites — the Mount of Olives, the Sea of Galilee, the tomb of the Virgin — suggest such a quest, as, more metaphorically, does his Christlike sojourn in the desert, "those mountains of the wilderness through which it is supposed that Our Saviour wandered for the forty days when the devil tempted him" (107). Yet reach as he might for spiritual revelation, the secular tourist remains just that: set apart from the fervor of Eastern pilgrims, he merely goes through the motions dictated by Baedeker, evincing no enlightenment in religious terms at all. Spiritual interiority is demonstrably vacuous: just as he cannot delve beneath his traveling companion's costume or the alienating appearance of the foreign nationals he meets, so Jones is thrown insistently back onto the profane surface of his own body at every moment that he seeks to plumb the depths of a divinely ordained soul. For the tourist, at least, spiritual experience, like gender and racial identity, turns out to be skin deep.

At his visits to religious shrines, the English pilgrim finds his body a problematic intrusion, in part because of the contact he is forced to make with disconcerting foreign objects. First, in his visit to the chapel at the tomb of the Virgin, the narrator reports on nothing but the vaguely horrifying experience of shoving his way through a crowd of filthy "Eastern worshippers," and at the British ability for so doing. Such national differences are immediately linked to bodily form and hygiene:

> How is it that Englishmen can push themselves anywhere? These men were fierce-looking, and had murder and rapine . . . almost in their eyes. . . . Yet we did win our way through them, and apparently no man was angry with us. I doubt, after all, whether a ferocious eye and a strong smell and dirt are so efficacious in creating awe and obedience in others as an open brow and traces of soap and water. I know this, at least, — that a dirty Maronite would make very little progress if he attempted to shove his way unfairly through a crowd of Englishmen at the door of a London theatre. (115)

Absent is any account of what one might see in the tomb of the Virgin, or what such a sight might make a Christian feel. In light of the long history of the English Church condemning the stage, the comparison between the tomb and a theater seems particularly sacrilegious, even allowing for Protestant skepticism about Mary worship. The physical description of penetrating a crowd of fearsomely dirty foreigners lends debased material form to the would-be spiritual quest whose place it takes.

The account of subjective interiority as dispersed across the surface of the body reaches its climax when Trollope's narrator bathes in the Dead Sea and the river Jordan. Again he follows the prescription for Christian renewal, bathing at the very site at which Jesus himself was baptized; again Jones experiences repulsive embodiment, realizing only his own epidermal limits. He seeks to immerse himself in the water, but it resists him: "Everything is perfectly still, and the fluid seems hardly to be displaced by the entrance of the body. But the effect is that one's feet are tripped up, and that one falls prostrate on to the surface. . . . I was unable to keep enough of my body below the surface. . . . However, I had bathed in the Dead Sea, and was so far satisfied" (123). Like a figure for himself, the Dead Sea functions as pure surface: it cannot be penetrated, it seems, but no matter — whatever depths it holds are irrelevant to his feeling "satisfied." As the passage progresses, the water then penetrates and revolts *him*:

> Anything more abominable to the palate than this water, if it be water, I never had inside my mouth. I expected it to be extremely salt, and no doubt, if it were analyzed, such would be the result; but there is a flavor in it which kills the salt. No attempt can be

made at describing this taste. It may be imagined that I did not
drink heartily, merely taking up a drop or two with my tongue
from the palm of my hand; but it seemed to me as though I had
been drenched with it. Even brandy would not relieve me from it.
And then my whole body was in a mess, and I felt as though I had
been rubbed with pitch. Looking at my limbs I saw no sign on
them of the fluid. They seemed to dry from this as they usually do
from any other water; but still the feeling remained. (123)

Jones locates phenomenal experience as a surface effect, which, if it
reaches past the cutaneous layer, does so by osmosis, as corrosive infection. Within the narration, the putrid liquid moves in the opposite direction — from inside out — jumping from palate and tongue to the hand
and the full extent of the skin. The water not only abrades the surface of
Jones's body but also, as he imagines, darkens it like pitch to effect a
quasi-racial debasement.[7] As though to reinforce and exaggerate his disgust, the narrator finds himself still more repulsed by dipping in the river
Jordan next. Upon leaving the river, he states: "I was forced to wade out
through the dirt and slush, so that I found it difficult to make my feet
and legs clean enough for my shoes and stockings; and then, moreover,
the flies plagued me most unmercifully. I should have thought that the
filthy flavour from the Dead Sea would have saved me from that nui-
sance; but the mosquitoes thereabouts are probably used to it" (125). As
he returns to proper European costume, the story alludes to the biblical
plague, but in being evacuated of any spiritual content, the experience is
again set entirely on the surface of the body. Beneath the epidermis seems
to lie not spiritual depth but simply more body, ever more capable of
physical distress.

The narrative emphasizes not only dirt on the surface of the body but
the pains and pleasures available to the skin as well. A Turkish saddle, for
example, penetrates the surface of the so-called Christian body to reach
not its soul but its gore, even as it supplies the occasion for potentially
erotic touching. "Of what material is formed the nether man of a Turk I
have never been informed," the narrator states, elaborating a fantasy of
Eastern male sexuality,

but I am sure that it is not flesh and blood. No flesh and blood —
simply flesh and blood — could withstand the wear and tear of a
Turkish saddle.... There is no part of the Christian body with
which the Turkish saddle comes in contact that does not become
more or less macerated. I have sat in one for days, but I left it a
flayed man; and therefore I was sorry for Smith.

I explained this to him, taking hold of his leg by the calf to
show how the leather would chafe him; but it seemed to me that
he did not quite like my interference. (112–13)[8]

To be Western and Christian is thus to have specially sensitive skin. Yet
Smith exhibits less discomfort than the narrator predicts, perhaps because her "nether man" does not impede her. "That confounded Turkish
saddle has already galled your skin," he tells her later. "I see how it is:
I shall have to doctor you with a little brandy — externally applied, my
friend" (118). Even the mildly obscene prospect of rubbing the thighs of
his friend suggests a transposition of the remedy (brandy) from its proper
location inside the body to the exterior integument. The texture of the
surface has both racial and sexual determinants: by contrast with the apparent roughness and dirtiness of the foreigners, Jones perceives the
"womanly softness" of Smith's skin: "He then put out his hand to me, and
I pressed it in token of my friendship. My own hand was hot and rough
with the heat and sand; but his was soft and cool almost as a woman's"
(127–28). Such an intimate tactile exchange affects both subject and object; if it touches an emotional interior, its vehicle is the skin. In a similar
way, powerfully repellent olfactory sensations reach inside: the pilgrims'
"strong smell and dirt" and their "savour[ing] strongly of Oriental life
and of Oriental dirt" signify a frightening foreignness that pervades the
sensitive nose of the Englishman. By contrast with visual apprehension,
which accentuates distance, hierarchy, and difference, the proximate
senses, which physically incorporate the outside world into the subject,
occur on the sensitive, inscribing surface of the body.

In the narrator's description of Eastern Christian worshipers, distress is again embodied, but pain is also excluded from effecting a spiritual transformation. He witnesses "a caravan of pilgrims coming up from
Jordan" (119), who, unlike himself, appear to be impelled by an abiding
religious faith, at which he can only wonder. Like his tourism, however,
he portrays their religious exercise as wholly formal, as far as his from
modifying any interior essence. Of "these strange people," he says, "The
benefit expected was not to be immediately spiritual. . . . To these members of the Greek Christian Church it had been handed down from father
to son that washing in Jordan once during life was efficacious towards
salvation. And therefore the journey had been made at terrible cost and
terrible risk" (120). As unthinkingly driven to go through their religious
paces as he is through his sightseeing, the pilgrims seem to suffer bodily
pain as an end in itself. Yet among them, Jones witnesses a figure to

whom, as Forrester demonstrates, he is particularly drawn, and with whom he vividly identifies:[9]

> Some few there are, undoubtedly, more ecstatic in this great deed of their religion. One man I especially noticed on this day. He had bound himself to make the pilgrimage from Jerusalem to the river with one foot bare. He was of a better class, and was even nobly dressed, as though it were a part of his vow to show to all men that he did this deed, wealthy and great though he was. He was a fine man, perhaps thirty years of age, with a well-grown beard descending on his breast, and at his girdle he carried a brace of pistols. But never in my life had I seen bodily pain so plainly written in a man's face. The sweat was falling from his brow, and his eyes were strained and bloodshot with agony. He had no stick, his vow, I presume, debarring him from such assistance, and he limped along, putting to the ground the heel of the unprotected foot. I could see it, and it was a mass of blood, and sores, and broken skin. An Irish girl would walk from Jerusalem to Jericho without shoes, and be not a penny the worse for it. This poor fellow clearly suffered so much that I was almost inclined to think that in the performance of his penance he had done something to aggravate his pain. Those around him paid no attention to him, and the dragoman seemed to think nothing of the affair whatever. (120–21)

To a point, Jones identifies with and is attracted to this figure, for he stands out among the pilgrims by virtue of his bearing and his armed potency. The narrator combines admiration for the pilgrim's self-abasing devotion with disgust at his excess; yet mingled with these reactions is also a sense of sheer bewilderment at the form this piety takes. As the passage continues, the very connection between spiritual ardor and bodily prostration that Jones reads in the pilgrim's pain effects a *dis*identification with him. Just as his own physical abasement affords no spiritual apotheosis, so the penance he witnesses here remains incomprehensible because he cannot imagine how altering the surface might affect religious depth. At the moment in which the tale comes closest to representing masochism, it is important that the narrator regards, but does not himself experience, such physical abjection. For masochism, whose gratifications may be religious as well as sexual, depends on a rigorous connection between the surface of the body and an interior emotional, spiritual, or mental entity, in all of which Jones seems to be deficient. As soon as he registers the fullness of the pilgrim's agony and its probable justification, he disavows his initial identification (on the basis of class and appearance) by introducing the otherwise unaccountable allusion to the Irish girl. Even as the comparison distinguishes the refined pilgrim from the stereotyped Celt, it also differentiates him from Jones, both by insidiously feminizing the pilgrim and by relegating him to the status of a colonial subject. Jones's potency and superiority are, though momentarily relaxed by regard of this figure, ultimately reinforced by the distinctions, for he, unlike the suffering barefoot pilgrim, stays entirely on the surface. He lacks the depth — here conceived of as spirituality, albeit a negated entity — to warrant a masochistic harrowing of the outside.

Trollope's tale presents relations between the surface of the body and its depth in comic and ironic terms. Another, more strictly psychological account of such material is also available, although the story itself modifies this theory. That the narrative's perplexities about gender, nationality, and religion are projected onto the surface of the body suggests the utility of Didier Anzieu's work *The Skin Ego* (1985), the most sustained discussion of the skin in relation to the psyche. Anzieu's theory develops the psychical topography that Freud outlines in *The Ego and the Id* (1923), at whose center is the proposition that the ego is "first and foremost a bodily ego" — which is to say, precisely mapped onto the surface of the body.[10] Anzieu's theory elaborates for the skin ego "three functions: as a containing, unifying envelope for the Self; as a protective barrier for the psyche; and as a filter of exchanges and a surface of inscription for the first traces, a function which makes representation possible. To these three functions, there correspond three representations: the sac, the screen and the sieve."[11] These functions resonate with the depiction of skin in Trollope's story as both a porous container of, and an entity contiguous with, the narrator's ego. The outer surface of the skin, Anzieu shows, protects the self and situates it in the world, operations that Jones is at pains to reinforce. He must shore up his psychical integrity by securing the surface of his own skin as well as his comprehension of others', both of which seem frequently to be in danger of dissolution. Yet the story departs from the psychological ruptures of the skin ego, on which Anzieu focuses his theoretical and clinical accounts in terms of narcissism, masochism, and castration. Trollope's story dramatizes such threats — as well as the necessity to reestablish the containing and protecting functions of the skin ego — by making them external, through the narrator's racial and sexual subjugation of others and his inflation of himself. He aims to secure the wholeness of his integument as much for cultural as for psychological reasons.

To Jones's dismay, the outer surface of his body, rather than simply containing him and differentiating him from others, is a permeable barrier. This surface has a double capacity, for even as it holds his insides within, it permits interaction with, and intrusions from, the exterior world. The spiritual experience from which, as the story shows, he is barred, assumes the form of dermatological trauma: desiccation, contusion, and avulsion of the skin, both experienced and witnessed. Erotic contact with Smith, though suggested, is made impossibly distant, consigned to a comic, seemingly unconscious homoeroticism, which is then recuperated as a heterosexual flirtation, itself made unavailable by the narrator's prior marriage. Like the spiritual quest emptied of deep content by its expression as epidermal abrasion, the romance is rewritten as laceration and so is equally relegated to the surface of the flesh. Yet the psychological distress expressed in the skin is compensated to some degree by its cultural valuation, for by comparing the surface of his skin — its color, hygiene, and texture — to those he perceives as fundamentally different from himself (by race, nationality, and religion), Jones establishes a sense of his own value and integrity. This is the point at which Trollope's story necessitates adaptation, in cultural terms, of Anzieu's narrowly Oedipal frame of reference.

Although psychoanalytic theory in the main attributes psychical formations to developmental experiences, at its roots are physiological processes that orient the psyche. Freud's theory of drives and the development of the ego ultimately finds its basis in the body, an insight that Anzieu pursues and expands. While Anzieu focuses on the etiology and pathology of subjects' mental conceptions of themselves in relation to the surface of their bodies, he has nothing to say about the social determinants of the skin: that the skin is a sign of racial classification receives no attention in Anzieu's discussion of the psychical consequences of human subjects' embodiment in flesh. It is easy enough to fault Anzieu for ignoring race, but to suggest that the skin is socially as well as psychologically encoded is not merely to argue for a more culturally attentive account; it modifies the psychology itself, since skin color, in the modern West, contributes at least as much to the constitution of the ego as any of its other attributes.

Within a system of epidermal discrimination, in which rights have been distributed on the basis of pigmentation, the skin always functions both individually and socially, as a cover and a surface. Skin color, as the physical embodiment and visual evidence of otherwise unverifiable racial difference, assumes the importance of making moral distinctions among people.[12] In combination with its psychological qualities as sac, screen, and sieve (envelope, barrier, and medium), the skin has not only functions but *significations* as well. Frantz Fanon, the preeminent psychoanalytic theorist of race, makes this point by showing how a psychological or phenomenological account of ego formation is inadequate to a subject marked, at the surface of the body, as "colored." He indicates the necessity of supplementing this "corporeal schema" with a historical and political description of a body that operates in the socially delimited world (the "racial epidermal schema") within which the ego necessarily forms:

> A slow composition of my *self* as a body in the middle of a spatial and temporal world — such seems to be the schema. It does not impose itself on me; it is, rather, a definitive structuring of the self and of the world — definitive because it creates a real dialectic between my body and the world.... Below the corporeal schema I had sketched a historico-racial schema. The elements that I used had been provided for me not by "residual sensations and perceptions primarily of a tactile, vestibular, kinesthetic, and visual character" [Lhermitte], but by the other, the white man, who had woven me out of a thousand details, anecdotes, stories... and above all *historicity*.... Assailed at various points, the corporeal schema crumbled, its place taken by a racial epidermal schema.[13]

Using Fanon's analysis of race in combination with Anzieu's notion of the skin ego allows us to see how Trollope's narrator has his internal integrity threatened through the experiences of dermatological abrasion (bathing in the Dead Sea, witnessing the bloody foot and the bruised leg) and yet secures that surface by contrasting its purity and cleanliness with the rough, dark, and dirty skins he encounters on his tour. These are not discrete processes — one internal (psychological, spiritual, or erotic), the other external (social or political) — but in fact belong to the same "schema," at once "corporeal" and "racial epidermal," by which the self is constituted at the body's surface and also brought into contact with the world. In giving these processes narrative form, the story parcels them out, but moments like the one in which Jones says he feels *himself* "rubbed with pitch" by his bathing illustrate how the language of racial coloring extends to that of psychological self-perception. Moreover, we can now see that, in narrating the effects of the skin on soul or self, the story connects the gender plot itself to the exotic setting: by portraying abrasions at the surface of the body, the tale provides a somatic vehicle for translating between the realm of racial/national distinction and that of sexual/gender confusion. The distressed skin is a metaphor for each mode of establishing difference, but it is also metonymically linked to both, for these distinctions are themselves bodily. The repeated collapse of surface and depth, interior and exterior, enables the valued inside to assume a privileged form (integrity, consistency, purity, and cleanliness) through projection onto the outside.

In this raising of interior qualities to the surface, dirtiness and dark skin are made to stand for each other. That having dark skin is imagined to be tantamount to having dirt *on* the skin suggests, on the one hand, the transitive possibility of racial infection and, on the other, the fantasy that racial distinction might be washed away: it is, in either sense, a resolutely superficial phenomenon. The link between dirty and dark skin is not incidental: as Anne McClintock has shown in an analysis of Victorian advertising iconography, the idealized domestic sphere, in which soap prevails, and the fearsome colonial one, in which dirt abounds, are mutually dependent.[14] Trollope's narrator gets dirty and so fears becoming like one of the savage "dusky" natives described in the adjoining story about New Zealand; at the same time, he witnesses pilgrims from across the Mideast and determines, on the basis of their appearance, that they are ontologically dirty. Perhaps the strangest aspect of this fantasy is that he feels himself to be dirtiest — not in some deep, metaphysical way but, again, on the surface — when he bathes. Hardly purifying his soul, the double baptism instead threatens to taint or tarnish his skin.

One can appreciate the significance of this oddity when it is placed back in the historical context of widespread Victorian concerns with dirt and sanitation. Trollope's story was published in a periodical called the *London Review:* with the sweep of its imperial gaze, this journal takes in the whole world, but it originates in the metropolitan capital. In that cosmopolitan context, around 1861, the depiction of filthy, infectious water could not but remind readers of the repulsive state of the river Thames. By the 1850s, England's urban waterways had become horrifically polluted, and widespread debates about the necessity of installing modern sewer systems ensued. During the summers of the late 1850s, hot, dry weather made the unembanked Thames so putrescent that passersby were overcome and Parliament, situated on the river, nearly had to close. Trollope may be thinking more of England's dirty water than of Palestine's in his tale, for similarly disgusting rivers appear in roughly contemporary texts, including Thomas Chadwick's *Report on the Sanitary Condition of the Labouring Population of Great Britain* (1842), Charles Dickens's *Bleak House* (1852–53) and *Our Mutual Friend* (1864–65), Charles Kingsley's *Yeast* (1848–50) and *The Water-Babies* (1863), Friedrich Engels's *Condition of the Working Class in England* (1845), and Henry Mayhew's *London Labour and the London Poor* (1851). These works uniformly portray dirty water in an urban English context, where sewage gets mixed up with drinking water, threatening disease and social decay. They fully exploit its potency as a metaphor, signifying infectious circulation among bodies, classes, and commodities.[15]

Trollope's use of the pollution metaphor to link *foreign* brutes and filthy waters is also not unprecedented: popular reports about the disgusting condition of London's waterways are frequently drawn to the same equation. In fact, the connection might have seemed inevitable as, in 1858, newspaper stories about alarm over the dirty river run beside reports of the sepoy uprising in India, an epochal rebellion against British imperialism and the decisive event in putting India under direct control of the British government. An editorial in the *Times* about the repulsive state of the Thames makes the connection explicit:

> The stench of June was only the last ounce of our burden, or rather it was an accidental flash of light which brought a great fact before our eyes. That hot fortnight did for the sanitary administration of the Metropolis what the Bengal mutinies did for the administration of India. It showed us more clearly and forcibly than before on what a volcano we were reposing. It proved to us that the Thames had become a huge sewer, not only figuratively but actually; that we had made it, of the two, rather worse than a regular drain; and that, if we did not set our city in order at once, there was no telling what might befall us.[16]

How is a colonial uprising like a stinking river? Both are filthy, frightening, and potentially lethal to the ruling class, requiring powerful, civilizing state intervention; both threaten to explode (in this heap of metaphors) like a flash of lightning or a long-dormant volcano — the one into mutinous bloodshed, the other into toxic cholera. If, during the so-called Great Stink of 1858, the Thames, like a retributive slave, threatened at last to rise

up (in the nostrils of the public) and kill off English citizens with its pestif-
erous vapors, so the fatal uprising in India had hygienic dimensions as
well. As reports came in to the British press about the rebellion in South
Asia, fantastic stories of rape, dismemberment, and torture circulated.
Prominent among these graphic accounts, whether based in fact or fantasy, were tales of English womanhood fatally besmirched by native
hands; even more pointedly, the event that became the central symbol in
English memory of the uprising — the wholesale murder of innocents in
the Bibighar compound in Cawnpore — was a crime of, among other
things, infection and impurity. Hundreds of British women and children
captives were hacked to death, their bodies dumped in the Ganges River
or stuffed down a well, which served as the emblem of the mutiny and
the rallying cry for its brutal suppression by colonial forces.[17] Here was
water literally tainted by blood, and purity not only stained but itself a
source of uncleanliness. Such symbolism facilitated the superimposition
of national and racial distinctions on those of hygiene and purity.

The military-sanitary analogy serves to taint the colonies with an
offense to cleanliness while at the same time attributing bloodshed to the
river pollution. Yet hygienic distinction was invoked on both sides of the
colonial conflict. The uprising was supposed to have been provoked by
the transgression of native hygiene practices: the rumor that new gun
cartridges were greased with the fat from cows and pigs, which violated
religious and caste prohibitions, was said to have sparked the Indian sol-
diers' revolt. Indian scruples about the touch of unholy animal matter
might have seemed absurd to the English, but in the midst of the sanitary
crisis, they must also have seemed familiar. The shared terror of incorporating filthy matter enables the analogy — between fears of urban miasma
and religious prohibitions against defilement — to be acknowledged overtly:
Punch, in its "Essence of Parliament" of July 10, 1858, reports, "The Thames
and the Ganges again divided the attention of the Commons. . . . To which
is offered the largest number of Human Sacrifices?" In this implied allegory, urban sanitary degeneration converges on uncivilized religious fa-
naticism: the ineffectual government of the metropolis is as callously indifferent to human life as barbarians who deliberately sacrifice it. While
Parliament neglects the health of the populace, the crazed Hindus — like
the hyperdevout Eastern Christian pilgrims portrayed in "The Banks of
the Jordan" — squander preservation of the body in favor of deep, interior spiritual life.[18]

Through the coincidence of the Thames crisis and the sepoy uprising, a local urban problem is displaced onto a connection between filth and foreignness, which makes its way into Trollope's story as a failed spiritual quest: it is no wonder the narrator finds his baptism so utterly unenlightening, for the foul water seems to speak more to English sanitary conditions than to affirming Christian faith. The link between a bathing that dirties and epidermal transformation becomes clearer still in one further piece of evidence from the period, which shows how the concatenation of mid-Victorian sanitary and imperial administrations necessitates a skin consciousness to keep them distinct. However filthy the metropolis may be, it is still not so bad as the colonies, the logic runs, where dirty subjects require blanching by the British administration. Figurative though it may sound, *Punch* makes this racist imagery altogether literal. The issue of July 17, 1858, contains a mock parliamentary hearing on the state of the Thames, which parodies legislative paralysis by showing every piece of expert advice to be contradicted by another. At the bottom of the same page, a small item titled "Ineffectual Ablution" reads: "His Highness the Maharajah JUNG BAHADOOR has been created a Knight of the Bath. A similar experiment has been tried before. JUNG BAHADOOR is a gentleman of a dark red complexion. The Bath will not render it white." A corresponding illustration at the top of the page, titled "Washing the Blackamoor White. Sir Jung Bahadoor and His Knights Companions of the Bath," shows the unhappy maharajah plunged in a steaming tub, white men in knights' armor scrubbing him vigorously.

The items about the maharajah, who was being rewarded for his role in suppressing the sepoy rebellion, literally surround the story of Parliament's inaction over the stinking river. This graphic arrangement makes explicit the analogy between the metropolis and the colonies: like the infectious waterway, dark skin is an impurity that requires violent purgation. The English claim for racial superiority, and the aspiration for whiteness imputed to the Indian (alternately "of a dark red complexion" and a "Blackamoor"), indicate in the idiom of ethnicity how degrading Londoners find it to have reached such an appalling level of sanitary degeneracy. Such reasoning equates dark skin, the bodily integument of the Indian figure, with the pollution that reaches inside and disturbs the English one. In this racist fantasy, one is ontologically dirty, visibly stained on the outside; the other is situationally infected by a miasma that carries the putrescence within, making the domestic subject *feel* unclean. The

WASHING THE BLACKAMOOR WHITE.

SIR JUNG BAHADOOR AND HIS KNIGHTS COMPANIONS OF THE BATH.

Punch, July 17, 1858. Courtesy of Special Collections, University of
Maryland Libraries.

danger for Trollope's narrator is that he, like *Punch*'s maharajah, might
not be able to scrub off the uncivilizing dirt that adheres to, and threatens to become, his skin.

In the context of Victorian sanitary reform, the tale's ironic desublimation of ritual cleansing seems even more irreducibly corporeal. In both
historical and phenomenological terms, the paradoxically defiling baths
help to repudiate a traditional spiritual account of the body as merely the
vessel for an ethereal essence. Once the body's visceral depths are revealed — its sexual cravings, its odors and filth, the gore exposed by mac-
erating saddles and contaminated waters — it too exhibits an interior.
This inside is no less material than the outside, only more horrifying,
and the narrator's failure throughout the story to move beneath the sur-

face seems, if not wise, then efficient. The reparations of the skin ego, he suggests, can take place only dermatologically, not internally.

The story thus proposes that while one is foolish to stay on the surface, because it can so easily deceive, there may be nothing *but* surface beneath. The final word on the matter comes at the moment in this desert tale when the epitome of deceptive appearance, a mirage, arises — or rather, fails to appear. "We have often heard, and some of us have seen, how effects of light and shade together will produce so vivid an appearance of water where there is no water, as to deceive the most experienced. But the reverse was the case here. There was the lake, and there it had been before our eyes for the last two hours; and yet it looked, then and now, as though it were an image of a lake and not real water" (121–22). Like the touch of its water, the appearance of the Dead Sea confounds expectations: it recedes when approached, just as it sullies rather than cleansing. While a mirage is a hallucination of an absent object, the phenomenon described in this moment *denies* the material existence of an actual object. A mirage signals desire and imagination; this counter-mirage indicates negation and distorted perception. Like the cross-dressed young woman, the Dead Sea hides in plain sight; as elsewhere, Jones does not interrogate the smooth exterior before him, just as the physical surface of the sea keeps buoying him up when he tries to dive beneath it. He fails to go below the surface, not so much because of his arrogance and prejudices, which are many, but because, Trollope suggests, there is nothing else: efforts to penetrate result not in the revelation of deep truths but in a further gliding along the surface of the skin.

4

Senses

Face and Feeling in
Hardy's The Return of the Native

Although it can never have been very tempting to read Thomas Hardy as a psychological realist, few critics have gone so far in the other direction as Gilles Deleuze, who states that Hardy's characters "are not people or subjects, they are collections of intensive sensations."[1] Deleuze identifies in Hardy what he calls "individuation without a subject," which might be thought of as depsychologized character. This is to suggest not that Hardy is uninterested in people but that he is interested in them as material objects, as agents of sensory interaction with the world rather than as beings that transcend it. To read Hardy's portrayal of sensory experience as part of an antihumanist impulse allows one to attend to his interest in people, landscapes, and the relations between them without succumbing to what Peter Widdowson has characterized as the literary-critical institutionalization of Hardy as a humanist and realist.[2] John Paterson and Elaine Scarry, among other critics, have noticed how Hardy's attention to people works against the establishment of deep, round characters with vivid inner lives. But none has been so suggestive as Deleuze about the ways in which Hardy's presentation of the human body as a mobile process can undermine the idea of intangible subjective interiority.[3]

Writing with Félix Guattari in *A Thousand Plateaus*, Deleuze elaborates the notion of *faciality*, which can help us understand Hardy's conception of the body. Hardy's writing can in turn clarify faciality, a difficult concept in a book of notoriously difficult concepts. As so often in *A Thousand Plateaus*, Deleuze and Guattari work against common sense, in this case the idea that the human face is an index of an expressive, interior essence — that it is a sign of subjective agency and the capacity for communicative interaction. Instead they present faciality as a system, or an "assemblage," that provides the illusion of individual coherence, psychological interiority, unitary being, and communicability.[4] For Deleuze and Guattari, the face is one of the registers through which modern society regulates and routinizes human behavior: masklike, it generates conventional signs, but it does not therefore hide some deep truth. The face must thus be prized away from its normalizing functions and instead understood as an unpredictable process of sensation and becoming. In its ordinary functioning, the face — or, more properly, the system they call faciality — belongs to the orders of "signifiance and subjectification" (167), of meaning making and subject making, which Deleuze and Guattari see as mystifications and to which they are consistently hostile. Their project of so-called schizoanalysis seeks to disrupt these processes, which are at odds with their exuberant values of multiplicity, flow, and becoming.[5]

A principal target of Deleuze and Guattari is the tendency of ordinary thinking about the face to subsume other parts of the body, indeed to obscure embodiment itself. Nineteenth-century physiological psychologists would have found this bodily materialism congenial, however different their motives for advocating it. Just as Victorian writers like Maudsley and Lewes pay little heed to religious and philosophical notions of soul or mind, so Deleuze and Guattari suggest that faciality belongs to a dualist opposition between body and mind, which reduces the body to a mere container of an interior self:

> The face is produced only when the head ceases to be a part of the body, when it ceases to be coded by the body, when it ceases to have a multidimensional, polyvocal corporeal code — when the body, head included, has been decoded and has to be *overcoded* by something we shall call the Face. This amounts to saying that the head, all the volume-cavity elements of the head, have to be facialized. What accomplishes this is ... the abstract machine producing faciality. (170)

Deleuze and Guattari show how the body is, to use their term, "territorialized" by the dominant order of faciality. I argue that the face can be reclaimed from the "abstract machine" of faciality by being put back in the body, specifically by means of the senses; the face would then be fully corporeal, not simply expressive of a conventional vocabulary of preconceived emotions or characteristics. They indicate a strategy of *bodily* means by which "to escape the face, to dismantle the face and facializations ... by strange true becomings" (171). Hardy demonstrates how the body can reterritorialize the face, for by emphasizing the function of the face both as an inlet for bodily sensation and as a material entity inseparable from the world of objects, he, like Deleuze and Guattari, resists its absorption into the univocality of facialized determinants.

Hardy's conception of the materiality of inner qualities was particularly influenced by Herbert Spencer, whose work on physiology gives perception a prominent role as a channel of communication between inner states and external environments.[6] Hardy focuses his material account of perception and interiority in his portrayal of the human face, a process he undertakes most rigorously in *The Return of the Native* (1878). This novel depicts the multiple functions of the face, as a screen onto which thoughts and feelings are projected and as a physiological receptacle for sensory encounters with the world. In this representation, Hardy, like Spencer and other Victorian physiological psychologists, contests the practices of physiognomy, the most celebrated form of face reading in the nineteenth century. Physiognomy — the system of evaluating individuals' characters on the basis of their facial features — gained popularity after the publication in 1783 of the Swiss pastor Johann Caspar Lavater's *Essays on Physiognomy*. While physiognomy might appear to be a materialist science of the body, it originated in Lavater's theological argument for facial expression as a manifestation of the soul and an affirmation of divine creation. By contrast, British proto-psychologists of the later nineteenth century argued that facial expression derived from physiological and evolutionary conditions, not from a divine essence.[7] Hardy's treatment of the face affirms this view, for which he found support in a statement of Lewes's that he copied into his notebook while preparing to compose *The Return of the Native:* "Physiology began to disclose that all the mental processes were (mathematically speaking) *functions* of physical processes, i.e. — varying with the variations of bodily states; & this was declared enough to banish for ever the conception of a Soul, except as a term simply expressing certain functions."[8] Both Hardy and the physiological psychologists advocate this material basis for mental and emotional processes, implicitly opposing the spiritual tenets of physiognomy.

Hardy's views, along with those of the Victorian materialists now largely consigned to the history of science, prefigure in striking ways Deleuze and Guattari's theories of body, subject, and sensation. Deleuze and Guattari's materialism is in one sense a reaction against a different legacy of the Enlightenment, the Cartesian premise of disembodied reason; the body, though never a static entity, is in their account the source and location of consciousness and subjectivity. In their emphasis on the power of embodied experience to challenge any abstract notion of human essence, Deleuze and Guattari implicitly revive elements of Merleau-Ponty's phenomenology, which might also be understood to supply an account of depsychologized character. The phenomenological discussion of perception as embodied experience and of the body as the untranscendable location of subjectivity parallels the concerns of Victorian writers in the materialist tradition and specifically of Hardy. Deleuze and Guattari share with Hardy a foundational situating of the human in the experience of a body made permeable to the world by its senses.

In discussing *The Return of the Native*, I suggest three main areas in which Hardy gives voice to a materialist insistence on the primacy of the body. He does this first in an account of the face as not only the object of perception but also its active subject, which, perhaps paradoxically, dramatizes the resistance of the face to being read as epiphenomenal to psychological depth. In line with contemporary physiological psychologists, Hardy understands perception as equally mental and physical and as located primarily in the sensory apparatus of the face. Second, by invoking synesthesia in striking ways, Hardy explores the variety of sensory incorporations, stressing the embodiment of subjectivity. Bringing together conventionally discrete sensory modalities enables him to dramatize the physiology of perceptual processes. Third, Hardy suggests that these perceptually permeable bodies are contiguous with the natural world, that landscape is in turn a percipient body, and that the two bodies exist in a mutually constitutive relation. By animating landscape and, at the same time, showing the porousness of human beings to nonhuman entities, Hardy erodes distinctions between subjects and objects. Elaborating on a conception of people as first and foremost in their bodies — and of these bodies as part of and open to the world through their senses — Hardy presents a vision of body, face, and location that belongs to a tradition of understanding human subjectivity as material. As one of the principal literary exemplars of this tradition, Hardy can clarify the phenomenological theory of embodiment that culminates in Deleuze and Guattari, who reciprocally help to elucidate his ideas.

While much of Hardy's fiction evinces scrupulous interest in the bodies, and especially the faces, of characters, none of his other novels approaches *The Return of the Native* in its sustained attention to the human countenance. The apparent intentions behind the work explain this distinction. The novel followed *The Hand of Ethelberta* (1876), a satiric, cosmopolitan work that Hardy wrote to counter the public perception of him, based on his early pastoral fiction, as strictly a regional novelist. When *The Hand of Ethelberta* was received poorly, Hardy took a yearlong hiatus from writing to pursue an extensive course of study in criticism, natural history, philosophy, and other fields — much of which found its way into *The Return of the Native* — as well as an investigation of portrait and landscape painting.[9] He returned to his native territory for the setting of this novel with a new seriousness of aesthetic purpose and design; in it, he aimed to show himself, as he had put it in an earlier letter to Leslie Stephen, "a great stickler for the proper artistic balance of the completed work."[10] Hardy's self-conscious attention to aesthetic form, his renewed commitment to the Wessex landscape, and his amplified knowledge of philosophy, physiology, and portraiture combined with unique intensity in this novel.

Although Hardy's attention to the formal features of the face has been widely noted, critics tend to treat the face as the object rather than the subject of visual consumption. In *The Expressive Eye*, a major study of Hardy's work in relation to painting and visual perception, for example, J. M. Bullen observes, "Again and again in *[The Return of the Native]*, characters are introduced into the story in terms of the appearance of their faces. Their presence is always anticipated by fragments of physiognomy or glimpses of facial features. . . . All the major characters enter the story in mysterious circumstances, and each of those circumstances heightens the desire to see the face."[11] Clym Yeobright's face, for instance, is first registered as an obscure object in other characters' imaginations, then in a comparison by the narrator to a Rembrandt painting. When Eustacia Vye is introduced, the celebrated description of her face aligns the portrait, as David DeLaura suggests, with Walter Pater's evocation of *La Gioconda*.[12] Instead of being the distillation of a pictorial art, however, this initial description of Eustacia resists facial conventions through its collection of idiosyncratic, unclassifiable, and disjunctive features that seem to make her a collection of natural forces. Indeed, the "Queen of Night" anatomizes what Deleuze and Guattari call the "*faciality traits* [that] themselves finally elude the organization of the face — freckles dashing toward the horizon, hair carried off by the wind, eyes you traverse instead of seeing yourself in or gazing into in those glum face-to-face encounters between signifying subjectivities" (171). These fanciful "traits" work against the *system* of faciality; they are just the sort of features that Hardy emphasizes in his depiction of Eustacia, which emphatically fails to undertake a physiognomic analysis:

> To see her hair was to fancy that a whole winter did not contain
> darkness enough to form its shadow: it closed over her forehead
> like nightfall extinguishing the western glow.
>
> Her nerves extended into those tresses, and her temper could
> always be softened by stroking them down.[13]

For all the rhetorical echoes of Pater, Hardy's character is less a person or
a picture of a person than a dynamic force, at once human and not. The
group of facial features can be resolved into a portrait only by domesticating the vast, animated landscape that is her face, including the palpable,
dark motion of her hair, a "nightfall" and an extension beyond the body's
surface of its capacity for touch. "The mouth seemed formed less to
speak than to quiver, less to quiver than to kiss. Some might have added,
less to kiss than to curl.... So fine were the lines of her lips that, though
full, each corner of her mouth was as clearly cut as the point of a spear"
(119). "The mouth" — already a depersonalized object — is led in the series
of negations through movement, from speech to quivering, to kissing and
curling, to cutting. The intentions and desires conveyed by this movement — flirtation, eroticism, contempt — are subordinated to the narrative's sheer wonder at the variability of its fleshy, sensual form.[14]

For Hardy, I suggest, the face is a tissue of interwoven strata through
which physical forms encounter and transform mental and spiritual
entities.[15] The face is a fungible medium in which the subject's ethereal
thoughts or feelings are given the material shape of an object. Hardy
explicitly invokes this notion of the face as medium in a passage describing Clym Yeobright's countenance as a marked surface:

> The face was well shaped, even excellently. But the mind within
> was beginning to use it as a mere waste tablet whereon to trace its
> idiosyncrasies as they developed themselves. The beauty here vis-
> ible would in no long time be ruthlessly overrun by its parasite,
> thought, which might just as well have fed upon a plainer exterior
> where there was nothing it could harm. Had Heaven preserved
> Yeobright from a wearing habit of meditation, people would have
> said, "A handsome man." Had his brain unfolded under sharper
> contours they would have said, "A thoughtful man." But an inner
> strenuousness was preying upon an outer symmetry, and they
> rated his look as singular. (194)

The theory of embodiment subtending this passage presumes that the
face is a vessel for mental contents, which drain or wear it; the physical
needs of life, however, compete with these less tangible demands on the

body. Clym's internal struggles thus come to be recorded or reflected in his face.[16] Here the face is an object for others — those hypothetical observers who would take Clym to be handsome or thoughtful — but it is also a subject of intellect and sensation. The face is not a text that might be read for its singular, extractable meaning but a palpable surface (the "waste tablet") molded by mental and physical experiences alike. Hardy goes on to elaborate and generalize the notion of thought as a "parasite" that feeds on the outer form:

> Hence people who began by beholding him ended by perusing him. His countenance was overlaid with legible meanings. . . . He already showed that thought is a disease of flesh, and indirectly bore evidence that ideal physical beauty is incompatible with emotional development and a full recognition of the coil of things. Mental luminousness must be fed with the oil of life, even though there is already a physical need for it; and the pitiful sight of two demands on one supply was just showing itself here.
>
> When standing before certain men the philosopher regrets that thinkers are but perishable tissue, the artist that perishable tissue has to think. Thus to deplore, each from his point of view, the mutually destructive interdependence of spirit and flesh would have been instinctive with these in critically observing Yeobright. (194–95)

Weirdly, the flesh that is the body contains the contending forces of "spirit and flesh." Because both drink at the same well, modifying the external form has interior effects. Extending this idea of face and mind as mutually inscribing surfaces, Hardy later writes that Clym's "sorrows had made some change in his outward appearance; and yet the alteration was chiefly within. It might have been said that he had a wrinkled mind" (448). Supplying a morphological account of otherwise invisible internal changes, in showing them to be recorded on the facial plane, Hardy presents thought as a physical process, which draws on bodily resources. This notion substantiates Deleuze's claim that Hardy's characters are sensate individuals without quite being subjects: interior being, Hardy suggests, is not transcendental but is another form of physical existence.

Hardy's literary notebooks provide evidence that, while composing *The Return of the Native*, he was reading Herbert Spencer's *Principles of Biology* (1864–67).[17] As I suggested in chapter 1, Spencer locates at the center of his inquiry the relations between fleshy surfaces and depths. Read in this context, Hardy's concept of the wrinkled mind or of the face as a waste tablet of the mind seems less anomalous. Like Spencer, Hardy emphasizes the material qualities of the interior, stressing in *The Return of the Native* the expressive capacities of the face and its role at the center of human sensory perception. If the face brings emotions to the surface, it also introjects external material by means of perception. The face, then, is both an inlet and an outlet, like the skin or the alimentary canal in Spencer's account.[18] Clym's "countenance," as Hardy says, may be "overlaid with legible meanings," but these meanings are unstable and flickering, not the singular signifiance into which facialization would resolve them.

The idea that the face can serve as both record and screen on which layers of conflicting meaning might variously arise is developed in a series of meditations on its function in *The Return of the Native*. In an early scene, Diggory Venn, the reddleman, transports Thomasin Yeobright, whose wedding has just been aborted and who is now asleep in the back of his van. Diggory reveals the sleeping figure to her aunt, holding a lantern to illuminate the scene, and the reader follows Mrs. Yeobright's eyes:

> A fair, sweet, and honest country face was revealed, reposing in a nest of wavy chestnut hair. It was between pretty and beautiful. Though her eyes were closed, one could easily imagine the light necessarily shining in them as the culmination of the luminous workmanship around. The groundwork of the face was hopefulness; but over it now lay like a foreign substance a film of anxiety and grief. The grief had been there so shortly as to have abstracted nothing of the bloom, and had as yet but given a dignity to what it might eventually undermine. The scarlet of her lips had not had time to abate, and just now it appeared still more intense by the absence of the neighbouring and more transient colour of her cheek. (89)

Although it provides a verbal portrait of Thomasin's face, this passage works more like cinema or like time-lapse photography, for the face is mobile: as with Clym's face, emotions move across it, like clouds in a landscape, but with the ability to effect permanent change. Hopefulness is the "groundwork" of this face, while anxiety and grief come from outside to overlay the facial stratum. The movement of unconscious affect across the surface is embodied in the form of fluid, variable shading, suggesting that what begins as coloration might eventually dig ruts and creases into the surface on which it flows. As Hardy writes later of Eustacia: "In respect of character a face may make certain admissions by its outline; but it fully confesses only in its changes. So much is this the case that what is called the play of the features often helps more in understanding a man or woman than the earnest labours of all the other members together" (107).

Yet if Thomasin's mobile face is to be seen as an object — a membrane that registers commerce between the interior and the exterior — it is crucial that we know we see her through Mrs. Yeobright's eyes and by virtue of Diggory's lantern. Thomasin's face is an object, then, but an object for or to particular subjects. Like Clym's, Thomasin's countenance faces both inside and out, functioning at once as object and subject. It is not only looked on by her aunt, her admirer, and the reader; even when her eyes are closed, an observer can "easily imagine the light necessarily shining in them" — which is to say, one imagines Thomasin looking back. In fact, as the passage continues, the subjectivity of this object mounts increasingly until the eyes being looked on themselves start to see:

> One thing at least was obvious: she was not made to be looked at thus. The reddleman had appeared conscious of as much, and, while Mrs. Yeobright looked in upon her, he cast his eyes aside with a delicacy which well became him. The sleeper apparently thought so too, for the next moment she opened her own.
>
> The lips then parted with something of anticipation, something more of doubt; and her several thoughts and fractions of thoughts, as signalled by the changes on her face, were exhibited by the light to the utmost nicety. An ingenuous, transparent life was disclosed; as if the flow of her existence could be seen passing within her. She understood the scene in a moment. (89)

Here the idea of "life" shifts from the one looking to the one looked at, as the signal of this life is the capacity for looking. Paintings do not look back, do not see themselves being seen, as the object in this passage does.[19]

The face, I propose, is so frequently an *object* of narrative attention in this work because it is the primary vehicle of the *subjective* agency through which attention is paid. The face is the body's principal repository of perception, the influx and outflow of physical sensation, with which affective and intellectual impressions are frequently conflated, as the word *feeling* testifies. Hardy's attention to the palpable, material qualities of perception often leads him to substitute one sensory modality for another, a shift that generally moves in the direction of greater direct contact between percipient subject and perceived objects. While Clym is principally associated with vision and its failures in the novel, Eustacia is often linked to hearing. The synesthesia that enables connections among the senses is both described and enacted in a passage where Hardy writes of Eustacia eavesdropping:

> She strained her eyes to see them, but was unable. Such was her intentness, however, that it seemed as if her ears were performing the functions of seeing as well as hearing. This extension of power can almost be believed in at such moments. The deaf Dr. Kitto was probably under the influence of a parallel fancy when he described his body as having become, by long endeavour, so sensitive to vibrations that he had gained the power of perceiving by it as by ears. (171–72)

In discussing how Eustacia's ears stand in for her eyes, the narrative, through a train of sensory regression, marshals an example in which the sense of touch assumes the function of hearing. The strangeness of this so-called parallel highlights the ineluctable corporeality of perceptual experience: the nerves (receptacles for vibrations) have become a diffuse ear that sheathes the whole body. Alternatively, the image might suggest an interior cavity (the auricular canal) folded inside out, now become the exterior surface of the skin. This is the opposite of facialization: here the face is affirmatively put back in the body, where, in Deleuze and Guattari's terms, it can display "a multidimensional, polyvocal corporeal code." That Eustacia's name evokes the eustachian tube, a vital organ of the auditory apparatus, makes the allusion to "the deaf Dr. Kitto" seem particularly apt. Clym's name also has relevant connotations, suggesting eyebright, an herb long used in England as a remedy for visual ailments.[20] When Clym loses his sight later in the story, he reenacts Eustacia's procedures: "The life of this sweet cousin [Thomasin], her baby, and her servants, came to Clym's senses only in the form of sounds through a wood partition as he sat over books of exceptionally large type; but his ear became at last so accustomed to these slight noises from the other part of the house that he almost could witness the scenes they signified" (449). In the absence of the sense classically ranked highest, sight, these characters cultivate other sensory modalities, senses that, to Hardy's way of thinking, permit greater direct contact between subjects and objects than vision does. Or rather, Hardy reconceives sight along the lines of what some critics, adopting Merleau-Ponty's phenomenology, call haptic visuality, whereby looking ceases to be remote and distant, becoming instead proximate and intersubjective. Hardy's reference to Dr. Kitto was gleaned from Spencer's *Principles of Biology*,[21] a text in which the eyes are shown to have evolved from the outer layers of skin: "Marvellous as the fact appears," Spencer writes, "the eye considered as an optical apparatus is wholly produced by metamorphoses of the skin."[22] Touch, sight, and sound do not merely substitute for one another but also substantially overlap in the fleshy field of the face.[23]

In Hardy's imagination, deprivation of one sense is thus less a debility than an opportunity for cultivating alternative means of intellection.[24] Invocations of synesthesia are often induced by perceptions of the natural world, for in the process of making connections among different sensory modalities, Hardy erases distinctions between the human body and its exterior surroundings. In writing of the wind, for instance, Hardy shows the organic phenomenon to interpenetrate the human subjects it encounters:

> Its tone was indeed solemn and pervasive. Compound utterances addressed themselves to [the inhabitants'] senses, and it was possible to view by ear the features of the neighbourhood. Acoustic pictures were returned from the darkened scenery; they could hear where the tracts of heather began and ended; where the furze was growing stalky and tall; where it had been recently cut; in what direction the fir-clump lay, and how near was the pit in which the hollies grew; for these differing features had their voices no less than their shapes and colours. (139)

The notion of "acoustic pictures" spatially and temporally reorganizes the relation between perceiving subject and object, turning a distant visual mode of sensation into an incorporative and dynamic auditory one, while making the natural object — the wind passing over the heath — the agent of sensation and the human ear the passive recipient of an aural image.[25] This is one of many passages documenting the auditory qualities of the heath, to which Eustacia is particularly attuned. The fullest of these, lasting several pages (at the beginning of book 1, chapter 6), opens with Eustacia on the barrow awaiting a sign from her lover, and the description of the sound of the wind on the heath moves in and out of her perception of it.[26] The wind moves across, around, and through her body, entering it in the form of music that arises from desiccated heath bells, which are themselves described as if they were little ears that impress on her ear:

> So low was an individual sound from these that a combination of hundreds only just emerged from silence, and the myriads of the whole declivity reached the woman's ear but as a shrivelled and

> intermittent recitative. Yet scarcely a single accent among the many
> afloat tonight could have such power to impress a listener with
> thoughts of its origin. One inwardly saw the infinity of those com-
> bined multitudes; and perceived that each of the tiny trumpets
> was seized on, entered, scoured and emerged from by the wind as
> thoroughly as if it were as vast as a crater. (105–6)

The tactile description of the heath music as a process, whereby air rubs
against a surface, produces that inward picture. Showing how such
sounds "laid hold of [Eustacia's] attention," Hardy recursively makes
the percipient body and the natural origin of the sound stand for each
other. It is a music perceptible in a body, which is itself an object in nature,
and a music recognizable as such because it sounds so much like the
voice that comes *from* a human body: it is a "linguistic peculiarity of the
heath" that this sound "bore a great resemblance to the ruins of human
song which remain to the throat of fourscore and ten." As often happens
in Hardy, the reciprocal exchange here depicted in specifically aural form
finds a model in the sense of touch: "It was a worn whisper, dry and
papery, and it brushed so distinctly across the ear that, by the accustomed, the material minutiae in which it originated could be realized as
by touch." The sound is a sort of material that lifts from the heath's own
ground — "mummied heath-bells . . . now . . . dried to dead skins" (105) —
and pushes into Eustacia's tubes, themselves seeming more like an im-
pressible surface than a hollow receptacle. In auditory terms, there is no
sharp distinction between speaker and listener, human and landscape:

> Suddenly, on the barrow, there mingled with all this wild rhetoric
> of night a sound which modulated so naturally into the rest that
> its beginning and ending were hardly to be distinguished. The
> bluffs, and the bushes, and the heather-bells had broken silence; at
> last, so did the woman; and her articulation was but as another
> phrase of the same discourse as theirs. Thrown out on the winds it
> became twined in with them, and with them it flew away.
>   What she uttered was a lengthened sighing, apparently at
> something in her mind which had led to her presence here. There
> was a spasmodic abandonment about it as if, in allowing herself
> to utter the sound, the woman's brain had authorized what it could
> not regulate. (106)

When Eustacia sighs, she becomes the agent of the wind, not only its recipient; "twined" together, her body and the heath are indistinguishable
as sources of that sound: they are "phrase[s] of the same discourse."
What Deleuze and Guattari consider the false promise of a facialized

subjectivity — the promise of a unique, transcendent humanity — is un-done by the sensory production that makes subjects and objects similarly fragmentary and overlapping.

Whatever its sensory modality, landscape description in Hardy relies on a homology with the human body. The features of the landscape that he notes implicitly require a human presence to be perceived; processes of human perception and intention, in turn, become organic features of the natural world. Beyond the inroads that sensory perception makes on faciality, then, it can also extend across the body to the natural world — so relentlessly dwelled on in *The Return of the Native* — that commingles with human forms. The almost reflexive connection between landscape and body in Hardy illuminates a similarly mutual relation that Deleuze and Guattari posit:

> This machine is called the faciality machine because it is the social production of face, because it performs the facialization of the entire body and all its surroundings and objects, and the land-scapification of all worlds and milieus. The deterritorialization of the body implies a reterritorialization on the face; the decoding of the body implies an overcoding by the face; the collapse of corpo-real coordinates or milieus implies the constitution of a landscape. The semiotic of the signifier and the subjective never operates through bodies. It is absurd to claim to relate the signifier to the body. At any rate it can be related only to a body that has already been entirely facialized. (181)

If the face — or at any rate the *facialized,* that is, the face constituted as such through semiosis and subjectivity — is ordered, systematized, and regulated by odious social "machines," then the disordered, unpredictable process of *becoming* is associated with the body (the so-called Body without Organs). While this body can be subsumed by facialization, it also, I suggest, has the potential to disrupt or deterritorialize the face. That the principal metaphor for this process in Deleuze and Guattari is *geography* (deterritorialization and reterritorialization) suggests to them a series of parallels between face and landscape, both of which are at odds with the fragmented and disruptive body they celebrate — a body, I am propos-ing, whose fluid process of becoming is most evident in the mechanisms of sensory incorporation. They write: "We could say that [the face] is an *absolute* deterritorialization: it is no longer relative because it removes the head from the stratum of the organism, human or animal, and con-

nects it to other strata, such as signifiance and subjectification. Now the
face has a correlate of great importance: the landscape, which is not just a
milieu but a deterritorialized world. There are a number of face-landscape
correlations, on this 'higher' level" (172). Deleuze and Guattari go on to
enumerate these correlations in painting, architecture, film, and literature, showing how face and landscape correspond and how "each of the
two terms reterritorializes on the other" (174). Yet while they seem to
function in similarly conventional ways, face and landscape can, in their
reciprocity, help to undo the facialization machine. Hardy likewise emphasizes the correspondence between human and landscape faces, but
by presenting them as interpenetrating through the sensory body, he
effects a proto-Deleuzian deterritorialization of both. By means of the
senses, in other words, Hardy breaks down sharp distinctions between
human subject and objective world.

In *The Return of the Native,* which famously exaggerates even Hardy's
usual devotion to landscape description, the natural surroundings of the
heath intrude on, and become inseparable from, the bodies of its inhabitants. In combination with the emphasis Hardy places on the face as
repository for sensation, its continuity with the landscape serves further
to dismantle any incorporeal idea of human subjectivity. Having seen
how Hardy emphasizes the status of the face and its orifices as sensory
receptacles and how this procedure serves, in Eustacia's case, to make
auditory perception inseparable from the wind itself, we can turn to the
novel's opening portrait — perhaps the most famous description of landscape in British fiction — to consider how it too adduces embodied experience. Indeed, attending to embodiment and sensation in the opening
chapter requires revision of two critical commonplaces about the heath:
that it is an uninhabited wasteland on which human beings only gradually
and obscurely appear, and that it functions as a character in the story.
The novel encourages the first of these misreadings: its bravura opening
description of the barren landscape is called "A Face on Which Time
Makes But Little Impression" (53), and the following chapter is titled
"Humanity Appears upon the Scene, Hand in Hand with Trouble" (58).[27]
But the description provides less an objective representation of natural
phenomena than a subjective "impression" that posits an apperceptive,
embodied human presence. The second paragraph states:

> The heaven being spread with this pallid screen and the earth
> with the darkest vegetation, their meeting-line at the horizon was
> clearly marked.... Looking upwards, a furze-cutter would have

been inclined to continue work; looking down, he would have decided to finish his faggot and go home.... The face of the heath by its mere complexion added half an hour to evening; it could in like manner retard the dawn, sadden noon, anticipate the frowning of storms scarcely generated, and intensify the opacity of a moonless midnight to a cause of shaking dread. (53)

The personification of landscape is common in Hardy's writing: the heath has a face and a complexion; it retards, saddens, anticipates, and so on. Yet such images personify not only in attributing human features to the natural world but also in evoking the sensory capabilities of one who would receive them. In this opening moment, Hardy almost immediately insinuates a human figure (the furze-cutter), ensuring that someone in particular consumes the scene's emotional and visual impressions (such as the heath's appearing to absorb sunlight). That the furze-cutter is not, or not yet, a character (it eventually comes to be Clym) can lead plot-hungry readers to disregard the human presence in a rush to story and incident. But the setting is already predicated on human sensation, even if the inseparability of person and environment tends to obscure the act of perception: the land actively enfolds the human being within it; the observer both emanates from and absorbs into himself the natural topography. While the actions ("anticipates," "intensifies") belong grammatically to the heath, experientially they pertain to someone in the scene (thus "shaking dread"). Described as a face, the heath is not simply a personification but — like the other faces portrayed — a dynamic field of human perception. This is not making a "character" of the heath, unless we understand the term in the Deleuzian sense as a collection of "intensive sensations." We might better say that Hardy makes a *body* of the heath.

The land does more than supply the occasion for the percipience that designates the human, however. Later in the opening chapter, Hardy writes that the heath is "a place perfectly accordant with man's nature ... like man, slighted and enduring; and withal singularly colossal and mysterious in its swarthy monotony. As with some persons who have long lived apart, solitude seemed to look out of its countenance. It had a lonely face, suggesting tragical possibilities" (55). In being "like man," the landscape stands in a reciprocal relation to the human: each serves as a figure for the other. Yet they are not only symbols of each other, for they also overlap and interact directly.[28] The relation between the heath and human sentience is at once symbolic, embodied, and continuous — which is to say, the landscape is a metaphor for, is metaphorized by, and is metonymic with the human. This is not simply a question of whether the heath darkens if no one sees it; Hardy's concern is not to determine if all knowledge is subjective but rather to insist that all subjectivity is perceptual.[29] The face is the feature shared by the human being and the heath; it is also the feature that opens them to each other.

Critics such as Bullen, Michael Irwin, and Sheila Berger have emphasized the visual aspects of perception in Hardy, and the intensively visual landscape in this opening chapter certainly reads like portraiture. But there are also sensory aspects of it that elude the eyes: "In fact, precisely at this transitional point of its nightly roll into darkness the great and particular glory of the Egdon waste began, and nobody could be said to understand the heath who had not been there at such a time. It could best be felt when it could not clearly be seen, its complete effect and explanation lying in this and the succeeding hours before the next dawn: then, and only then, did it tell its true tale" (53). By insisting that the landscape is better felt than seen — which is to say, apprehended in the dark — Hardy suggests a synesthetic transfer of sensations contingent on embodiment for the scene's apprehension. This is saying more than that the sense of touch provides a truer impression of the place than sight; Hardy presents an interpenetration of subject and object until the distinction itself is eradicated. Like the reference to the furze-cutter, this allusion to situational blindness presages Clym's embodied experience of the heath; as we learn later, he is almost literally inseparable from it: "He was permeated with its scenes, with its substance, and with its odours. He might be said to be its product" (231). We have seen how auditory experience enacts such a breakdown with Eustacia when her sighs and the wind intermingle; at a later point, this character and the landscape overlap in even more materially explicit terms. Here Hardy portrays her eye not as a receptacle for visual images but as a source for tears, which effect a literal commingling with the environment: "Extreme unhappiness weighed visibly upon her. Between the drippings of the rain from her umbrella to her mantle, from her mantle to the heather, from the heather to the earth, very similar sounds could be heard coming from her lips; and the tearfulness of the outer scene was repeated upon her face" (421). This mixture of world and body — which resonates with Scarry's discussion of Hardy's representation of work — emblematizes Deleuzian "becoming": the landscape is a body, the body a landscape;

each is perceptible to the senses, each capable of sensory experience. For in addition to allegorizing the heath to the person, the "dripping" in this passage argues for the contiguity of the animate and the inanimate.[30] Landscape and human subject are requisite to each other's possibility, and the difference between them is eroded when crying and raining are indistinguishable. Perhaps because, more than anything, Eustacia longs to go to Paris, her rainy eyes can best be heard in French: *Il pleut comme elle pleure.*

If the landscape and the human body in *The Return of the Native* enact a mutually metaphorical relation — in that they not only stand for each other but actually mix and interpenetrate by means of the senses — it is an active, dynamic process, not a rigidly fixed one. Each of these two entities, which receive so much of the novel's attention, constantly adapts the other to itself, incorporating and making use of it. Eustacia and her lovers, for example, regularly appropriate natural phenomena as signals to each other. Early on, Wildeve indicates his presence by imitating the sound of a toad's jump by tossing a pebble into a pond; for Clym, a lunar eclipse "marked a preconcerted moment: for the remote celestial phenomenon had been pressed into sublunary service as a lover's signal" (254). Just as the heath is both like a person and perceived by people, so these apparently indifferent natural events, when their "sublunary" significance is perceived, become contiguous with the human: "overcoded" with human meanings, such phenomena come into characters' eyes or ears. If the eclipse functions in the register of signification as "a lover's signal," it also mixes with the perceiving subject's body, refusing to stay stably outside. In one sense, it gives objective form to Clym's clouded vision, so that, like some celestial cataract, it serves as another prevision of his blindness: "While he watched the far-removed landscape a tawny stain grew into being on the lower verge: the eclipse had begun" (254). In another aspect, however, the moon becomes not the thing seen but itself the agent of sight: "He flung himself down upon the barrow, his face towards the moon, which depicted a small image of herself in each of his eyes" (253). Rather than giving us either the moon as Clym sees it (a subjective view of the object) or a portrait of him seeing (an objective view of the subject), Hardy enacts a collapse of subject and object: we see the object of Clym's sight reflected in the optical apparatus that is his eyes. In an altogether denaturalized account of human vision, the moon is the agent of its own representation in his seeing eyes.[31]

The eclipse, then, functions as both a social sign, which brings lovers together, and an embodied experience, which brings human being and natural object together. Hardy elaborates on the conjunction in another scene of Eustacia finding a "lover's signal" in a natural object, this time one actively induced by her inamorata:

> The heath tonight appeared to be totally deserted: and Wildeve, after looking over Eustacia's garden gate for some little time, with a cigar in his mouth, was tempted by the fascination that emotional smuggling had for his nature to advance towards the window, which was not quite closed, the blind being only partly drawn down. He could see into the room, and Eustacia was sitting there alone. Wildeve contemplated her for a minute, and then retreating into the heath beat the ferns lightly, whereupon moths flew out alarmed. Securing one, he returned to the window, and holding the moth to the chink, opened his hand. The moth made towards the candle upon Eustacia's table, hovered round it two or three times, and flew into the flame.
>
> Eustacia started up. This had been a well-known signal in old times when Wildeve had used to come secretly wooing to Mistover. She at once knew that Wildeve was outside, but before she could consider what to do her husband came in from upstairs. Eustacia's face burnt crimson at the animation that it too frequently lacked. (330–31)

The play of illumination is instructive: Wildeve, with his presumably glowing cigar, and Eustacia, with her candle, are versions of each other; by sending the moth into her room, he intends to draw her out to him, just as the insect flies toward the flame. When her candle goes out, her momentary blindness seems spontaneously to invoke the appearance of her husband, Clym, by now nearly blind, and, at the same time, to transfer onto her body the properties of the candle itself: her "face burnt crimson." Like the moon, which directs its reflection off Clym's eyes, the moth is here the agent of a meaningful darkness. The natural occurrence of a moth flying into a flame is rendered fully social in being adapted as a sign between lovers, even as the scene's narration illustrates the contiguity between animate and inanimate objects: people, moths, and candles all fall along a tactile continuum of brightness.[32]

Insects function transitionally between human forms of social organization and the natural world in Hardy's novel, suggesting a relation that Deleuze and Guattari call "becoming-animal" (233). Like the heath, insects both allegorize human beings and overlap with them through direct contact.[33] Once blind and laboring, Clym himself appears to be like a moth: "The silent being who thus occupied himself seemed to be of no more account in life than an insect. He appeared as a mere parasite of the heath, fretting its surface in his daily labour as a moth frets a garment, entirely engrossed with its products, having no knowledge of anything in the world but fern, furze, heath, lichens, and moss" (339). This might merely be an analogy but for two considerations: first, the word "parasite" returns us to the earlier statement that thought feeds on the beauty of his face (194), suggesting that just as mental entities are materially contiguous with outer forms, so this outer form is in turn contiguous with the landscape; and second, Clym is immersed in an actual insect universe: "His daily life was of a curious microscopic sort, his whole world being limited to a circuit of a few feet from his person. His familiars were creeping and winged things, and they seemed to enroll him in their band. Bees hummed around his ears with an intimate air, and tugged at the heath and furze-flowers at his side in such numbers as to weigh them down to the sod" (312). These relations between man and insect might be read as symbolizing the smallness of human endeavor, but one would not want thereby to miss the forms of direct, consequential contact between them. Likewise, the moth's instinct for the flame could be taken as an emblem of love's ephemeral nature (at least in the case of Wildeve and Eustacia). But allegorical reading should not efface the insects' material lives, which get so much of Hardy's attention: the moth may be a sign (to Eustacia) and a symbol (of rapidly exhausted desire), but it is, first of all, a creature that flies into a candle. It brings the outdoors inside, it transforms the social through the natural, and it helps to make light itself a palpable object of perception.

On Egdon Heath, human beings interact meaningfully with insects: in Clym's case, the insect world is both an allegory of his narrow, sightless labor and the literal element in which he works; for Eustacia and Wildeve, the moth elucidates by spreading darkness. Similarly, when Wildeve and Diggory play a game of dice on the heath for the fortune that Mrs. Yeobright has sent to her niece, their play is interrupted when "a large death's head moth" flies into their lantern and puts out the light (292). If in thus depriving sight, insects draw attention to both the material sources and organs of vision (flames and eyes), they also make a tactile entity of light by serving as literal sources of illumination. The two gamblers, undaunted, find that "it happened to be that season of the year at which glowworms put forth their greatest brilliancy, and the light they yielded was more than ample for the purpose, since it is possible on such nights to read the handwriting of a letter by the light of two or three" (293). This scene distills Hardy's concerns, bringing together an extraordinary natural phenomenon with a consequential game of chance — that element of the arbitrary and inhuman within human lives. While the incident is loaded with symbolic content, Hardy underwrites the scene with the interaction between human and animal in vividly perceptual terms. One insect brings darkness, another miraculously provides light; like the heath, whose fading incandescence in the opening portrait is part of its embodiment, the glowworms are an animate form of illumination. In the original three-volume edition of the novel, Hardy confesses to recognizing just how weird a scene he has concocted here: "The incongruity between the men's deeds and their environment was striking. The soft juicy vegetation of the hollow in which they sat, gently rustling in the warm air, the uninhabited solitude, the chink of guineas, the rattle of the dice, the exclamations of the players, combined to form such a bizarre exhibition of circumstances as had never before met on those hills since they first arose out of the deep."[34] Although the admission that the moment is "striking" and "bizarre" is cut from later versions, the synesthesia associated with the animate light source, and its extension to the tactile and auditory dimensions of the narration, remains.

The topics I have been discussing — sensory perception, a human commingling with the environment, and the deterritorialized face — all finally converge on one figure. Probably the strangest and most memorable collapse of external world and sensate individual in the novel — if not in all of Hardy's fiction — occurs in the cumulously rubicund environment of Diggory Venn. A number of features contribute to Venn's singularity. First, his trade in red dye is anachronistic: his "vocation . . . was to supply farmers with redding for their sheep. He was one of a class rapidly becoming extinct in Wessex, filling at present in the rural world the place which, during the last century, the dodo occupied in the world of animals" (59). Second, even if his profession were not obsolete, he would have scant business on the heath, which supports no agriculture beyond furze cutting: "Not a plough had ever disturbed a grain of that stubborn soil. In the heath's barrenness to the farmer lay its fertility to the historian. There had been no obliteration, because there had been no tending" (66). Venn, the reader learns, haunts the heath not to ply his trade but to keep an eye on Thomasin and Eustacia, which explains his practical irrelevance.[35] But the most striking thing about Venn — and the reason Hardy is willing to go to such lengths of improbability to get him on the scene — is the fact of his "lurid" redness (58). His itinerant vocation may explain his crimson appearance, but it does nothing to diminish the mystical and symbolic overtones: "That blood-coloured figure was a sublimation of all the horrid dreams which had afflicted the juvenile spirit since imagination began" (131).[36]

Like the reddle that "spreads its lively hues over everything it lights on" (131), Diggory, by dint of his peripatetic trade, is dispersed and diffused across the heath; he is both identified with and an element of it. Clym "might be said to be [the] product" of the landscape (231), but Diggory is literally saturated with it, for his skin is impregnated with rufous material dug out of the earth. Like that of the other characters, Diggory's face receives its due paragraph of narrative attention, but in addition to the play of thought and emotion across his face — which in this respect resembles Clym's and Thomasin's — it also imbibes elements of nature. It does not, like Eustacia's face, evoke wild tempests or invoke classical allusions; it is simply that the ruddy material has worked its way into his pores. Like Clym's, his face is more attractive than it strictly needs to be; as elsewhere, an imagined observer shepherds the transition from object to subject of visual perception:

> The reddleman who had entered Egdon that afternoon was an instance of the pleasing being wasted to form the ground-work of the singular, when an ugly foundation would have done just as well for that purpose. The one point that was forbidding about this reddleman was his colour. Freed from that he would have been as agreeable a specimen of rustic manhood as one would often see. A keen observer might have been inclined to think... that he had relinquished his proper station in life for want of interest in it....
>
> While he darned the stocking his face became rigid with thought. Softer expressions followed this, and then again recurred the tender sadness which had sat upon him during his drive along the highway that afternoon. (132)

Charted like the landscape that Diggory traverses, his countenance exhibits all the features of Hardy's facial lexicon: an inseparability of face from environment, a fluid shift between roles as object and subject, and an inscribed record of the encounter between external phenomena and subjective emotions. While for Thomasin and Clym, mental and emotional processes are etched onto the appealing "groundwork" of the face, in Diggory the substance that mars his countenance is unambiguously material. His eye too becomes an object of visual interest as much as a subject of perception, but the vermilion saturation of his face dramatically highlights the influx and outflow: "He lifted the lantern to his face, and the light shone into the whites of his eyes...which, in contrast with the red surrounding, lent him a startling aspect enough to the gaze of a juvenile" (127).[37] Just as we saw the variable shading of Thomasin's sleeping face through Diggory's eyes, so we see his face — a repetition of the lantern that illuminates it — through the "gaze" of the boy. Diggory's visage is a porous screen on which the landscape leaves its traces and across which emotions, like the candlelight, dance and flicker until they too leave their marks; it condenses the various functions that Hardy assigns to the face in *The Return of the Native*. The face is a shifting series of surfaces, affective and material, which work in parallel and overlapping ways, a structure that embodies Deleuze and Guattari's "strange true becomings." More than a mirror of the soul, this face is a sensate record of flows and intensities.

Hardy's account of face, sensation, and landscape helps to explicate the sometimes baffling logic of Deleuze and Guattari: it suggests how the percipient body supplies some means of resistance to the conventions of faciality, how sensation intermingles the body and the landscape, and how interior entities, such as thought and feeling, might be understood in material terms. No doubt Hardy sometimes writes for the sheer pleasure of evoking specific geographic locations and rendering the sensuous particulars of a given perceptual experience.[38] By amalgamating subject and object, person and landscape, interior and exterior, however, Hardy works toward larger goals as well: of moving agency away from individuals and showing how human beings have a palpable, categorical connection with the natural world. Putting the human in contact with a material location may not require a diminution of psychological motives, but it tends to have that effect. In its insistence that will or motive is always embodied, Hardy's narrative links nineteenth-century physiological theories of mind, soul, and body to twentieth-century philosophical concepts of sensation and becoming. By means of sensory perception, Hardy demonstrates the continuity between an extremely wide spatiotemporal vantage on human action — that of the geological, the epochal, the historical — and the minute one supplied by the individual body.

5

Soul

Inside Hopkins

Like the other writers I have discussed, the poet and Jesuit priest Gerard Manley Hopkins posits a continuity between the external form of natural objects and their effects on human subjects' interiors. Like them too, Hopkins extends this continuity so far as to muddy the boundaries of agency and existence between subject and object, a proposition summarized epigrammatically in a phrase from his journals: "What you look hard at seems to look hard at you."[1] While Hopkins emphasizes sensory experience in ways akin to his contemporaries, however, he, unlike the others, believes that the external world possesses a divinely ordained form of perfection, which enters the human body through its sensory channels as well as through a peculiarly embodied form of language; once there, it interacts with and helps to perfect the human spirit, also divinely charged. In his efforts to replicate this embodiment in language, he arrives at a materialist conception of human interiority by means of, rather than against, a spiritual one. Hopkins focuses on physical, especially sensory, experience because he sees it as the means of access to the divine, and in this way his approach contrasts with that of the others I have considered: Brontë's self-abnegating Protestantism; Dickens's benign, essentially secular sentimentalism; Hardy's vigorous animism; and, most starkly, Trollope's active desublimation of religious faith. Hopkins thus returns us to the spiritual concerns whose repudiation, I have argued, was the historical corollary of the nineteenth century's embrace of materialist sciences of the mind and the self. While Hopkins's religious motives oppose the essentially skeptical and secular origins of this emergent science and the literary culture growing under its influence, the two views concur to a remarkable extent on the centrality of bodily experience to the inner life.

Even before his conversion, at twenty-two, to Roman Catholicism and his decision to enter the Jesuit priesthood, Hopkins was already uneasy with the materialist turn in contemporary psychology. In his undergraduate essay "The Probable Future of Metaphysics," he explicitly deprecates these developments, writing: "Material explanation cannot be refined into explaining thought and it is all to no purpose to show an organ for each faculty and a nerve vibrating for each idea, because this only shows in the last detail what broadly no one doubted, to wit that the activities of the spirit are conveyed in those of the body as scent is conveyed in spirits of wine, remaining still inexplicably distinct" (118). This sentence epitomizes Hopkins's approach to the question of materialism: he opposes it philosophically, and yet the terms in which he does so are inescapably material. He gives voice to the immateriality of spirit by describing it with the simile of an olfactory sensation — which is to say, of a sensory experience that brings the perceived object into the body of the subject. After his conversion, this uneasy preservation of the material as both source and evidence of an idealist principle was sublated in a conception of the divine as at once immanent in and transcendent of fleshly human existence. As Daniel Brown has established, Hopkins's training in British idealist philosophy served as a basis for these arguments,[2] which were augmented by his later discovery of the work of the medieval theologian Duns Scotus and by his own highly inventive prosody. This combination of intellectual interests, religious beliefs, and poetic practices enabled Hopkins to partake of the broader cultural strains of Victorian materialism I have been tracing and, at the same time, to appear to repudiate it — often by sublimating it into ecstatic, sometimes agonized, spiritual revelation. Yet throughout his writing, even when he seems most resolutely to abjure the flesh in favor of the spirit, Hopkins does not evade the sensuous terms of embodiment.

Jesuit practice supplies Hopkins with a means of reconciling the conflicting impulses in his account of human interiority toward, on the one hand, an ethereal spiritualism and, on the other, the manifest physicality of bodily sensation. In the letter he writes to his father announcing his conversion, Hopkins declares that at the core of his decision lies the dogma of transubstantiation, which captures this doubleness: the "literal truth of our Lord's words by which I learn that the least fragment of the consecrated elements in the Blessed Sacrament of the Altar is the whole Body of Christ."[3] Through the doctrine of Incarnation, which receives even greater attention in his oeuvre than transubstantiation, Hopkins works out the paradox of a God at once divine and embodied, and a humanity both transcendent and substantial. He elaborates on the relation of bodily form to spiritual essence in a later letter to Robert Bridges: "For though even bodily beauty... is from the soul, in the sense, as we Aristotelian Catholics say, that the soul is the form of the body, yet the soul may have no other beauty, so to speak, than that which it expresses in the symmetry of the body — barring those blurs in the cast which wd. not be found in the die or the mould."[4] Hopkins articulates one of the tenets of the materialist position: that "the soul is the form of the body." He means this in a sense akin to Freud's later proposition that the ego is "first and foremost a bodily ego" — that is, the subject's conception of his interior self conforms precisely to the contours of his external morphology. But Hopkins also makes the stranger suggestion that the soul is the die from which the body is cast — in other words, that the subject as embodied takes its form as an impression from a type of Platonic ideal, one conventionally imagined as formless. The mystery of Incarnation and its replication in the sacrament of the Eucharist encompass for Hopkins the inextricability of spirit from matter, indicating that the soul lends form to the flesh as much as the reverse. Understood in relation to the tradition I have been tracing, Hopkins's devotion to the divine, perhaps surprisingly, does nothing to diminish the primacy of the material.

In his poetic theory, Hopkins places special pressure on the space of the inside with the concept of "inscape." W. H. Gardner describes inscape as "a name for that 'individually-distinctive' form (made up of various sense-data) which constitutes the rich and revealing 'oneness' of the natural object."[5] In the movement between the inscape of an object and the human apperception of it through "instress" — and through the materialization and recapitulation of this process within poetic language itself — Hopkins identifies a tangible contiguity between human subjects and the world, interiority and the exterior. These features of Hopkins's weltanschauung, familiar to readers acquainted with his poetry and prosody, are also manifest in his theological pronouncements. Yet despite overwhelming evidence that Hopkins conceives of instress as a somatic experience, critics have had little to say about its location within the human body, except to note that instress often involves the senses.[6] To the extent that the human body in Hopkins's work has received attention recently, it has tended to be discussed in terms of repressed or sublimated sexuality.[7]

In this chapter, I focus on Hopkins's understanding of the interior, and its interaction with the external world, as irreducibly corporeal. For Hopkins the body's material form limits — sometimes even degrades — spiritual existence, yet it is also the agency that enables experience of the divinely charged world, for the perceptual encounter of instress would be unimaginable without it. After establishing this doubleness, which generates the poet's alternately despairing and joyous account of embodiment, I turn to his depiction of sensory experience, which provides the means of mediating the problem of the body. Hopkins, I argue, attends to the sensory routes to the interior because they do three things: they bring the world into the body; they suggest ways of imagining objects in the world themselves *as* percipient bodies; and they make the human body itself an object of sensory apprehension. In short, bodily sensation affirms the status of the human subject as an object in the world — albeit a privileged one — which is both contiguous with other objects and mutually pervious to them. The reversibility of subjects and objects is key to Hopkins's poetic practice, his theology, and his implicit theory of knowledge, for it dramatizes the primacy of the body in human experience — even experience of the divine — and simultaneously elevates inanimate objects into agents integral to the human. While incorporation through the senses is a key theme in works like "The Windhover," the "Kingfishers" sonnet, and the other poems for which Hopkins is best known, I extend the argument to the journals in which he records observations of nature and philosophical speculations. The journal entries expand on problems distilled in the poems while shifting our attention from the theological and prosodic concerns predominant in the poetry. I focus on excerpts from the journals, reading them in tandem with Hopkins's poetry and spiritual exercises, to demonstrate how, in a relatively secular context, Hopkins understands sensory experience to break down boundaries between inside and outside and between subject and object. Such writings extend the fusion of spirit and matter, grounded in Catholic doctrine, manifest in his poetry.

My discussion of Hopkins's formulations — of perception as a physical encounter with the world, of visual sensation in particular in tactile terms, and of perceiving human subjects themselves as objects — relies implicitly on twentieth-century phenomenology's account of such concepts and specifically on the ideas of Maurice Merleau-Ponty, which I have outlined in chapter 1. Hopkins's conception of embodiment shares with Merleau-Ponty's an argument against the tradition of Cartesian rationalism, which posits a dualistic distinction between mind and body; Hopkins also shares with Merleau-Ponty an assessment of knowledge, in even its most abstract forms, as rooted in the body. For both writers, the sense of sight is deprivileged, partly through an emphasis on other senses, which bring the world into or onto the body directly, and partly through a reimagination of sight itself as a form of incorporation and touching. While Hopkins's theory of sensation bears affinities to Merleau-Ponty's, in always taking perception to be a form of proximate contact, Hopkins takes the eye itself as an object of visual and visceral interest — an interest that suggests productive connections with Bataille as well. Hopkins presents an account of the human subject that resembles Bataille's insofar as that subject's material substance yields an exalted debasement, a savoring of degradation (physical, emotional, and spiritual), and an explosion outward of inner matter. Hopkins at times anticipates and illustrates Bataille's notion of a subject not just threatened but shattered by the fact of his own substantial being; both writers find resources for a paradoxically derealized psychological and spiritual subjectivity in the very degradation they feel embodiment to entail. Rather than the spiritual transcendence of a devotional Hopkins — or even the radically sensual one who, as Julia Saville has argued, turns ascetic renunciation into a form of sexual ecstasy — this is Hopkins understood as fully embodied, both elevated and unmade by the material conditions of his existence.[8]

Hopkins's frame of reference for the enclosure of spirit within corporeal forms varies widely, with allegories of embodiment ranging from the contracted (a prison) to the expansive (a landscape).[9] In the poem "The Caged Skylark," for example, the analogy between bodily and spatial enclosure is positively carceral. Just as the bird is trapped in its cage, so human "spirits" are imprisoned in their bodies:

> As a dare-gale skylark scanted in a dúll cáge,
> 　　Man's mounting spirit in his bone-house, mean house, dwells —
> 　　That bird beyond the remembering hís free fells,
> 　This in drudgery, day-labouring-out life's age. (122)[10]

Enclosure is negative through most of this poem, imagined in terms of cage, cell, and prison; the body, through the kenning in line 2, is the "house" for both "spirit" and "bone." The cage is "dull"; its inmates "droop deadly sómetimes in their cells / Or wring their barriers in bursts of fear or rage." Although the outdoors, too, can form an enclosure, Hop-

kins nearly always prefers it to "being indoors," for the immediate connections the outdoors allows to natural forms. Some of the most famous
lines in the Hopkins corpus (from the "Kingfishers" sonnet) reiterate the
language of spatial inhabitation as a figure for the inscape of spiritual
qualities within material frames: "Each mortal thing does one thing and
the same: / Deals out that being indoors each one dwells" (115). Similarly pressing on the conventional terms in which a soul is imagined as
imprisoned in the body, an entry from Hopkins's journal of 1873 describes a nightmare in which he feels paralyzed: "The feeling is terrible:
the body no longer swayed as a piece by the nervous and muscular instress seems to fall in and hang like a dead weight on the chest. I cried on
the holy name and by degrees recovered myself as I thought to do. It
made me think that this was how the souls in hell would be imprisoned
in their bodies as in prisons" (238).[11] The passage is both evocative and
involuted: somehow "the body" itself "weigh[s] on the chest," the whole
obstructing the part. Likewise, if condemned souls are "imprisoned in
their bodies as in prisons," then the body is at once actually a prison and
the figure for a prison. Explicitly linking the image of spiritual imprisonment within the body to the theory of instress, these lines implicitly
point to the body as the channel to (and agent for) its spiritual contents:
when denied the flexibility and movement of the corporeal frame, the
soul is condemned to its enclosure, like the wretched in hell.

The body is the route through which human beings encounter the
godhead; the problem is that the body also incarcerates the soul, corrupting it through the occasions the body supplies for taint and temptation.
Moreover, even if, for degraded mortals like the poet, the body impedes
spiritual liberty, it is necessary to the doctrine of Incarnation: by assum-
ing the material form of human flesh, Christ fulfilled his divine function
as embodied.[12] This paradox explains the turn taken in the last lines of
"The Caged Skylark," which shift from calling the body a cage to proposing that it houses the "best" of man:

> Man's spirit will be flesh-bound when found at best,
>   But úncúmberèd: meadow-dówn is nót distréssed
>   For a ráinbow fóoting it nor hé for his bónes rísen.

Although human subjects may be ineluctably embodied, it is possible,
Hopkins suggests, with Christ as a model, for the "flesh-bound" "spirit"
to inhabit the body "uncumbered" — which is to say, to be in the body
but not wholly *of* the body. While most of the poem dwells on the caged

bird as a figure for the enclosure of human souls, this condensed final stanza extends the allegory in two directions, one lower, the other higher. Man's spirit is bound to his flesh but need not be hindered by it, these lines state, just as the meadow is not "distressed" by the rainbow that appears to set a foot down on it (a verbal image that personifies, and so lends bodily form to, the inanimate), and just as Christ does not regret the necessity of coming to earth in bodily human form, from which he arose (that is, was bodily resurrected). The poet holds out hope that rather than being the prison house of the soul, the body might be its portal.

If the body is the untranscendable vessel bearing the human soul, then the body's own portals — its sensory openings — are the means of both material and spiritual ingress to the subject. Like "The Caged Skylark," "The Candle Indoors" draws an analogy between human embodiment and an inhabited dwelling, linking them through the image of interior illumination, both visible and sacred. The sonnet opens:

> Some candle clear burns somewhere I come by.
> I muse at how its being puts blissful back
> With yellowy moisture mild night's blear-all black
> Or to-fro tender trambeams truckle at the eye. (133)

The body is the absent, implied connection between the image, rendered in spatial terms (illumination shines within a physical container), and its spiritual meaning: the candle illuminates a house just as divine truth illuminates a soul. The soul, however, resides within a body, as is indicated by the realization of "I," the speaker, in the "eye," whose placement at the end of sentence, line, and quatrain emphasizes the word. If the human body is only suggested in the allegory between house and soul, it returns as the perceptual medium for receiving light: the embodied subject of this vision is engaged in a dialectical exchange of reflection and refraction with the shimmering candle flame.[13] The sonnet's apostrophic second half invites the addressee into an illuminated "indoors," whose light might mend the dimming internal flame of faith:

> Come you indoors, come home; your fading fire
> Mend first and vital candle in close heart's vault;
> You there are master, do your own desire;
>
> What hinders?

Hopkins's innovation on the traditional figure of divine inspiration as light is to emphasize its sensory apprehension through a visual apparatus ("trambeams," "beam-blind") that takes vivid tactile metaphors. The result is an account of seeing as a proximate sensation: with its "yellowy moisture," the candle pushes away the blinding blackness of the night. Hopkins prefigures Merleau-Ponty in employing a model of what has come to be called haptic visuality, of seeing modeled on the example of touch, the sense whose reciprocal and reversible qualities are most immediately evident. Describing vision as "palpation of the eye," Merleau-Ponty, like Hopkins, lends it the tactile qualities of propinquity and direct contact.[14] Rather than supplying the subject mastery over what he sees, such embodied sight renders him an object, to himself and to others, even as it permits him to experience the other — equally embodied — as a subject as well.

Hopkins is alternately jubilant and fearful about the possibilities the senses hold for enlightenment. The piety of Hopkins's works and their intensely devotional resolutions are rooted in the sensual apprehension of the world. At times, this sensitivity is ecstatic, insofar as "The world is charged with the grándeur of God" ("God's Grandeur," 139): the poet celebrates the earthly wonders that make tangible the promise of divine redemption. Hopkins's poems celebrating sensory experience of the natural world date from early in his extant work, beginning with "The Habit of Perfection" (77) — an extended apophasis that provides a sensuous account of forswearing each of the organs of perception in favor of the intangible sensations of divinity — and culminating in "The Windhover" (120), whose sensory and verbal achievements are inextricably bound together.[15] Such accounts of body and soul richly appreciate the human perceptual appurtenances as inlets for beauty, pleasure, and intellection. Although the poet sometimes reproves himself for savoring his apprehension of the natural world, his eyes fix on the divine even when his hands are in the mud.

One consequence of Hopkins's emphasis on perceiving simultaneously divine and sublunary objects is that the relation between the subject and the object of perception blurs, and the observer's process of observation itself becomes as central a focus of reflection as the objects that prompt it. The effect resonates with Merleau-Ponty's "double sensation" and "flesh," the idea of a reciprocity entailed by the embodied subject becoming an object of perception, which is exemplified by the way in which a hand that touches is itself always simultaneously touched. Hopkins addresses related concepts in a passage from the first of the Ignatian spiritual exercises he wrote on retreat in 1880. This passage makes distinctions between what lies within human beings — whether in bodily, mental, or spiritual

terms — and what lies outside; that these distinctions are fluid and shifting rather than absolute leads him to consider the means of communication, as well as boundary transgression, between inside and outside:

> Part of this world of objects, this object-world, is also part of the
> very self in question, as in man's case his own body, which each
> man not only feels in and acts with but also feels and acts on. If
> the centre of reference spoken of has concentric circles round it,
> one of these, the inmost, say, is its own, is óf it, the rest are tó it
> only. Within a certain bounding line all will be self, outside of it
> nothing: with it self begins from one side and ends from the other.
> I look through my eye and the window and the air; the eye is my
> eye and of me and me, the windowpane is my windowpane but
> not of me nor me. A self then will consist of a centre *and* a surround-
> ing area or circumference, of a point of reference *and* a belonging
> field, the latter set out, as surveyors etc say, from the former; of
> two elements which we may call the inset and the outsetting or
> the display.[16]

The subject of perception has become its own object: "man's . . . own body"
is the "centre of reference" in which perception, both sensual and spiritual, originates — but this "self" is perceptible *to* itself as well.[17] Much in
Hopkins's account depends on prepositions, as he seeks to make syntac-
tical sense of the overlapping, relational articulation between subject and
world. When he reaches for a figure by which to represent this process,
he imagines himself indoors, looking through a window at an outside
scene and taking it back in, through windowpane and eye, to the centered
self. Window and eye are like each other — each is a transparent medium
through which an exterior object can reach the inner self — but the eye, as
part of the body ("the eye is my eye and of me and me"), lies within that
"certain bounding line" where "all will be self," while the window, its
representation, lies beyond it ("not of me nor me"). This passage portrays the distinction between self and world by invoking an inside/out-
side body boundary superimposed on that of indoors/outdoors: Hopkins instinctively equates "external" with an outside landscape (as the
reference to "surveyors" indicates), where the invisible (but for him, palpable) "air" is located. Instressing — or, to use the terms he here coins,
taking to the "inset" the "outset" scene — is seeing his own eye seeing. If
this is an exploration of "the very self" of man, it is an emphatically embodied self.[18]

This perceptual theory informs a passage from a very early journal,
dated January 23, 1866. The journals' apparently casual notation of sense

impressions, particularly of natural forms, is often exceedingly complex and evocative; as J. Hillis Miller has suggested, these entries deserve to be approached as a species of prose poetry.[19] This particular entry richly meditates on relations between subjective interiors and the form of objects. In explicating it, one encounters a welter of implied connections between an apperceptive human body and the sense impressions made on it by the natural world — of instress in process. The passage opens by naming a trivial phenomenon or object, "drops of rain hanging on rails," and then, in an apparent effort to evoke the visual experience, proceeds through an elaborate series of associations inspired by both the object and the process of perceiving it. In its entirety, the entry reads:

> Drops of rain hanging on rails etc seen with only the lower rim lighted like nails (of fingers). Screws of brooks and twines. Soft chalky look with more shadowy middles of the globes of cloud on a night with a moon faint or concealed. Mealy clouds with a not brilliant moon. Blunt buds of the ash. Pencil buds of the beech. Lobes of the trees. Cups of the eyes. Gathering back the lightly hinged eyelids. Bows of the eyelids. Pencil of eyelashes. Juices of the eyeball. Eyelids like leaves, petals, caps, tufted hats, handkerchiefs, sleeves, gloves. Also of the bones sleeved in flesh. Juices of the sunrise. Joins and veins of the same. Vermilion look of the hand held against a candle with the darker parts as the middles of the fingers and especially the knuckles covered with ash. (72)

By following the logic of this passage, we can witness Hopkins's imagination at work as it moves progressively deeper into the body. The prose advances through a series of associations, filling in some steps that the poetry, with its customary layering of condensed images and metaphors, often elides; but it shares with the poetry a conception of objects known through their effects on the interior of the observing subject.

After notation of the thing he has observed ("drops of rain"), the particular illumination of these drops leads Hopkins to assimilate the visual phenomenon to another object, "nails," and then to specify that he means a part of the human body, "(of fingers)." It may be that "rails" elicits "nails" simply because of rhyme, for the sequence of sounds throughout the phrase makes it seem as if he were trying out sounds and images together: rain/hanging/fingers, rain/rails/rim, only/lower/lighted/like, and all the long vowels (rain, seen, only, lower, lighted, like).[20] The link to the next image — "screws of brooks and twines" — is unclear: certainly there is a play of light on water in both; perhaps from nails (before they are human nails) to screws (things that fasten); or by an implied analogy between watery natural objects and human, or human-made, ones: raindrops are to fingernails as brooks are to twines. The association within the compound "brooks and twines" itself is the spiral ("screw") pattern common to whirlpools in running water and bound thread. From these two image sets to the following description of faintly illuminated clouds at night, the bridge is the impression of texture created by light, as with nails in raindrops or shapes of running water. All three imply an inscape, an embodied essence in material objects: the perfection of shape the raindrops assume, the curling into "screws" of winding flows, and the interior of the cloud pushing out to its surface ("soft chalky look with more shadowy middles"). As in the poetry, the language in this line mimics and instantiates the objects' inscape with its bounding rhythm and condensed internal rhymes (soft/chalky/look, shadowy/globes, chalky/shadowy, more/middle, etc.). "Mealy clouds with a not brilliant moon" stays with nighttime clouds and reflected illumination, documenting the perceived textural consequence of a change in light, from chalky to mealy. As with the opening line, the refraction of light in water gives rise to a series of associations; clouds are a perennial favorite object of observation in Hopkins's journals.

Even beyond the potential spiritual allegories of light and water, as the passage progresses the subject of sensation begins to move forward in the description of the perceptual encounter in ways that suggestively illuminate other parts of Hopkins's corpus. The next phrase makes a leap in object — "blunt buds of the ash" — but it remains focused on the haptic impression made through visual perception of a natural object. Describing how the buds look — "blunt" — supplies an indication of how they might feel, and the name of the tree ("ash") resonates with the "chalky, mealy" clouds above, and with what follows. Moving from one variety of tree bud to another, Hopkins goes to "pencil buds of the beech," whose long, pointed, tipped buds indeed resemble pencils. He then pulls back to a more distant view of the tree as a whole and, at the same time, to the generic form: "lobes of the trees." But with "cups of the eyes," a surprising shift occurs. While the genitive syntax remains the same (x of the y), there is an important change in substance. In concentrating on the process of visual perception, Hopkins here moves from the perceived object to the perceiving agent. More precisely, he shifts to seeing the subject as itself an object, by reflexively considering the eyes, which are likened to, and reflect, the object (the trees) they see: the trees have lobes, the eyes have cups. Perhaps the trees are like ears in having lobes, indicating a move from one sensory organ to another. The "cups" are eyelids, which both protect and blind the viewer, literally (perceptually) as well as figuratively: as in "The Habit of Perfection," apprehension in the everyday world impedes transcendental perception of the "uncreated light." Hopkins now stays with the eyes, fascinated with the eyelids, strange cups that fold: "Gathering back the lightly hinged eyelids. Bows of the eyelids." He focuses intensively on the appearance of the eyelids themselves, anatomizing their mechanics and appreciating their form.

How, then, do we get from eyes back to pencils? From an object that is a container ("cups") to one that is a perimeter ("bows"), Hopkins moves to the outer edge with "pencil of eyelashes." The "lashes" sound like "ashes," both the preceding tree and the ash that ends the entry. The *OED* lists one relevant definition for *pencil*, "a small tuft of hairs, bristles, feathers, or the like, springing from or close to a point on a surface," noting that, from the nineteenth century on, it is only used in natural history. It may be that Hopkins intends the word in this sense, but both the earlier use of it in this passage ("pencil buds") and its common meaning — difficult as they are to reconcile with this context — are relevant. Hopkins, who not only wrote with a pencil but was accomplished at drawing with one too, here seems to move around the eyes to sketch them (from lids to lashes) and then puts the pencil itself — the instrument for rendering the image — *into* the picture.[21] The identification and mutual dependency between, on the one hand, the interior energy realized in the outward form of phenomenal objects and, on the other, the incorporative abilities of human sensory apprehension break down the boundaries between subject and object. This peculiar "pencil" reaches back to the "pencil buds of the beech" and moves beyond the merely metaphoric relation to secure the connection between trees and eyes — not least because pencils are made from trees, are trees remade into an object accommodated to the human hand, which recursively serves to record the image of trees for the consumption of the eye.

The surprise is that the process moves still further in: having penetrated the image, the pencil now seems to puncture the eye itself. And inside the body, Hopkins discovers — more body: "juices of the eyeball." Grotesquely literal as it seems, this reading is authorized by his poetry. In "Binsey Poplars," eyes and trees are associated metaphorically (being

likened to eyes makes the fallen poplars seem fragile), as well as through
the dialectical relation between perceiving subject and object:

> "Ó if we but knéw whát we do
>   Whén we delve or hew —
>   Háck and rack the growing green!
>   Since Country is so tender
>   To tóuch, her béing só slénder,
>   That, like this sleek and seeing ball
>   But a prick will make no eye at all,
>   Whére we, even where we mean
>   To mend her we end her,
>   Whén we hew or delve. (130)

Through the analogy between cutting down trees and puncturing an eye,
the natural scene comes to be like a body, damaged irretrievably by even
the most apparently insignificant alteration. "This sleek and seeing ball"
may be not just the eye but the globe of the earth, capable of being
"pricked" as well by such changes.[22] As a heuristic, we might think of
Hopkins's process of sensation as stages of transformation: from "eyes see
trees" (subject perceives object) to "eyes are like trees" (subject resembles,
and so becomes, an object), to "trees puncture eyes" (object enters subject); his body is the switch point between self and world, immaterial and
material ways of being.

Placing such pressure on the phenomenology of vision brings Hopkins to the disgusting innards of the human body, as his poetical exercises
in spiritual degradation (the "terrible sonnets") do later in his career.
Seeking to unlock the mystery of seeing as a practice of literal incorporation, he arrives at one of the human body's deepest material secrets, the
vitreous humor. This vile jelly is the medium within the eyeball through
which light passes on its way from lens to retina. If we return to Hopkins's spiritual exercise of 1880, where he uses the figure of a man looking
out a window as an allegory for the constitution of the self in relation to
the world, then the vitreous humor might be represented by the air — the
usually invisible intermediary between windowpane (metaphoric lens)
and eye (metaphoric self). The horror of puncturing the eye and releasing
this fluid arises from the imagined violence to the body's integrity, from
the revelation of the sanctified sense of sight's dependence on viscous
bodily substances, and perhaps from the inherent disgustingness of
imagining encountering sticky things.[23] Bataille similarly understands
the powerful revulsion that attaches to the eye perceived as an object — a

charge he exploits through scenes not only of ocular enucleation but also of the ingestion and eroticization of the orb. While Bataille perversely celebrates such mutilation and disfigurement,[24] Hopkins tends to treat it as a curious thought experiment — an effort at anatomizing vision — until, as we will see, he later finds the body a source of unmitigated disgust and yet of possibility, a corporeal realization of his spiritual degradation in the face of an unknowable, retributive divinity.

The unfinished poem "Ashboughs" extends the link that Hopkins posits between eyes and trees in his journal and in "Binsey Poplars." Read in the context of these works, the picture in "Ashboughs" of tree limbs breaking into the sky conjures up an image of them simultaneously breaking into the viewer's perceptual field, if not the eye itself:

> Not of all my eyes see, wándering on the world,
> Is ánything a mílk to the mínd so, só sìghs déep
> Poetry tó it, as a tree whose boughs brèak in the sky.
> Say it is áshboughs: whether on a December day and furled
> Fast ór they in clammyish láshtender còmbs créep
> Apárt wìde and new-nestle at héaven most hígh.
> They touch, they tabour on it, hover on it; here, there hurled,
> With talons sweep
> The smouldering enormous winter welkin. Eye,
> But more cheer is when May
> Mells blue with snowwhite through their fringe and fray
> Of greenery and old earth gropes for, grasps at steep
> Heaven with it whom she childs things by. (170)[25]

The trees penetrate at once the sky, the mind, and the eye, for the speaker's instressed vision of their form flows into all three. By contrast with the destructive "prick" of the hewn poplars or the tree that dies into a pencil, the liquid, nutritive image of milk here suggests that both the mind and the visual apparatus function by analogy with a gustatory process, incorporating and deriving sustenance from external objects. Now the "juices of the eyeball" seem less in danger of flowing out than of battening on the beautiful form embodied in the tree limbs; even in winter dormancy, live trees in the landscape nurture the poet, unlike the dead forms that threaten sight with violent puncturing. Reaching inside the speaking subject's mind and body through a combination of sensory modalities (including the tactile "gropes for, grasps at"), the tree exhales its own poetic qualities into the poet's eye and mind ("só sìghs déep / Poetry tó it"). By the poem's end, these ashboughs, breaking into springtime regeneration, seem not only to lie behind the journal's "blunt buds of the ash" but to explain some of its fecund associations among trees, buds, eyes, juices, and pencils.

The punctured and leaky eye is one of the points at which the boundary between interior, affective selfhood and external being seems to dissolve. In a related journal entry from December 23, 1869, Hopkins is led from a consideration of the sources of dreams (attributing them largely to what Freud would call "daily residue") to a discussion of dream images themselves, then to a comparison with images phenomenally perceived.[26] Dream images, he postulates, are seen "'between our eyelids and our eyes' ... [and] are brought upon that dark field, as I imagine, by a reverse action of the visual nerves" (194). Following this meditation on the physiology of visual perception, he recounts an episode of emotion welling up and resulting in an unexpected flood of tears, which he analogizes to a piercing of the flesh:

> They were reading in the refectory Sister Emmerich's account of the Agony in the Garden and I suddenly began to cry and sob and could not stop.... Neither the weight nor the stress of sorrow... by themselves move us or bring the tears as a sharp knife does not cut for being pressed as long as it is pressed without any shaking of the hand but there is always one touch, something striking sideways and unlooked for, which in both cases undoes resistance and pierces, and this may be so delicate that the pathos seems to have gone directly to the body and cleared the understanding in its passage. On the other hand the pathetic touch by itself, as in dramatic pathos, will only draw slight tears if its matter is not important or not of import to us, the strong emotion coming from a force which was gathered before it was discharged: in this way a knife may pierce the flesh which it had happened only to graze and only grazing will go no deeper. (195)

After the discussion of imaginary visions that the dreamer feels literally impressed on his eyes, this entry extends the embodying logic even further: first, in its argument that an unexpected charge of pathos can pierce the body and induce a spasmodic emotional response, physically manifested in the evidence of tears; second, in the grotesque analogy it draws between this process and that of a sharp knife pressing on, and then cutting into, the flesh. The hinge between these two meanings is the heteronym *tears*, which might be read as both the salty water that drips from the eyes and the ripping into flesh performed by the knife.[27] Unlike "Binsey Poplars," this passage does not feature a punctured eyeball, but it does draw blood, and the lachrymose response it recounts suggests an affectively pierced eye that leaks when it takes in too much or too suddenly. The oddity of the comparison between knife and pathos is that it suggests that deep wounding, whether physical or emotional, is a matter of slight or unanticipated cuts: here is a penetration that moves incrementally, like the flow of liquid.

Hopkins's notion of perceptual processes, with its attention to blood, milk, tears, and the "juices of the eyeball," thus draws as much from an idea of fluid mechanics as from puncturing. In presenting a self whose integrity is in flux and exchange with the world of objects, Hopkins makes it paradoxically nonidentical to itself; the self is therefore capable of being both subject and object of perception. On the penetration model, one is both stabber and stabbed; on the liquefaction model, subject and object melt into each other. In an 1881 sermon on the Sacred Heart, he brings together the puncturing of an organ and the deliquescence of distinctions between inside and outside: in an effort to elicit compassion among his hearers for Christ's metaphoric heart, Hopkins discusses the piercing of the bodily heart. Focusing on the significance of God's physical incarnation in man, Hopkins shows how Christ's embodiment is the necessary condition of redemptive death and resurrection.[28] Although Hopkins makes a distinction between solid and liquid parts of the body, the heart is of special interest to him because it contains the properties of both: "The body consists of solid parts which are permanent or changed slowly and of liquid parts which move to and fro, and are fast renewed. The heart is one of these solid parts, of these pieces of flesh, and is a vessel of the liquid blood" (101). Beating, the heart is the solid form that rhythmically keeps life's liquid essence, the blood, in fluxion; punctured, the heart bleeds, its solidity dissolving into the liquescence that stills it.[29] By focusing on the particular qualities of the body's materiality — its alternating states of solidity and liquidity, and even horrible in-between states, such as putrescence — Hopkins at once articulates the inescapability of embodiment to selfhood and relishes the humbling effects the body has on its tenant, the soul.

Returning to the journal entry "Drops of rain...," we can now see how, having shifted from the observed object to the seeing subject, Hopkins imagines going *inside* that subject, making a physically embodied object of it. Robert Boyle has discussed how significantly the eye in "The Windhover" stands for a theologically suffused subjective consciousness, in part through an *eye/I* homonymy never lost on Hopkins's ear (and, one might add, through their shared capacity for sight).[30] The images we have been considering materialize sight-oriented consciousness, and although the punctured eye is jarring, "juice," with its tactile and gustatory evocations, has positive connotations in Hopkins's lexicon.[31] The dual meaning of the "leaky" eye reiterates the simultaneous abjuration and celebration of the body as a whole, whose depth both stands for and displaces spiritual interiority. Focusing on the contents of the eyeball is an admittedly strange exercise, which not only emphasizes the substantiality of ordinarily sealed-off bodily insides but (as "Binsey Poplars" demonstrates) suggests their susceptibility to leaking out as well. It therefore makes sense that when we continue following Hopkins's journal notes, we find him returning to the eyelids, drawing out associations on things that cover and contain: "eyelids like leaves, petals, caps, tufted hats, handkerchiefs, sleeves, gloves." Eyelids are likened to organic forms of membranes (leaves, petals), then to textiles that cover the body, in a sequence that shifts down from the head (with caps and hats), to the handkerchief, then to arms with sleeves and finally to gloves.[32] Interested in the idea of covering, and in the means by which the body covers itself (and so keeps its wet insides securely contained), Hopkins shifts to a grimmer image: "Also of the bones sleeved in flesh." With his instinctive assimilation of everything in its proximity to the human form itself, he moves from the cloth that lies atop the flesh to the flesh itself as a covering: the "juicy" exterior flesh encloses an inner, dry body made of bones (even when bony excrescences, in the form of fingernails or eyelashes, stick out).

Hopkins affiliates juiciness with vibrant tactility (sometimes even with overripeness); through its connection with the tactile, juice is also associated with vision, which, as we have seen, Hopkins tends to render as a form of touching. In a startling way, the end of the passage reverses this process, showing touch itself to be a mode of sight. From the juices within the body, he now indicates "juices of the sunrise," returning to the theme of illumination, which both renders texture visible and alludes to divine revelation. The juices in the eye make vision possible, while, reciprocally, the juices emitted by the source of celestial light enable human eyes to see. As before, the gustatory connotation of "juices" makes light itself a material presence incorporated into the observing subject, as if one drank by seeing. Continuing the liquid associations, the sunrise itself then becomes a body: "Joins and veins of the same." Like the perceptible images it produces, the sunrise has the anatomical features of a body: it has veins, through which flows the blood-colored early morning light; it has "joins" too, perhaps articulated joints. Although syntactically a noun, "joins" also functions as a verb, suggesting the sun's production of shadow and light that visually joins objects together (as, mechanically, do nails and screws).

From the natural illumination of the sun, this passage finally moves back to an indoors or nighttime setting with its description of a candle, in an image that sums up much of what precedes it: "Vermilion look of the hand held against a candle with the darker parts as the middles of the fingers and especially the knuckles covered with ash." The blood-red image of the sunrise with its veins now becomes blood itself, pulsing through a hand, which looks "vermilion" when illuminated, its interior juices appearing to rise to the surface. Recalling the earlier impression of raindrops that look "like nails (of fingers)" "seen with only the lower rim lighted," Hopkins here interests himself in *seeing through* his body, seeing down beneath the integument, to arrive at the bones that are "sleeved in flesh." In describing these bones on the inside as, paradoxically, covering the outside with ash, he renders deep interiority (in this case, anatomical) in terms of its superficial visual effects. In so doing, he also alludes to the grave, to burning out the candle, the source of light, as the "ash" links his body to the trees once more ("Blunt buds of the ash"). The extraordinary experiment of looking through his hand (the hand that touches, draws, and writes) is a wholly embodied model for observing the subject of sensation, of reaching inside the body as if to discover there the propulsive secrets of perception itself. As the passage progresses, both the subject and the object of sensation shift significantly from eye to hand: not only is the visual tactile, but the means of touching has now become a way of seeing.

The conjunction of candle, sun, eye, light, juice, tree, and bone produces a compact series of images: of sources and objects, airy and substantial, of the means of seeing and what is seen, of the inside and the outside of the world and the body.[33] Hopkins's poetry imbues these images with theological meanings; even in the relatively uninflected form of natural observation, they echo with suggestions of the divine (light),[34] Incarnation (bones), the Passion (tree as cross), and other Christian images. The journal's ending meditation on the idea of the body as built up, flesh upon bone, is recast in a devotional context in the opening stanza of "The Wreck of the Deutschland":

Thou mastering me
God! giver of breath and bread;
Wórld's stránd, swáy of the séa;
Lord of living and dead;
Thou hast bóund bónes and véins in me, fástened me flésh,
And áfter it álmost únmade, what with dréad,
Thy doing: and dost thou touch me afresh?
Óver agáin I féel thy fínger and fínd thée. (101, st. 1)

Just as in the journal the bones and blood lie at the core of being — and yet, by dint of the candle's illusion, rise to the body's surface — so the "me" of this stanza both contains and is indissoluble from the bones, veins, and flesh. The difference is that the self of the poem is explicitly created matter; the contiguity of body and soul, rather than being presumed, is made strange by the language of binding, fastening, and unmaking. The apostrophized divine agency of this making and unmaking gives a theological significance to embodiment itself, suggesting that the perceptual experiments of the journal, like the corporeality of these lines, replays the mystery of Christ's Incarnation. The embodiment of the divine, and the inseparability of human body from soul, are both miraculous and excruciating phenomena whose materiality is brought forward in the self-consciousness of self-perception. Even the creator, who gives form to man and man's form to Christ, is here embodied; God's agency as maker and master is in a relation of reciprocal incarnation ("Over again") with man, dramatized by the exchange of touches. The speaker "feels" the "touch" of God, whose principal organ of touch (the finger) in turn feels the lump of flesh.

In portraying the reciprocity of God's touch and man's, and the inextricability of body from soul, the stanza also recapitulates in its language the fastening of self in body — which is to say, of meaning in matter. The interlocking of sounds between and within lines is characteristically tight. The incantatory, propulsive rhythm pushes against the masculine rhyme of the end-stopped lines, whose *ababcbca* pattern encloses lexical variation among terms that emphasize substantiality (including bread, dead, and flesh) within a scheme that starts with "me" and ends with "thee"; internally, the lines are wound together by alliteration patterned on the Anglo-Saxon model. The aural form of the words exemplifies the lines' thematic exploration of the ways in which matter is not simply the vessel for the sacred but is rather its very being. The language in Hopkins's journal similarly reinforces through sound the tight web of connection among objects (vermilion/look, hand/held/against/candle, etc.). Where the journal works through a thought experiment concerning the relation of vision to touch, however, the poetry makes the reader's body (ear and tongue) perform the fusion of its spiritual and formal aspects. The reciprocal relation of sound and sense is allegorized by the mutual touching (feeling and being felt) of God and man — a theologically suffused version of Merleau-Ponty's "double sensation."

The works I have been discussing are appreciative of, and sometimes ecstatic about, the infusion of divine perfection in the natural world. In perceiving the external world, the poet is drawn inside his body, both to its own capacities for perception and as itself a natural object of perceptual interest. A search for a specifically spiritual interior pervades the writing, but because — like the materialist psychologists he deprecated — Hopkins always finds more of his body on the inside, this spirit seems either to be located elsewhere or to be comprehensible only by analogy with the processes of his self-regarding physical system. When Hopkins's consideration of the embodied inscape of natural objects focuses on the regarding human subject himself, its register can sometimes turn sharply from astonished wonderment into disgust. Even while recognizing that the body makes bliss possible, Hopkins often notes at moments of profound theological insight that all human flesh is destined for necrosis. "Carrion Comfort," for example, opens with the poet tempted to descend into a vision of worldly existence as vile, corruptible matter:

> Not, I'll not, carrion comfort, Despair, not feast on thee;
> Not untwist — slack they may be — these last strands of man
> In me. (159)

In seeming to consume himself, the poet approaches perhaps the most horrifying end of taking the body as an object: self-cannibalization, a radical form of incorporation. The antidote, the speaker knows, is paradoxically to keep the material and immaterial aspects of his humanity "twisted" together, rather than unbounded as distinct subject and object.[35] The untwisting of syntax here, even more than usual, performs the disintegrative effect of unbinding essence from matter.

The putrescence of embodiment is one of the features that make Hopkins's "terrible sonnets" so profoundly despairing. In these poems, incorporation is not simply the state of mortal existence, nor do the poems hold out the joyful, if fearsome, promise of redemption in the Eucharist, itself a cannibalistic sacrament. Instead, the body seems to be taken inside the self in a way that repels and disgusts. "I wake and feel the fell of dark" makes self-consumption a specifically gustatory process. Humiliating himself and counting himself desperately low in his body, the speaker states:

> I am gall, I am heartburn. God's most deep decree
> Bitter would have me taste: my taste was me;
> Bones built in me, flesh filled, blood brimmed the curse.
> Selfyeast of spirit a dull dough sours. I see
> The lost are like this, and their scourge to be
> As I am mine, their sweating selves; but worse. (155)

Less the external observer of his own objectified embodiment than in the journal, the poet here writes of being, and being in, his body, felt from the inside out: he identifies himself with degrading processes of digestion and acrid flavors, as if feasting on his own rotten insides ("my taste was me"). The juices native to and incorporated within the body, previously celebrated, have now become sweaty and bilious. "God's most deep decree" is implanted in his flesh, driving him below the viscera to the very bones, on which he then imagines the creator building up the body in its flesh and blood. The process is the same as in the opening lines of "The Wreck of the Deutschland," only here it elicits disgust at the human creation instead of awe of the divine creator. Rather than an imitation of divine Incarnation (or its recapitulation in the Eucharist), this awful but unavoidable condition of mortal embodiment shows scant evidence of the sacred; its unredeemed horror is condensed in the harrowing line "Selfyeast of spirit a dull dough sours."[36] The image suggests that the poet's impure spirit is the yeast that makes rise (and, like some starters, makes sour) the "dull dough" of his breadlike embodied self; the evocation of foul tastes produces a hyperbolically negative type of incarnation, which conveys both the necessity of the bodily vehicle for the soul and its degrading effects. The body, in this grim vision, feeds on and vulgarizes the divinely ordained spirit, which, like some benevolent virus, has insinuated itself within this feculent host, lending it some measure of sacredness while using the body to expand beyond itself.

For Hopkins the introjected sense impressions made by phenomenal objects, including his own body, are both untranscendably corporeal and deeply spiritual. He uses natural objects, as well as his own subjective perception, as the occasion for reflecting on this divine fusion of the physical and metaphysical. In turning to a final prose passage, to which many critics have looked for its intensively expressed notions of selfhood, we find Hopkins meditating on embodiment, again in an experimental mode of self-exploration rather than the despairing one of the sonnets' excoriating cannibalism. In this Ignatian spiritual exercise of 1880, Hopkins describes his invisible, interior consciousness as knowable primarily through the experience of sense data. Contemplating the question of creation and its source, he attempts to account for his own intense personal sense of self and to differentiate it from that of human nature in general:

> When I consider my selfbeing, my consciousness and feeling of myself, that taste of myself, of *I* and *me* above and in all things, which is more distinctive than the taste of ale or alum, more distinctive than the smell of walnutleaf or camphor, and is incommunicable by any means to another man (as when I was a child I used to ask myself: What must it be to be someone else?). Nothing else in nature comes near this unspeakable stress of pitch, distinctiveness, and selving, this selfbeing of my own. Nothing explains it or resembles it, except so far as this, that other men to themselves have the same feeling. But this only multiplies the phenomena to be explained so far as the cases are like and do resemble. But to me there is no resemblance: searching nature I taste *self* but at one tankard, that of my own being. The development, refinement, condensation of nothing shews any sign of being able to match this to me or give me another taste of it, a taste even resembling it.[37]

To "consider... selfbeing" is for Hopkins a process of bodily ingestion, as he relies on the two most incorporative sensory modalities, taste and smell. To know himself is to taste himself, to taste the taste of himself, and thus to be both taster and tasted. It is an unusual way to construe this sense, transferring to it the attributes of touch, which is more ordinarily understood as simultaneously subjective and objective. As Hopkins writes elsewhere, "Seeing is believing but touch is the truth, the saying goes."[38] He here shows his understanding even of abstract subjectivity and consciousness — knowledge of the self and the world — to be grounded in the sensory experience of the body. While it shares with "Carrion Comfort" and "I wake and feel the fell of dark" a sense of self rooted in the experience of tasting himself, this passage employs a perceptual exercise to test the internal boundaries of subjectivity without courting the abject threat of self-devouring. For Hopkins, to encounter himself as an object — the classic exercise of self-consciousness — is instinctively a sensory experience and, crucially, an internal one: to be conscious is physically to inhabit his own body and to perceive that inhabitation to such an extent that imagining himself in someone else's body is impossible. It is demonstrably a spiritual exercise, and in the same measure a poetic and sensory one, too. He takes himself perceptibly within himself, even as he rubs up against the materiality of language, presenting the world of possible tastes as ranging from "ale" to "alum": a verbal feature (alliteration), rather than a gustatory one, explains the oddity of this selection among all available flavors. Grasping for the sensation on his palate of what it tastes like to be himself, Hopkins finds that words themselves shape his mouth and ordain the objects he imagines inhabiting it. Language itself is the substance on his tongue.

Hopkins's attempts to know himself, like his efforts to represent sensory encounters with the natural world, serve his faith in divine grace. While such exercises are nominally spiritual, this does not mean that they are immaterial: they are manifestly physical, both as he receives them through his body's sense organs and as he represents them in a tactile language that mimetically reproduces somatic experience. While the theological goals of Hopkins's writings seem a long way from those of the other writers I have considered, the poet shares with them a commitment to the irreducibility of embodiment. Dickens, Brontë, Trollope, and Hardy suggest that experience of and through the senses constitutes subjective interiority; to the extent that they imagine a spiritual interior as disembodied, they thereby tend to discount it. Hopkins uses the same means to show that embodied selfhood *is* spiritual existence, which enacts communion with the divine.

Conclusion

Breath through a keyhole, water-defiled skin, rain on the face, a pencil in the eye: let these events serve as emblems for the type of embodiment from which the argument of this book has proceeded. They are some of the fractured moments that provide glimpses of the body unmaking any abstract idea of the human. They do so by highlighting the contiguous and reciprocal contact between body and world and by focusing on sensory influx and corporeal outflow; in short, they draw attention to the conditions of embodiment itself. When the body obtrudes on the self and cannot be regarded merely as its container, we are shocked into a recognition of the fullness of bodily existence. Such a recognition registers the primacy of the material that *is* the human and, at the same time, prevents that material from becoming fixed and left behind by an idea of ethereal, transcendent, or universal personhood.

Despite the presence of such moments, one might object that the dominant drive of many Victorian literary works is precisely to secure the consolidation and transcendence of their human subjects, in the form of narrative or lyric closure. The antihumanist dimensions of these texts admittedly run athwart such overt aims. But to make a claim on behalf of the materialist aspects of such works is not to attempt to capture them in their totality; rather, it is to address their counternormative energy, to draw out those elements that seem to push against a beneficent humanism. Nor is this to deny the spiritual aspirations of the writers, many of whom adhere to religious beliefs that uphold an idea of transcendence, such as a Christian afterlife and an immortal soul. Particularly for Charlotte Brontë and Gerard Manley Hopkins, the material conditions of embodied existence are a primary vehicle through which they arrive at their conclusions about transcendence. Still, the body is hardly disposable; it is the inescapable condition of possibility for human existence, here if not hereafter, and their writing dwells tenaciously in the life of the flesh.

The argument of this book might entail another risk as well: the charge of materialist reductivism. Yet to think of a human subject in terms of embodiment is not necessarily to fix or contain either self or body at the boundaries of the skin: permeable and pervious to the world through our senses, our bodies are, according to this model, dynamic selves. In making this suggestion about embodiment, I draw on a number of currents of contemporary thought. Posthumanism is one name for an understanding of the human as simultaneously located in its materiality and as attachable to (and coextensive with) other materialities — those, for instance, of machines, animals, and the environment.[1] From the vantage point of microbiology, the individual human being cannot be strictly differentiated from its surroundings, with which, at a microbial level, it is literally contiguous; in an extreme version of this perspective, the human body might be thought of as the vehicle whereby microbes travel and interact.[2] By contrast with a picture of contained, discretely bounded individuals, the body, on such a model — no less than the self or the mind — is fungible and variable. Teresa Brennan suggestively argues that affects are themselves transmissible between people, by material means, through sensory apparatuses like olfaction. Taking the individual subject as the only meaningful unit, Brennan writes, obscures the evidence for such affective transmission.[3]

A description of embodied subjectivity as open to possibility, adaptation, permutation — even infection — dovetails with the accounts offered by Merleau-Ponty, Deleuze and Guattari, and Bataille of the body as a material entity that is always in process. Recent work by Gayle Salamon and Sarah Ahmed has productively brought together phenomenological philosophy and queer theory, demonstrating the possibilities made available in both arenas by an understanding of subjectivity as embodied. While phenomenology takes embodied, particularly perceptual, experience as foundational, Salamon explains that "to be real, in this [phenomenological] sense, is to hold one's body and one's self open to the possibilities of what one *cannot* know or anticipate in advance. It is to be situated at materiality's threshold of possibility rather than caught within a materiality that is at its core constricted, constrictive, and determining."[4] This is an important challenge to any account of materialism that takes it to be strictly deterministic or reductive. The notion of body as process, in this sense, derives from Merleau-Ponty's intervention in the philosophical contest between versions of idealism (the world is knowable only through concepts, of which the body is but one) and of materialism (the world exists objectively as matter, and concepts themselves arise from physical processes in the body). Merleau-Ponty, as Salamon writes, suggests that "the body is an amalgam: not only matter and not wholly ideality, but found somewhere in the relation between the two. . . . It can only be located in the juncture between the psychic and the physiological. It is this hinge between the material and the phantasmatic . . . that is . . . the site at which the embodied subject emerges."[5] The "embodied subject," then, is material at the same time that it is ideational; its concepts are flesh and its flesh is a concept.

The Victorian literary texts I have considered disorient conceptions of the human in relation to the body in ways that prefigure such formulations. What contribution might they, so considered, make to contemporary cultural criticism? In one sense, they speak to the concern in much recent scholarship to provide accounts of embodied experience that are differentiated on the basis of identities. Bodily differences — of, for instance, race, gender, sexuality, or disability — are often understood as the ground for identities, and scholarship focused on identity formation can in part be credited with the critical attention that the body has received. Yet the phenomenological approach I have adopted in this book shifts the focus from a subject's coming-into-being through an externally displayed or attributed identity, addressing itself instead to the *derealization* of subjectivity as corporeally experienced, through the senses, from within. While such an approach does not diminish the political efficacy of identity formations, it stresses their subjective and experiential dimensions.

Queer theory has provided some tools for conceptualizing the body and subjectivity in terms that complicate notions of identity formation. Queerness (often by contrast with homosexuality) has been proposed as an anti-identity — as a form of embodiment or a mode of relation antithetical to the coherence and containment of humanist subjectivity itself. In its most radically anti-identitarian form, queer theory, as Lee Edelman has articulated it, construes "the queer" as the excluded and unassimilable remainder requisite to the constitution of the human. Rather than affirming a minority sexual identity, Edelman presents queerness as an effect of psychical and ideological structures inherent in ideas of the human itself.[6] While queerness is a position against which identities become fixed and unfixed, the approach I have pursued discovers, in the work of the writers I have considered, a related derealization of the human, but it does so on the basis of the body's materiality, rather than the sexual constitution of the subject. The materiality of the body, in conflict with any transcendent notion of the human, is a modality by which subjects are made and unmade. Of course, even to state things this way implies the existence of an immaterial subject prior to its unmaking by the body. Instead, in the works I have discussed, the constitution of the subject in (and of) a body is — to argue along the dialectical lines that Judith Butler has suggested — coincident with the disintegration of that subject by the very means of its materiality.[7]

The critique of "the human" — with its phantasmatic completeness and integrity — that arises from queer theory thus looks somewhat different than that of phenomenology. Some examples from the Victorian material I have discussed can help to clarify the distinction. Most obviously, the biographical status of Hopkins as quasi- or proto-homosexual has sometimes supplied an impetus to read his work as encoding or enacting gay themes. In the phenomenological account, the queerness of this writing would lie more in its representation of subjectivity as misaligned with, and undermined by, the agency of the flesh. In several other works, instances of what might, from a contemporary perspective, be called queerness also arise. *David Copperfield, The Professor,* and "The Banks of the Jordan" all contain episodes of manifestly perverse, sometimes same-sex eroticism. Yet the readings I have offered, which foreground embodiment, suggest that if such episodes merit being called queer, it is not just because of their sexual counterorthodoxy. Rather, they present the openness of the body to the world by the senses as a type of permeability, or penetrability, that is not reducible to heterosexuality — nor is it even limited to the realm of the sexual. Such a form of embodiment is interactive and dynamic, and it is by means of the flesh that it works to defeat the coherence of personhood. If this form of embodiment is queer — in lying outside normative sexual formations — then it may be beyond sexuality itself; it is, in this sense, a queerness *of* the body. Even Hardy's writing exhibits a strain of emphasis on the materiality of the human that, by these criteria, might be called queer; while lacking Hopkins's theism, Hardy also depicts the fluid exchange between the body and the natural world. To label such elements queer, however, is to court confusion by implying that there is something sexual about them; better, then, to call this a type of antihumanism.

The more recently emerging field of disability studies can also help to throw light on the relation of embodiment to the human. This field has not tended to articulate disability in the agonistic, anti-identity terms that Edelman and others have with queerness, in part because disability studies does not share the same theoretical origins in psychoanalysis. But disability studies has the potential to denaturalize any presumption of stability and uniformity in the idea of the body itself. It suggests that embodiment is the principle of making and unmaking subjectivity without necessarily becoming the marker of a realized identity — though disability studies, and the disability rights movement from which the field emerged, have understandably advocated for "disabled" as a minority identity category.[8]

Understood as encompassing a range of physical possibilities, disability speaks to many of the concerns of this book, including the boundaries of the body, its extensions, and its openness.[9] Recall, for example, Harriet Martineau with her ear trumpet — a prosthesis that, in Hawthorne's description, becomes part of a body/machine couple. Although her deafness may be a disability, it is many things besides: it is linked to other aspects of Martineau's embodiment, such as her ill health, her sexuality, her celibacy, and her childlessness; it is a character trait connected to her charms, her fears, her passions, and her wants; and it contributes to her atheism and to her professional career as a writer. Collins's Miss Finch might likewise be accounted disabled, but the novel works, in both plot and theme, to show that her blindness is an asset (in enhancing her ability to form a nearly electrical circuit of desire with her blue lover) and that she regrets ever having attempted to "cure" it. Moreover, as I argued in chapter 1, she can be understood to belong to an embodied dyad, one aspect of which appears blue on the outside, while the other, which is barred from the surface, has special access to inner matter; she thus becomes a sort of transindividual character, like the fusion of Heathcliff and Cathy in *Wuthering Heights,* realized in sensory terms. Moving beyond bodies conventionally marked as disabled, we can see that all the corporeal forms I have investigated demonstrate ways of challenging cohesive subjectivity on the basis of embodiment: from the physical contiguity of Hardy's characters with the heath and of Trollope's with water that dirties, from David Copperfield's oral incorporations to Hopkins's visual, tactile, and olfactory ones, these are bodies that, through their porousness and lack of containment, open a range of possibilities for engagement with, and belonging in, the world. Victorian writers rendered this process of estrangement and demystification so vigorously in part as a result of their encounter with what they recognized as a newly and sometimes frighteningly secular world, denuded of spiritual dimensions.

Embodiment supplies a way of suspending subjectivity, of forestalling the fantasy of completeness that inheres in the concept of the human, without necessitating transcendence of the material. Embodiment understood in phenomenological or Deleuzian terms — as process, as becoming, as plural and permeable — is a force of subjective derealization, of undoing the imaginary coherence of the self by estranging it from its material form. If this account of embodied subjectivity synthesizes idealism and materialism, it also supplies a model for preserving the centrality of embodied difference on which critical domains invested in identity have insisted. This insight, I have proposed, is not a new one: it is something that writers like Charlotte Brontë, Thomas Hardy, and Gerard Manley Hopkins, among others, recognize in the embodied experiences they represent and evoke. It is the "double-faced unity" of which Bain writes, and it appears, at particular moments, as a significant dimension of literary representation. Oscar Wilde expresses the transitivity and generativity of the body in *The Picture of Dorian Gray* by giving the soul itself material qualities: "To project one's soul into some gracious form, and let it tarry there for a moment; to hear one's own intellectual views echoed back to one with all the added music of passion and youth; to convey one's temperament into another as though it were a subtle fluid or a strange perfume: there was a real joy in that — perhaps the most satisfying joy left to us."[10] This is a transitivity beyond the boundedness of self, soul, or indeed body itself, a material form of existence whose porousness puts it both outside and at the center of what it means to be human.

Notes

1. Subject

1. On Victorian discussions of the fate of physical remains as inextricably mixed up with meditations over the fate of the soul, see Christopher Hamlin, "Good and Intimate Filth," in *Filth: Dirt, Disgust, and Modern Life*, ed. William A. Cohen and Ryan Johnson (Minneapolis: University of Minnesota Press, 2005), 3–29.

2. Drew Leder, *The Absent Body* (Chicago: University of Chicago Press, 1990), deconstructs Cartesian rationalism from the perspective of twentieth-century phenomenology. For recent philosophical investigations of dualism and the mind-body problem, see Kevin Corcoran, ed., *Soul, Body, and Survival: Essays on the Metaphysics of Human Persons* (Ithaca, N.Y.: Cornell University Press, 2001).

3. Roy Porter, *Flesh in the Age of Reason* (New York: Norton, 2004).

4. In *The Body Economic: Life, Death, and Sensation in Political Economy and the Victorian Novel* (Princeton, N.J.: Princeton University Press, 2006), Catherine Gallagher writes of "a development in which political economists and their Romantic and early Victorian critics jointly relocated the idea of ultimate value from a realm of transcendent spiritual meanings to organic 'Life' itself and made human sensations — especially pleasure and pain — the sources and signs of that value" (3). The shift in emphasis, from spirit to living matter (particularly as measured in physiological terms) as the locus of value, that Gallagher takes as a historical given is likewise a basis on which my argument rests. On the many meanings of *materiality* and a rich discussion of its relation to the novel tradition, see Daniel Hack, *The Material Interests of the Victorian Novel* (Charlottesville: University of Virginia Press, 2005), esp. 1–10.

5. Michael S. Kearns observes that the concept of the mind as a substantial entity was common to mid-Victorian proto-psychologists otherwise as diverse as William B. Carpenter, Alexander Bain, and Herbert Spencer. Kearns, *Metaphors of Mind in Fiction and Psychology* (Lexington: University Press of Kentucky, 1987), chap. 4. See also Edward S. Reed, *From Soul to Mind: The Emergence of Psychology from Erasmus Darwin to William James* (New

Haven, Conn.: Yale University Press, 1997), which outlines various nineteenth-century versions of materialism; Reed observes that the "view of the distributed soul serves to undermine the Cartesian separation of soul and body, especially the key Cartesian assumption that the mind is in contact only with states of the brain. For many nineteenth-century thinkers, this theory of the distributed soul placed it dangerously close to the 'animal' aspects of the world and tended to make the soul indistinguishable from our viscera" (6). In *Charlotte Brontë and Victorian Psychology* (Cambridge: Cambridge University Press, 1996), Sally Shuttleworth writes that unlike in earlier periods, "The novelist and physician shared similar ground in mid-Victorian culture.... They shared ... the same central metaphors for their proceedings, drawn, pre-eminently, from the sphere of science: surgical dissection, and penetration of the inner recesses of mind and body" (14–15). For an illustration of this point, see Richard Menke, "Fiction as Vivisection: G. H. Lewes and George Eliot," *ELH* 67 (Summer 2000): 617–53. Menke's "Victorian Interiors: The Embodiment of Subjectivity in English Fiction, 1836–1901" (Ph.D. diss., Stanford University, 1999) is especially relevant in its account of embodied subjectivity (by which he means mind); the focus is specifically on realist fiction and situated in a context of narrative theory on consciousness.

6. As Rick Rylance has argued in his history of the development of psychology, the concept of mind was an evolving one in the nineteenth century, which cannot be sharply delineated from either a religious idea of soul or medical notions about the body and the brain; these concepts were being worked out not in a single discourse but in simultaneous, overlapping, sometimes competing realms of physiology, religion, medicine, and philosophy. See Rylance, *Victorian Psychology and British Culture, 1850–1880* (Oxford: Oxford University Press, 2000). A survey of ideas in the history of psychology (overlapping with philosophy of mind) and its ceaseless effort to distinguish the material from immaterial contents of being can be found in Robert H. Wozniak, *Mind and Body: René Descartes to William James* (Bethesda, Md.: National Library of Medicine, 1992); see also Robert M. Young, *Mind, Brain, and Adaptation in the Nineteenth Century: Cerebral Localization and Its Biological Context from Gall to Ferrier* (Oxford: Clarendon, 1970). In introducing *Embodied Selves: An Anthology of Psychological Texts, 1830–1890* (Oxford: Clarendon, 1998), Jenny Bourne Taylor and Sally Shuttleworth describe mental science as "a materialist science of the self which rejected the dualistic division between mind and body" and show how psychology moved progressively away from disembodied metaphysics and toward physiology over the course of the nineteenth century (xiv).

7. Henry Maudsley, *Body and Mind: An Inquiry into Their Connection and Mutual Influence, Specially in Reference to Mental Disorders* (1870), 3d ed. (New York: Appleton, 1885), 12–13. Maudsley is sometimes defensive in his corpo-

real materialism: "I have no wish whatever to exalt unduly the body; I have, if possible, still less desire to degrade the mind; but I do protest, with all the energy I dare use, against the unjust and most unscientific practice of declaring the body vile and despicable, of looking down upon the highest and most wonderful contrivance of creative skill as something of which man dare venture to feel ashamed" (95).

8. Taylor and Shuttleworth, *Embodied Selves*, 93.

9. Rylance, *Victorian Psychology*, supplies a nuanced account of the positions of the major players, including objections from clergy and philosophers such as James Martineau and Samuel Taylor Coleridge. See also Young, *Mind, Brain, and Adaptation*.

10. Alexander Bain, *Mind and Body: The Theories of Their Relation*, reprinted as vol. 4 of the International Scientific Series (New York: Appleton, 1901), 196; parts originally in *Fortnightly Review* (1865).

11. Herbert Spencer, *Principles of Biology*, 2 vols. (1867 ed.; reprint, New York: Appleton, 1897), 1:80 (italics in original). Hereafter cited in the text.

12. For example, Thomas Hardy writes in *The Woodlanders* (1887; Oxford: Oxford University Press, 2005): "The darkness was intense, seeming to touch her pupils like a substance. She only now became aware how heavy the rainfall had been and was; the dripping of the eaves splashed like a fountain. She stood listening with parted lips, and holding the door in one hand, till her eyes growing accustomed to the obscurity she discerned the wild brandishing of their arms by the adjoining trees" (278). Hardy frequently concatenates visual, tactile, and auditory sensations, as here with a darkness palpable by the eyes (although, oddly, what it touches is an emptiness, the pupils), and sounds perceived by mouth rather than ear ("She stood listening with parted lips"). For another example, in the famous passage in *Middlemarch* (1871–72; New York: Penguin, 1994) about Dorothea's experience of Rome on her honeymoon, George Eliot describes the heroine's future mental picture of Saint Peter's (decorated with "red drapery...for Christmas") as "spreading itself everywhere like a disease of the retina" (194) — which is to say, she does not retain an image of the object seen, but instead an impression that her organ of seeing has degenerated.

13. Herbert Spencer, *Principles of Psychology* (1855), 3d ed. (London: Williams and Norgate, 1881). In *Hopkins's Idealism: Philosophy, Physics, Poetry* (Oxford: Clarendon, 1997), Daniel Brown writes of Spencer: "The functionalist psychology of the evolutionists is a version of physiological reductionism, a form of materialism: 'we are here primarily concerned,' writes Spencer at the beginning of the *Principles [of Psychology]*, 'with psychological phenomena as phenomena of Evolution; and, under their objective aspect, these, reduced to their lowest terms, are incidents in the continuous redistribution of Matter and Motion'" (4).

14. Herbert Spencer, "The Physiology of Laughter," *Macmillan's Magazine*, March 1860, 395–402 (reprinted in *Essays* [London, 1901]); Freud cites this article in his 1905 book on jokes. In describing the effect of the "excitement of certain nerves" — by which he means ideational or emotional stimulus — Spencer writes: "There are three channels along which nerves in a state of tension may discharge themselves.... They may pass on the excitement to other nerves that have no direct connexions with the bodily members, and may so cause other feelings and ideas; or they may pass on the excitement to one or more of the motor nerves, and so cause muscular contractions; or they may pass on the excitement to the nerves which supply the viscera, and may so stimulate one or more of these" (396).

15. D. W. Hamlyn, *Sensation and Perception: A History of the Philosophy of Perception* (London: Routledge and Kegan Paul, 1961).

16. Daniel Cottom, *Cannibals and Philosophers: Bodies of Enlightenment* (Baltimore, Md.: Johns Hopkins University Press, 2001), xii.

17. In literary-historical terms, the emergence in the nineteenth-century novel of qualities affiliated with realistic characterization ("roundness," "depth") may also be understood as a question of interiority. Two studies of eighteenth-century English fiction demystify the purportedly natural evolution of characterological interiority by demonstrating the economic and social imperatives for privileging such modes of fictional representation. Deidre Shauna Lynch, in *The Economy of Character: Novels, Market Culture, and the Business of Inner Meaning* (Chicago: University of Chicago Press, 1998), argues that the valorization of characters' inner lives is contingent on market relations; Catherine Gallagher, in *Nobody's Story: The Vanishing Acts of Women Writers in the Marketplace, 1670–1820* (Berkeley: University of California Press, 1994), argues that such characterization depends on the nonreferentiality of fictional "nobodies." Critical works focused on Victorian fiction that address novel characters' outward performance of inner depth include Joseph Litvak, *Caught in the Act: Theatricality in the Nineteenth-Century English Novel* (Berkeley: University of California Press, 1992); and John Kucich, *Repression in Victorian Fiction: Charlotte Brontë, George Eliot, and Charles Dickens* (Berkeley: University of California Press, 1987). Dorrit Cohn, *Transparent Minds: Narrative Modes of Presenting Consciousness in Fiction* (Princeton, N.J.: Princeton University Press, 1978), supplies a helpful discussion, in the terms of narrative theory, of how fiction realistically represents characters' mental interiors.

18. Although the goal of this work is not to establish direct lines of influence from nineteenth-century scientific culture into literature, a number of excellent studies have done so. Models of such a critical enterprise are represented by Gillian Beer, *Darwin's Plots: Evolutionary Narrative in Darwin, George Eliot, and Nineteenth-Century Fiction,* 2nd ed. (Cambridge: Cambridge University Press, 2000); Sally Shuttleworth, *George Eliot and Nineteenth-Century*

Science: The Make-Believe of a Beginning (Cambridge: Cambridge University Press, 1984); Shuttleworth, *Charlotte Brontë and Victorian Psychology;* George Levine, *Darwin and the Novelists: Patterns of Science in Victorian Fiction* (Cambridge, Mass.: Harvard University Press, 1988); and Alan Richardson, *British Romanticism and the Science of the Mind* (Cambridge: Cambridge University Press, 2001). Kearns argues that in some cases novelists produced new models in advance of scientists: the language of the mind as a substantial entity "did not develop at the same rate in fiction and in psychology; new metaphors are quite visible in novels by the middle of the nineteenth century but do not emerge in psychological works until later" (*Metaphors of Mind,* 16). See also Rylance, *Victorian Psychology,* on Lewes and Eliot.

19. John Stuart Mill, *Autobiography and Literary Essays,* ed. John M. Robson and Jack Stillinger, vol. 1 of *Collected Works* (Toronto: University of Toronto Press, 1981), 37, 39.

20. See Rylance, *Victorian Psychology,* on Mill's defense in print of Bain's work in physiological psychology and of associationist psychology more generally.

21. Harriet Martineau, *Autobiography,* 3 vols. (London: Smith, Elder, 1877). Martineau completed this book in 1855, but it was not published until after her death. All quotations are from vol. 1.

22. See, for example, Mary Poovey, *Uneven Developments: The Ideological Work of Gender in Mid-Victorian England* (Chicago: University of Chicago Press, 1988); Thomas Laqueur, *Making Sex: Body and Gender from the Greeks to Freud* (Cambridge, Mass.: Harvard University Press, 1990); and John Bender, "Impersonal Violence: The Penetrating Gaze and the Field of Narration in *Caleb Williams,*" in *Vision and Textuality,* ed. Stephen Melville and Bill Readings (Durham, N.C.: Duke University Press, 1995), 256–81.

23. In a complex argument that has bearing on my own, Herbert F. Tucker, in "When the Soul Had Hips: Six Animadversions on Psyche and Gender in Nineteenth-Century Poetry," in *Sexualities in Victorian Britain,* ed. Andrew H. Miller and James Eli Adams (Bloomington: Indiana University Press, 1996), 157–86, investigates the poetic domain of writing about the soul in nineteenth-century England, focusing on the paradox of representing as bodily that which by definition has no form. He is particularly concerned with the consequences of mapping the body/soul dichotomy onto a female/male representational system, and although he focuses primarily on a theologically conceived soul, Tucker (like the poets he discusses) does not draw sharp distinctions among soul, spirit, and mind.

24. Martineau's brother James, a celebrated Unitarian minister, was a leading public opponent of physiological psychology from the point of view of religious commitment (Rylance, *Victorian Psychology*); by 1851 he had broken with Harriet on the grounds of her declared atheism.

25. *The English Notebooks, 1853–1856,* ed. Thomas Woodson and Bill Ellis, vol. 21 of *The Centenary Edition of the Works of Nathaniel Hawthorne* (Columbus: Ohio State University Press, 1997), 115–16.

26. Emily Brontë, *Wuthering Heights* (New York: Norton, 1972), 72. Hereafter cited in the text.

27. Leo Bersani, *A Future for Astyanax: Character and Desire in Literature* (Boston: Little, Brown, 1976), chap. 7.

28. Robert Browning, "Fra Lippo Lippi," in *Poetical Works* (Boston: Houghton Mifflin, 1974), 343–44. See Tucker, "When the Soul Had Hips," on the embodiment of the soul in Victorian poetry more generally.

29. Wilkie Collins, *Poor Miss Finch* (Oxford: Oxford University Press, 2000); for example, 89, 220.

30. The comparison is made explicitly in the narrative (for example, 117–18).

31. Oscar Wilde, *The Picture of Dorian Gray,* ed. Joseph Bristow, vol. 3 of *Complete Works* (Oxford: Oxford University Press, 2005), 184; further references are to this edition (1891 ed.). My discussion of Wilde is indebted to conversation with Kathryn Bond Stockton, for which I am grateful. Wilde explicitly worries over the relation of flesh to spirit throughout the novel; for example, Lord Henry muses: "Soul and body, body and soul — how mysterious they were! There was animalism in the soul, and the body had its moments of spirituality. The senses could refine, and the intellect could degrade. Who could say where the fleshly impulse ceased, or the psychical impulse began? How shallow were the arbitrary definitions of ordinary psychologists! And yet how difficult to decide between the claims of the various schools! Was the soul a shadow seated in the house of sin? Or was the body really in the soul, as Giordano Bruno thought? The separation of spirit from matter was a mystery, and the union of spirit with matter was a mystery also" (219).

32. On olfaction in *Dorian Gray* as a countervisual mode of knowledge connected to sexual disruption, see Paul Morrison, *The Explanation for Everything: Essays on Sexual Subjectivity* (New York: New York University Press, 2001), 36–40. In terms congenial to my approach, Kelly Hurley, in *The Gothic Body: Sexuality, Materialism, and Degeneration at the Fin de Siècle* (Cambridge: Cambridge University Press, 1996), discusses the materiality of the body as a late-nineteenth-century challenge to the sanctity of the human, both in science and in literature: "In place of a human body stable and integral . . . the *fin-de-siècle* Gothic offers the spectacle of a body metamorphic and undifferentiated; in place of the possibility of human transcendence, the prospect of an existence circumscribed within the realities of gross corporeality; in place of a unitary and securely bounded human subjectivity, one that is both fragmented and permeable" (3).

33. Maurice Merleau-Ponty, *The Primacy of Perception,* quoted in Elizabeth Grosz, *Volatile Bodies: Toward a Corporeal Feminism* (Bloomington: Indiana University Press, 1994), 87.

34. Grosz, *Volatile Bodies,* 86.

35. Maurice Merleau-Ponty, "The Intertwining — the Chiasm," chapter 4 of *The Visible and the Invisible,* ed. Claude Lefort, trans. Alphonso Lingis (Evanston, Ill.: Northwestern University Press, 1968), 137.

36. On haptic visuality, see Laura U. Marks, *The Skin of the Film: Intercultural Cinema, Embodiment, and the Senses* (Durham, N.C.: Duke University Press, 2000); and Marks, *Touch: Sensuous Theory and Multisensory Media* (Minneapolis: University of Minnesota Press, 2002). See also Eve Kosofsky Sedgwick, introduction to *Touching Feeling: Affect, Pedagogy, Performativity* (Durham, N.C.: Duke University Press, 2003). With reference to recent technologies for describing the relation between meaning and the human body, I am indebted to Kathryn Bond Stockton, "Prophylactics and Brains: *Beloved* in the Cybernetic Age of AIDS," in *Novel Gazing: Queer Readings in Fiction,* ed. Eve Kosofsky Sedgwick (Durham, N.C.: Duke University Press, 1997), 41–73: "For all of its crude explanation, meme theory runs with a point importantly implicit in Saussure, in his stress on 'the physiological transmission of the sound-image' out of someone's brain into someone else's ear. The point is this: a sign, in order to be a sign *to you,* must get inside your body. Actually, it must enter your body through an orifice" (58).

37. Merleau-Ponty was ambivalent about the radically anti-Cartesian strain in his own work; see Martin Jay, *Downcast Eyes: The Denigration of Vision in Twentieth-Century French Thought* (Berkeley: University of California Press, 1993), an intellectual history of modern French philosophy organized around the idea of "the denigration of vision," which explains some of the reasons for the turn away from phenomenology in the years just after Merleau-Ponty's death in 1961. Jay writes that *The Visible and the Invisible* can be read as "anticipating some of the themes of later contributors to the anti-ocularcentric discourse. First, his new emphasis on the 'flesh of the world' rather than the lived, perceiving body meant that the notion of vision itself began to assume a post-humanist inflection" (316) — it becomes "utterly impersonal" (319), outside subjectivity, and so, at its limit, resembles the models of Bataille and Foucault. This phenomenological model thus makes possible a deconstruction of the subject/object and inside/outside antinomies that structure Cartesian dualism, but without necessarily preserving a transcendental subject. See also Christopher Macann, *Four Phenomenological Philosophers: Husserl, Heidegger, Sartre, Merleau-Ponty* (London: Routledge, 1993), on Merleau-Ponty's "ambiguous" relation to the question of the transcendental subject, on which Husserl insisted (193–94). David Abram, *The Spell of the Sensuous: Perception and Language in a More-than-Human World* (New York:

Pantheon, 1996), shows how Husserl posited a transcendental subject, but how Merleau-Ponty's "body-subject" undid it.

38. See Grosz, *Volatile Bodies*, 100–103.

39. While my work draws in part from the phenomenological tradition, it does not attempt to resuscitate it as a mode of literary criticism. In its mid-twentieth-century incarnation, this approach, as Terry Eagleton writes, reduced a literary work "to a pure embodiment of the author's consciousness"; Eagleton condemns it for having "recovered and refurbished the old dream of classical bourgeois ideology." Eagleton, *Literary Theory: An Introduction* (Minneapolis: University of Minnesota Press, 1996), 58.

40. See Grosz, *Volatile Bodies*, 170.

41. Gilles Deleuze and Félix Guattari, *Capitalism and Schizophrenia*, vol. 2, *A Thousand Plateaus* (1980), trans. Brian Massumi (Minneapolis: University of Minnesota Press, 1987), 158. Hereafter cited in the text.

42. Georges Bataille, *Visions of Excess: Selected Writings, 1927–1939*, trans. Allan Stoekl et al. (Minneapolis: University of Minnesota Press, 1985), 74. For examples of literary criticism employing Bataille, see John Kucich, *Excess and Restraint in the Novels of Charles Dickens* (Athens: University of Georgia Press, 1981), which adapts Bataille's conceptions of erotism and *dépense;* and David Trotter, *Cooking with Mud: The Idea of Mess in Nineteenth-Century Art and Literature* (Oxford: Oxford University Press, 2000), which invokes Bataille's notion of *informe*. For an instructive anthropological application, see Joseph Roach, *Cities of the Dead: Circum-Atlantic Performance* (New York: Columbia University Press, 1996).

43. Bataille, *Visions of Excess,* 77.

44. See Peter Stallybrass and Allon White, *The Politics and Poetics of Transgression* (Ithaca, N.Y.: Cornell University Press, 1985).

45. Georges Bataille, *Story of the Eye*, trans. Joachim Neugroschel (San Francisco: City Lights, 1987), 92.

46. William Ian Miller, in *The Anatomy of Disgust* (Cambridge, Mass.: Harvard University Press, 1997), writes: "When our inside is understood as soul the orifices of the body become highly vulnerable areas that risk admitting the defiling from the outside. But when our inside is understood as vile jelly, viscous ooze, or a storage area for excrement the orifices become dangerous as points of emission of polluting matter, dangerous both to us and to others" (89).

47. This period of rapid urban and industrial expansion gave extraordinarily varied and diverse power to metaphors of filth, which shaped the terms in which poverty, sexuality, race, and urban life were imagined and discussed. With crises of public health, sanitation, and urban renovation facing nineteenth-century populations, filth — especially in its most psychologically powerful form, human waste — pervades public discourse, not least in a correlative literary language. The literary genealogy of Victorian filth includes a cluster of midcentury novels and nonfiction works notable for their thematic

focus on water pollution and urban pestilence. I make these arguments more fully in chapter 3 and in my introduction to *Filth;* see also essays in that volume by David L. Pike, David S. Barnes, and Pamela Gilbert. See Christopher Hamlin, *Public Health and Social Justice in the Age of Chadwick: Britain, 1800–1854* (Cambridge: Cambridge University Press, 1998); Frank Mort, *Dangerous Sexualities: Medico-Moral Politics in Britain since 1830* (London: Routledge, 1987); Mary Poovey, *Making a Social Body: British Cultural Formation, 1830–1864* (Chicago: University of Chicago Press, 1995); and Joseph Childers, *Novel Possibilities* (Philadelphia: University of Pennsylvania Press, 1995).

48. It is also worth noting that the works on which I focus in the following chapters all provoked controversy of some kind, often because of the ways they invoked the body: both Charlotte Brontë's first novel and Gerard Manley Hopkins's poetry could not be published in their lifetimes; once published, the Trollope story I discuss outraged readers; and Thomas Hardy's novels were invariably contentious. Many of the writers I have considered in this chapter — Martineau, Mill, Emily Brontë, Collins, and Wilde — were also subjects of controversy, and the reception of the physiological psychologists themselves was fraught with dissent and discord. In every case, the particular accounts that these works provide of human embodiment disturbed contemporary readers.

49. Nancy Armstrong, *Fiction in the Age of Photography: The Legacy of British Realism* (Cambridge, Mass.: Harvard University Press, 1999); Jonathan Crary, *Suspensions of Perception: Attention, Spectacle, and Modern Culture* (Cambridge, Mass.: MIT Press, 1999). On visual perception in relation to the body (as represented in science and art) in the eighteenth century, see also Barbara Stafford, *Body Criticism: Imaging the Unseen in Enlightenment Art and Medicine* (Cambridge, Mass.: MIT Press, 1991).

50. Such work on hearing includes: Steven Connor, *Dumbstruck: A Cultural History of Ventriloquism* (Oxford: Oxford University Press, 2000); Jonathan Rée, *I See a Voice: Deafness, Language, and the Senses — a Philosophical History* (New York: Henry Holt, 1999); Leigh Eric Schmidt, *Hearing Things: Religion, Illusion, and the American Enlightenment* (Cambridge, Mass.: Harvard University Press, 2000). John M. Picker, *Victorian Soundscapes* (New York: Oxford University Press, 2004), is also concerned with Victorian auditory experience in a New Historicist mode.

51. Hans J. Rindisbacher, *The Smell of Books: A Cultural-Historical Study of Olfactory Perception in Literature* (Ann Arbor: University of Michigan Press, 1992); Janice Carlisle, *Common Scents: Comparative Encounters in High-Victorian Fiction* (New York: Oxford University Press, 2004). See also Constance Classen, David Howes, and Anthony Synnott, *Aroma: The Cultural History of Smell* (London: Routledge, 1994); Piet Vroon, *Smell: The Secret Seducer,* trans. Paul Vincent (New York: Farrar, Straus and Giroux, 1997); Annick Le Guérer, *Scent: The Mysterious and Essential Powers of Smell,* trans. Richard Miller (New

York: Turtle Bay, 1992); and Alain Corbin, *The Foul and the Fragrant: Odor and the French Social Imagination*, trans. Mariam L. Kochan et al. (Cambridge, Mass.: Harvard University Press, 1986) (originally published as *Le miasme et la jonquille: L'odorat et l'imaginaire social, 18e–19e siècles* [1982]). Corbin writes of "the baffling poverty of the language" of odors (6) and cites Locke's emphasis on the problem in *An Essay concerning Human Understanding* (1755). On the senses generally in relation to poetry, see Susan Stewart, *Poetry and the Fate of the Senses* (Chicago: University of Chicago Press, 2002). Relevant discussions of the sense of touch can be found in Marks, *Touch*, and in works on the skin cited in chapter 3.

52. When interiority itself is taken as a subject of cultural studies, it is often treated merely as a synonym for subjectivity, denuded of material substance. For example, in *Strange Dislocations: Childhood and the Idea of Human Interiority, 1780–1930* (Cambridge, Mass.: Harvard University Press, 1995), Carolyn Steedman writes: "'Interiority' is a term quite widely used in modern literary and cultural history, and in literary criticism, to describe an interiorised subjectivity, a sense of the self *within* — a quite richly detailed self" (4). If interiority is understood as a wholly psychological concept, it is not clear what the term gains over "subjectivity" or "selfhood," since its placement *in* the interior receives no attention. Nicholas D. Paige, *Being Interior: Autobiography and the Contradictions of Modernity in Seventeenth-Century France* (Philadelphia: University of Pennsylvania Press, 2001), discusses the interior as a literary concept specifically tied to the emergence of autobiography as a genre; see the introduction for a critical history of the concept, albeit also in nonmaterial terms. Diana Fuss, *The Sense of an Interior: Four Writers and the Rooms That Shaped Them* (New York: Routledge, 2004), brings together architectural and psychological conceptions of the interior in an analysis of the literary imagination. On psychologically complex interiority in relation to theatrical display in an earlier period, see Katharine Eisaman Maus, *Inwardness and Theater in the English Renaissance* (Chicago: University of Chicago Press, 1995).

53. In "Making an Issue of Cultural Phenomenology," *Critical Quarterly* 42, no. 1 (Spring 2000): 2–7, Steven Connor proposes that "instead of readings of abstract social and psychological structures, functions and dynamics, cultural phenomenology would home in on substances, habits, organs, rituals, obsessions, pathologies, processes and patterns of feeling. Above all, whatever interpreting and explication cultural phenomenology managed to pull off might well be accomplished in the manner of its getting amid a given subject or problem, rather than the completeness with which it got on top of it. It would inherit from the phenomenological tradition an aspiration to articulate the worldliness and embodiedness of experience" (3). See also David Trotter, "The New Historicism and the Psychopathology of Everyday Modern Life," in the same issue (36–58), reprinted in *Filth;* and Connor's Web site, http://www.bbk.ac.uk/english/skc, which contains links to many relevant works.

An earlier use of the term, with different connotations, is employed in T. J. Csordas, "Embodiment and Cultural Phenomenology," in *Perspectives on Embodiment,* ed. Gail Weiss and Honi Haber (New York: Routledge, 1999), 143–62.

54. A number of Victorianists have expressed related dissatisfactions. See Mary Poovey, *A History of the Modern Fact* (Chicago: University of Chicago Press, 2000), the first chapter of which argues, from the point of view of "genealogy," against a privileged mode of literary criticism whose goal is the relentless "unmasking" of prejudices in earlier periods. Also relevant is the argument developed in Sedgwick, with Adam Frank, "Shame in the Cybernetic Fold: Reading Silvan Tomkins," in *Touching Feeling* (93–121), that the "theorization" of anything is equivalent to its "denaturalization" and that this is in itself a politically efficacious act.

55. Rey Chow, in the introduction to the special issue "Writing in the Realm of the Senses," *differences* 11, no. 2 (1999), makes a related argument for steering a middle course between historical and formalist approaches and for remaining theoretically engaged while responding to local concerns. She discourages "simply rehearsing 'ideas' or 'concepts' without being able to deal with formal and representational issues" as well as "claims to be 'historical' by facilely appealing to all kinds of marginalized experiences in the name of resisting high theory"; instead she advocates work that is "both theoretically astute and historically informed as to the ineluctable relationships between what may be loosely termed perceptive, sensorial, or affective phenomena, on the one hand, and the more concrete, because semiotically chartable, issues of representation, on the other" (7). This approach runs, if not at odds with, then aslant the wide assortment of scholarship on human bodies that falls within the tradition of Foucault's genealogical inquiry, which places a primary emphasis on power relations.

56. Michel Foucault, *Discipline and Punish: The Birth of the Prison,* trans. Alan Sheridan (New York: Vintage, 1979), 30. This is admittedly the most relentlessly "disciplinary" Foucault; this doctrine was both complicated and relaxed in his later work on the care of the self, which was signaled, toward the end of *The History of Sexuality,* vol. 1, trans. Robert Hurley (New York: Vintage, 1978), with the famously cryptic comments on the possibilities held out for "bodies and pleasures" (157, 159). Comparing Foucault and Merleau-Ponty, Gail Weiss argues that while on the one hand body images "are themselves subject to social construction . . . [and are the] disciplinary effects of existing power relationships as well as sources of bodily discipline," on the other, "too strong an emphasis on the social construction of our body images runs the danger of disembodying them by presenting them as merely the discursive effects of historical power relationships." Weiss, *Body Images: Embodiment as Intercorporeality* (New York: Routledge, 1999), 2.

57. See Sedgwick, *Touching Feeling,* 9–13. Sedgwick writes that Foucault's "analysis of the pseudodichotomy between repression and liberation has led,

in many cases, to its conceptual reimposition in the even more abstractly reified form of the hegemonic and the subversive" (12); she writes later of how "Foucauldian deprecations of 'the repressive hypothesis' . . . [are] transformed virtually instantaneously into binarized, highly moralistic allegories of the subversive versus the hegemonic, resistance versus power" (110).

58. On the construction of the body's materiality in relation to language and sexual subjectivity, see Judith Butler, *Bodies That Matter: On the Discursive Limits of "Sex"* (New York: Routledge, 1993), chap. 1.

2. Self

1. Distinctions between flat and round (or shallow and deep) characters often rely on E. M. Forster, *Aspects of the Novel* (New York: Harcourt, Brace, 1927). Alex Woloch expatiates on the distinction, usefully extending it to a discussion of major and minor characters in *The One vs. the Many: Minor Characters and the Space of the Protagonist in the Novel* (Princeton, N.J.: Princeton University Press, 2003). Like Forster, however, Woloch, rather than interrogating the constitutive elements of roundness, takes it for granted as an immediately evident psychological quality by which readers identify realistic (or major) characters.

2. A paradigmatic example is in Henry Fielding, *The History of Tom Jones, a Foundling* (1749; London: Penguin, 2005), book 1, chap. 8: "When Mr. *Allworthy* had retired to his Study with *Jenny Jones*, as hath been seen, Mrs. *Bridget*, with the good House-keeper, had betaken themselves to a Post next adjoining to the said Study; whence, through the Conveyance of a Key-hole, they sucked in at their Ears the instructive Lecture delivered by Mr. *Allworthy*, together with the Answers of *Jenny*, and indeed every other Particular which passed in the last Chapter" (55).

3. Charles Dickens, *Nicholas Nickleby* (London: Penguin, 1999), 633.

4. Anthony Trollope, *Barchester Towers* (New York: Oxford University Press, 1980), 166–67. Trollope invokes the conventional form, for example, in *Doctor Thorne* (1858; New York: Oxford University Press, 1980): " 'Step downstairs a moment,' said the doctor, turning to the servant, 'and wait till you are called for. I wish to speak to your master.' Joe, for a moment, looked up at the baronet's face, as though he wanted but the slightest encouragement to disobey the doctor's orders; but not seeing it, he slowly retired, and placed himself, of course, at the keyhole" (458); and in *The Way We Live Now* (1874–75; London: Penguin, 1994): "Mrs. Pipkin, however, quite conquered by a feeling of gratitude to her lodger, did not once look in through the door, nor did she pause a moment to listen at the keyhole" (741).

5. Audrey Jaffe provides the supplest reading of this issue in chapter 2 of *Vanishing Points: Dickens, Narrative, and the Subject of Omniscience* (Berke-

ley: University of California Press, 1991), showing how impersonal omniscience constantly slides toward personal narration, both in the framework of the narrative and in its plotted analogues: "The distance the narrator hopes to gain by choosing omniscient over personified narration is repeatedly undermined by the narrative's persistent focus on an analogous movement within the novel: figures who strive for, but cannot gain, positions outside scenes in which they are involved. *The Old Curiosity Shop* repeatedly focuses on observational activity, shifting from an unframed, central action to an observer on the periphery of that action" (53–54).

6. See Jaffe, *Vanishing Points*, and Ann Gaylin, *Eavesdropping in the Novel from Austen to Proust* (Cambridge: Cambridge University Press, 2002), on eavesdropping as a characterological model for readers' interests in story.

7. Charles Dickens, *The Old Curiosity Shop* (London: Penguin, 2001), 81. Further references are to this edition.

8. See Catherine Robson, *Men in Wonderland: The Lost Girlhood of the Victorian Gentleman* (Princeton, N.J.: Princeton University Press, 2001), chap. 2.

9. For example, Michael Slater, *Dickens and Women* (Stanford, Calif.: Stanford University Press, 1983): "The reader feels naturally somewhat disappointed that the vital, highly individualized figure of the Marchioness has 'dwindled into a wife' in this conventional way" (241).

10. Charles Dickens, *David Copperfield* (London: Penguin, 1985), 61. Further references are to this edition.

11. On texture, see Renu Bora, "Outing Texture," in *Novel Gazing: Queer Readings in Fiction,* ed. Eve Kosofsky Sedgwick (Durham, N.C.: Duke University Press, 1997), 94–127.

12. Mary Ann O'Farrell deftly reads these scenes, and bodies in *David Copperfield* more generally, in terms of their expressive capacities, in *Telling Complexions: The Nineteenth-Century English Novel and the Blush* (Durham, N.C.: Duke University Press, 1997).

13. See Oliver S. Buckton, "'The Reader Whom I Love': Homoerotic Secrets in *David Copperfield*," *ELH* 64, no. 1 (Spring 1997): 189–222. For another article that reads (and reflects on the reading of) modern sexual categories in Dickens, see Annamarie Jagose, "Remembering Miss Wade: *Little Dorrit* and the Historicising of Perversity," *GLQ* 4, no. 3 (1998): 423–51.

14. In a related analysis of the materiality of mind, Michael S. Kearns, in *Metaphors of Mind in Fiction and Psychology* (Lexington: University Press of Kentucky, 1987), writes: "Dickens' novels, like those of Brontë, tend to portray the mind as a being with a life, and his psychology, like hers, was limited by the mind-as-entity metaphor. He conceived of the mind as shaped (literally 'impressed') by the external world through the mechanism of the senses and according to the laws of association. His novels dramatize how an individual's mind is shaped in opposition to the urgings of the heart and how this shape, usually imaged as layers, can subsequently be stripped away to allow

the formation of a new shape that better suits the heart's best urges" (158). Athena Vrettos has a relevant discussion of realism, character, and Dickens's representation of mind in "Defining Habits: Dickens and the Psychology of Repetition," *Victorian Studies* 42, no. 3 (Spring 1999–2000): 399–426.

15. For instance, Wendy A. Craik writes: "[Charlotte Brontë's] first attempt, in a public, professional sense, at the novel...is undoubtedly minor. *The Professor* is not, within its limits, a failure; it has striking originalities and a few great scenes and passages, but it always remains on a lower level than her other three works. Smith and Elder were wise to reject it, and, since it drove Charlotte Brontë to write *Jane Eyre*, and since, had it been published, she could never have felt free to re-work and transmute its Belgian material and characters in *Villette*, readers must be grateful to them for doing so. *The Professor* must always remain the last read, as it was the last published, of the Brontë novels." Craik, "The Brontës," in *The Victorians*, ed. Arthur Pollard, vol. 6 of *The Penguin History of Literature* (London: Penguin, 1993), 151. Juliet Barker is similarly dismissive: "[The] determination to put Angria behind her and write about the real and the ordinary was somewhat marred in the execution.... Charlotte fell into her old bad habits of Gothic exaggeration.... Unable to write convincingly as a man, Charlotte retreated behind the comforting familiarity of the sarcastic and frequently flippant shell. In so doing, she destroyed the heart of the novel, for her central character is unreal. In her last novel, *Villette*, Charlotte was to prove that it was possible to have an embittered and uncharismatic but realistic first-person narrator." Barker, *The Brontës* (New York: St. Martin's, 1994), 500–501. For accounts of the novel's inconsistencies and inadequacies, see Judith Williams, "*The Professor:* Blocked Perceptions," in *Critical Essays on Charlotte Brontë*, ed. Barbara Timm Gates (Boston: G. K. Hall, 1990), 125–38; and, in the same volume, Annette Tromly, "*The Professor*," 103–25. In her own evaluation of *The Professor*, however, Brontë stated: "The middle and latter portion of the work...is as good as I can write; it contains more pith, more substance, more reality, in my judgment, than much of 'Jane Eyre.'" Letter to W. S. Williams, December 14, 1847, quoted in the introduction to *The Professor*, by Charlotte Brontë, ed. Margaret Smith and Herbert Rosengarten (Oxford: Clarendon, 1987), xix.

16. Charlotte Brontë, *The Professor*, ed. Margaret Smith and Herbert Rosengarten (Oxford: Oxford University Press, 1991), xvii–xviii. Smith admits that this description is "baldly stated," and she judiciously situates Brontë's composition of the novel in a range of biographical and literary contexts. In a later suggestion, however, Smith perpetuates the biographical explanation: "In transforming her life into her art, Charlotte to some extent controlled its pain by making herself — or at any rate her first person narrator — the master. She attributes to William the inward qualities she had looked for in M. Heger" (xxiii). Further references are to this edition.

17. On enclosure imagery, see Tromly, "*The Professor*" (107–8), which associates it with repression; see also John Kucich, *Repression in Victorian Fiction: Charlotte Brontë, George Eliot, and Charles Dickens* (Berkeley: University of California Press, 1987). In "Beloved Objects: Mourning, Materiality, and Charlotte Brontë's 'Never-Ending Story,'" *ELH* 65 (Spring 1998): 395–421, Kate E. Brown supplies a fascinating analysis of the value of objects, in relation to bodies and mourning, in Brontë's early compositions.

18. The epigraph alludes to John Bunyan's *Pilgrim's Progress* (1678) and more generally to the Protestant practice of locating value in self-degradation — a tradition of which the novel's French-speaking Catholic characters are oblivious. On the basis of Martin Luther's writings, Norman O. Brown argues for links among Freudian anality, Thanatos, the Protestant devil, and emergent capitalism in ways that resonate with Brontë's concerns; see Brown, *Life against Death: The Psychoanalytical Meaning of History* (New York: Vintage, 1959), esp. chap. 14. In later work, Brontë transforms psychological enclosure from metaphor into plot event to produce some of her most memorable scenes (Jane Eyre in the red room, Bertha Mason in the attic, Lucy Snowe in the deserted garret). In *Eros and Psyche: The Representation of Personality in Charlotte Brontë, Charles Dickens, and George Eliot* (New York: Methuen, 1984), Karen Chase supplies an analysis of Brontë's spatial metaphors of mind that is congenial to my own, including a discussion of Brontë's "tendency to transform concepts into conceits" (54).

19. As Catherine Robson pointed out to me, early in *Jane Eyre,* where the young protagonist retains traces of this (justifiably) paranoiac self-conception, she also conceives of her mind as filthy: "All John Reed's violent tyrannies, all his sisters' proud indifference, all his mother's aversion, all the servants' partiality, turned up in my disturbed mind like a dark deposit in a turbid well." Charlotte Brontë, *Jane Eyre,* ed. Jane Jack and Margaret Smith (Oxford: Clarendon, 1975), 12. I am indebted to Kathryn Bond Stockton, "Heaven's Bottom: Anal Economics and the Critical Debasement of Freud in Toni Morrison's *Sula,*" *Cultural Critique* (Spring 1993): 81–118, for a suggestive discussion of debasement, race, and anality in the context of Morrison's literary work and Freudian theory. In a provocative reference to Brontean anality, Eve Kosofsky Sedgwick, in "A Poem Is Being Written," *Tendencies* (Durham, N.C.: Duke University Press, 1993), 177–214, cites a letter from Brontë to W. S. Williams of April 12, 1850: "What throbs fast and full, though hidden, what the blood rushes through, what is the unseen seat of life and the sentient target of death" (210–11); but Kearns, in *Metaphors of Mind* (142), reads this passage as referring to the heart.

20. Sally Shuttleworth, *Charlotte Brontë and Victorian Psychology* (Cambridge: Cambridge University Press, 1996), chap. 7. In *Amnesiac Selves: Nostalgia, Forgetting, and British Fiction, 1810–1870* (Oxford: Oxford University

Press, 2001), Nicholas Dames undertakes a related analysis of Brontë, whom he treats as representative of a nineteenth-century practice privileging the external surface of the body over a model of depth psychology; Dames places particular weight on the visibility, and readability, of the body, as exemplified by phrenological practice. Like Shuttleworth, Dames associates vision (which Dames terms a "clinical gaze") with a disciplinary model of subject formation and regulation. In my reading, what is striking about "the gaze" in Brontë is that, unlike Panoptic prisoners, those who are looked at almost always look back, and this reciprocal process has tactile properties. For a view of Brontë focused on the embodiment of affect rather than a conflict between surface and depth, see John Hughes, "The Affective World of Charlotte Brontë's *Villette*," *Studies in English Literature, 1500–1900* 40, no. 4 (Autumn 2000): 711–26. Hughes writes, "For Deleuze, [Brontë's] writing is a milieu of affects and sensations which contest the closures and boundaries of social identity by evoking, in the reader's mind, echoes of the body's own inmost natural powers and movements" (724).

21. Shuttleworth, *Charlotte Brontë and Victorian Psychology*, 128. In equating "interiorized selfhood" with the mind as psychologists understood it, Shuttleworth sets aside the soul, which for Brontë, with her intense religious affinities, was at least in equal measure the content of the self. On the religious body of the Victorian soul, see Kathryn Bond Stockton, *God between Their Lips: Desire between Women in Irigaray, Brontë, and Eliot* (Stanford, Calif.: Stanford University Press, 1994).

22. The medical context that Shuttleworth supplies in the first half of *Charlotte Brontë and Victorian Psychology* invites an interpretation of this scene as Mlle Reuter's phrenological reading of Crimsworth. The directress feels and probes Crimsworth's mind in the way a phrenologist might manipulate the head, but psychological discourse cannot sufficiently account for Brontë's bizarre extension of the metaphors.

23. In the face of such language, normalizing conceptions of gender and sexuality sometimes hamper Brontë critics. Irene Tayler, for instance, describes this passage as an error on Brontë's part — it is an example of "gender-inappropriate metaphor" — and despite Crimsworth's explicit attestation of pleasure, she reads these images as "couched in the figurative language of male seduction or rape." Tayler, *Holy Ghosts: The Male Muses of Emily and Charlotte Brontë* (New York: Columbia University Press, 1990), 165.

24. For Freud's formulations, see "'A Child Is Being Beaten': A Contribution to the Study of the Origin of Sexual Perversions" (1919), in *The Standard Edition of the Complete Psychological Works of Sigmund Freud*, ed. and trans. James Strachey et al., 24 vols. (London: Hogarth Press and the Institute of Psycho-Analysis, 1953–74), 17:179–204; further references to Freud's works are to this edition. Jean Laplanche has a helpful discussion of aggression as the instinct on which, in the dimension of sexuality, sadistic drives are

"propped"; see Laplanche, *Life and Death in Psychoanalysis*, trans. Jeffrey Mehlman (Baltimore, Md.: Johns Hopkins University Press, 1976), chap. 5. Among the three basic types of masochism that Freud delineates, one is "feminine masochism" — which is to say, femininity itself. See "The Economic Problem of Masochism" (1924), in *Standard Edition*, 19:159–70. Extending Freud's reasoning, Julia Kristeva, in her discussion of the maternal "abject," revalues the subordinated female term itself while maintaining its gender determinism. Kristeva, *Powers of Horror: An Essay on Abjection*, trans. Leon S. Roudiez (New York: Columbia University Press, 1982). For the Deleuzian account, see Gilles Deleuze, "Coldness and Cruelty," in *Masochism*, trans. Jean McNeil (New York: Zone, 1991), which proposes that the subject of sadism is the male master (paradigmatically, Sade), while the slave in the sadistic scene is a feminine object unwittingly coerced for the master's erotic stimulation. The subject of masochism is the slave, also presumptively male; he must train the dominatrix, who consents to punish him in the prescribed ways. A comprehensive review of scholarship on masochism is in John Kucich, "Melancholy Magic: Masochism, Stevenson, Anti-Imperialism," *Nineteenth-Century Literature* 56, no. 3 (2001): 364–400.

25. Kucich, *Repression in Victorian Fiction*, 97, 109. Kucich states that the "consequence of master/slave reversals is that they pluralize and confuse the configurations of power to such a degree that contest — which defines isolation and distance — becomes endless and illimitable, rather than being frozen in a permanent structure of relationship. The reversibility of mastery and slavery makes them transient positions of combat" (106). While I largely concur with this analysis, it remains a question whether one should take it to mean that "no one is actually mastered" (106), as Kucich concludes. Janet Gezari addresses related concerns in a chapter on *The Professor* in *Charlotte Brontë and Defensive Conduct: The Author and the Body at Risk* (Philadelphia: University of Pennsylvania Press, 1992).

26. The reduplication of the protagonist occurs yet again at the novel's end with the appearance of his son. In describing the child's response to the death of a favorite dog, Crimsworth repeats the garden-and-graveyard imagery he employs to portray first his own development, then that of his wife: "I saw in the soil of his heart healthy and swelling germs of compassion, affection, fidelity — I discovered in the garden of his intellect a rich growth of wholesome principles — reason, justice, moral courage promised — if not blighted, a fertile bearing.... Yet I saw him the next day, laid on the mound under which Yorke [the dog] had been buried, his face covered with his hands" (244). With the analogy between human growth and crops that batten on feculent corpses, the narrative demonstrates how development comes about through incorporation of aversive matter.

27. Helene Moglen, in *Charlotte Brontë: The Self Conceived* (New York: Norton, 1976), notes the similarity among the novel's characters and supplies a

biographical explanation: "[Brontë] divides herself among the three central figures — Crimsworth, Frances, and Hunsden" (87).

28. "Monsieur wishes to know if I agree — if, in short, I wish to marry him?"

"Exactly."

"Will Monsieur be as good a husband as he has been a professor?" ...

... "smile at once shrewd and bashful" ...

"That is, Monsieur will always be a little obstinate, demanding, willful — ?"

29. In spite of Brontë's manifest identifications with the narrator, Judith Mitchell, in *The Stone and the Scorpion: The Female Subject of Desire in the Novels of Charlotte Brontë, George Eliot, and Thomas Hardy* (Westport, Conn.: Greenwood, 1994), attributes a stereotyped misogynistic male psyche to the narrator: "*The Professor* is in fact a novel of domination... of fear of the feminine and the resulting obsessional need of the male to control both Self and Other" (32).

30. Firdous Azim, in *The Colonial Rise of the Novel* (London: Routledge, 1993), writes of *The Professor:* "English imperialism is now personalised and sexualised into a little love story" (168).

31. For details, see Charlotte Brontë, *The Professor,* ed. Margaret Smith and Herbert Rosengarten (Oxford: Clarendon, 1987), 283, note to 215, and appendix iv.

32. See Rebecca Rodolff, "From the Ending of *The Professor* to the Conception of *Jane Eyre,*" *Philological Quarterly* 61, no. 1 (Winter 1982): 71–89, which marshals substantial evidence for the argument that "the Frances section" of *The Professor* "contains in embryo many of the elements developed at greater length in the novel *[Jane Eyre]* that [Brontë] began writing just a few weeks later" (73).

33. More than in most bildungsromans, the aims announced in *The Professor* are deliberately pedagogical: the narrator takes pains to detail "the system [he] pursued with regard to [his] classes," for such "experience may possibly be of use to others" (60). The narrative is at points explicitly didactic, as when Crimsworth states: "My narrative is not exciting and, above all, not marvellous — but it may interest some individuals, who, having toiled in the same vocation as myself, will find in my experience, frequent reflections of their own" (11). Still, the narrator-as-teacher has his sadistic impulses as well (for example, when he taunts his readers).

34. Deleuze, "Coldness and Cruelty," 20–21.

35. On the exaltation of visuality in this period of European culture generally, as well as its subsequent dethroning, see Martin Jay, *Downcast Eyes: The Denigration of Vision in Twentieth-Century French Thought* (Berkeley: University of California Press, 1993), whose exhaustive notes chart the extensive

critical literature on visuality. In *Charlotte Brontë and Victorian Psychology,* Shuttleworth emphasizes the disciplinary charge in Brontë's surveillance thematics; for example, "Crimsworth's language underscores the interdependence of theories of interiorized selfhood and external structures of surveillance. His sense of the primacy of a pre-existent realm of selfhood is illusory. As Foucault has argued, the modern interiorized subject is itself actively produced by the internalization of the social structures of surveillance" (127). In her introduction to *The Professor* (London: Penguin, 1989), Heather Glen describes the correspondence between Brontë's writing and Victorian surveillance: "This imagery of looking and being looked at runs throughout the novel. . . . In an extraordinarily precise and consistent way, Charlotte Brontë seems to be exposing and articulating the logic of a whole society — a society whose essential dynamics are the same as those that Jeremy Bentham had sought to enshrine and objectify in his great plan for a 'Panopticon' some fifty years before" (18). In an illuminating discussion of the novel's insistence on antagonism, refusal, and negation, however, Glen eschews reading it as wholly controlled by disciplinary thinking. Other compelling examples of Foucault-inflected discussions of disciplinarity in Brontë include Joseph Litvak, *Caught in the Act: Theatricality in the Nineteenth-Century English Novel* (Berkeley: University of California Press, 1992); and Bette London, "The Pleasures of Submission: *Jane Eyre* and the Production of the Text," *ELH* 58 (1991): 195–213.

36. For examples of Oedipal strands in readings of the novel, see John Maynard, *Charlotte Brontë and Sexuality* (Cambridge: Cambridge University Press, 1984); and Gezari, *Charlotte Brontë and Defensive Conduct.*

3. Skin

1. On the physiology and psychology of the skin, see Ashley Montagu, *Touching: The Human Significance of the Skin,* 2d ed. (New York: Harper and Row, 1978).

2. Anthony Trollope, "The Banks of the Jordan," in *Complete Short Stories,* vol. 3, *Tourists and Colonials,* ed. Betty Jane Slemp Breyer (Fort Worth: Texas Christian University Press, 1981), 114–15. References are to this edition, but quotations have been emended slightly to conform to the original journal publication.

3. *London Review and Weekly Journal of Politics, Literature, Art, and Society* 2, no. 29 (January 19, 1861): 54.

4. Ibid.

5. N. John Hall, *Trollope: A Biography* (Oxford: Clarendon, 1991), 207–8 (italics in original). Hall writes that an editor "wrote to Trollope . . . [and] quoted one of the 'mildest' of the many letters to their editor, this reader speaking of destroying the supplements in which the stories were printed

and giving up the paper, while inquiring whether the proprietors meant to appeal to men of 'intelligence & high moral feeling' or those of a 'morbid imagination & *a low tone of morals*'" (208). See also Mark Forrester, "Redressing the Empire: Anthony Trollope and British Gender Anxiety in 'The Banks of the Jordan,'" in *Imperial Desire: Dissident Sexualities and Colonial Literature,* ed. Philip Holden and Richard J. Ruppel (Minneapolis: University of Minnesota Press, 2003), 115–31.

6. In *The Bertrams* (1859; Stroud: Alan Sutton, 1993), whose early scenes occupy the same landscape as "The Banks of the Jordan," the alienating setting serves more straightforwardly as the site of seduction: the novel's hero, George Bertram, meets and falls in love with Caroline Waddington (the work's self-consciously announced "*donna primissima*") in Jerusalem, proposing to her on the Mount of Olives while gazing out on "the temple in which Jesus had taught" (120). This is the normative romance on which the later story plays, in its disguises and disruptions, as well as in its archetypal names and characters.

7. See Erin O'Connor, *Raw Material: Producing Pathology in Victorian Culture* (Durham, N.C.: Duke University Press, 2000), chap. 1, which supplies evidence for disease and factory work itself as blackening, and metaphorically racially degenerating, in the Victorian popular imagination.

8. With the allusion to flaying, Trollope's story here converges on the Greek myth of Marsyas (a mortal who inadvertently entered into competition with Apollo and was punished by being flayed alive), which Anzieu places at the center of his analysis of the skin ego. This appears to be one of the passages to which the *Cornhill* editors objected; for Trollope's response to the magazine's rejection of the tale, see his letter of August 9, 1860, to George Smith, in *The Letters of Anthony Trollope,* vol. 1, ed. N. John Hall with Nina Burgis (Stanford, Calif.: Stanford University Press, 1983), 116–17. Later in the letter, Trollope also rejects Smith's proposal to pare down the story, providing a fleshy allegory of the tale itself: "Did you ever buy your own meat? That cutting down of 30 pages to 20, is what you proposed to the butcher when you asked him to take off the bony bit at the end, & the skinny bit at the other. You must remember that the butcher told you that nature had produced the joint bone & skin as you saw it, & that it behoved him to sell what nature had thus produced" (117).

9. Forrester, in "Redressing the Empire," notes: "While Jones has been disgusted by (and yet drawn to) the filthy masses at the chapel, he is clearly drawn to (and yet repelled by) this solitary, suffering pilgrim. In terms of background and physical appearance, the pilgrim bears striking similarities to Jones (and to Trollope himself), and in that moment of self-reflection Jones begins to acknowledge a masculine (remember his 'brace of pistols') craving for submission and suffering" (126).

10. Sigmund Freud, *The Ego and the Id,* trans. Joan Riviere (New York:

Norton, 1960): "The ego is first and foremost a bodily ego; it is not merely a surface entity, but is itself the projection of a surface" (16). In a footnote to this passage added to the 1927 English translation, Freud writes: "I.e., the ego is ultimately derived from bodily sensations, chiefly from those springing from the surface of the body. It may thus be regarded as a mental projection of the surface of the body, besides, as we have seen above, representing the superficies of the mental apparatus." On the embodiment of the ego, see also Jean Laplanche, *Life and Death in Psychoanalysis,* trans. Jeffrey Mehlman (Baltimore, Md.: Johns Hopkins University Press, 1976); and Leo Bersani, *The Freudian Body: Psychoanalysis and Art* (New York: Columbia University Press, 1986).

11. Didier Anzieu, *The Skin Ego,* trans. Chris Turner (New Haven, Conn.: Yale University Press, 1989), 98. Anzieu's account is at base material and biological, and he elaborates these three functions (later expanded into nine) in greater detail at another point: "Every psychical activity is anaclitically dependent upon a biological function. The Skin Ego finds its support in the various functions of the skin. I shall proceed later to a more systematic study of these. For the moment, however, I shall briefly indicate three of the functions (the ones to which I restricted myself in my original article of 1974). The primary function of the skin is as the sac which contains and retains inside it the goodness and fullness accumulating there through feeding, care, the bathing in words. Its second function is as the interface which marks the boundary with the outside and keeps that outside out; it is the barrier which protects against penetration by the aggression and greed emanating from others, whether people or objects. Finally, the third function — which the skin shares with the mouth and which it performs at least as often — is as a site and a primary means of communicating with others, of establishing signifying relations; it is, moreover, an 'inscribing surface' for the marks left by those others" (40). More recent scholarship on skin that in some cases develops Anzieu's theories includes *Thinking Through the Skin,* ed. Sara Ahmed and Jackie Stacey (London: Routledge, 2001); Steven Connor, *The Book of Skin* (Ithaca, N.Y.: Cornell University Press, 2003); Laura U. Marks, *The Skin of the Film: Intercultural Cinema, Embodiment, and the Senses* (Durham, N.C.: Duke University Press, 2000); Marks, *Touch: Sensuous Theory and Multisensory Media* (Minneapolis: University of Minnesota Press, 2002); Jay Prosser, *Second Skins: The Body Narratives of Transsexuality* (New York: Columbia University Press, 1998); Claudia Benthien, *Skin: On the Cultural Border between Self and the World,* trans. Thomas Dunlap (New York: Columbia University Press, 2002); Shannon Sullivan, *Living across and through Skins: Transactional Bodies, Pragmatism, and Feminism* (Bloomington: Indiana University Press, 2001).

12. On the "economy of visibility," on which race and gender categories rely, see Robyn Wiegman, *American Anatomies: Theorizing Race and Gender* (Durham, N.C.: Duke University Press, 1995), chap. 1.

13. Frantz Fanon, *Black Skin, White Masks* (1952), trans. Charles Lam Markmann (New York: Grove, 1967), 111–12; italics in original. Fanon articulates this largely psychoanalytic account of racial distinction in the terms of Sartrean phenomenology, predominant in the period of the work's composition. See also Kaja Silverman, *The Threshold of the Visible World* (New York: Routledge, 1996), chap. 1; and Kalpana Seshadri-Crooks, *Desiring Whiteness: A Lacanian Analysis of Race* (London: Routledge, 2000).

14. Anne McClintock, *Imperial Leather: Race, Gender and Sexuality in the Colonial Contest* (New York: Routledge, 1995), chap. 5. See also Warwick Anderson, "Excremental Colonialism: Public Health and the Poetics of Pollution," *Critical Inquiry* 21 (Spring 1995): 640–69, on the medical representation of human waste in a colonial context (in this case, the Philippines of the early twentieth century).

15. On the relation between spiritual conceptions of bodily waste and Victorian sanitary policy, see Christopher Hamlin, "Providence and Putrefaction: Victorian Sanitarians and the Natural Theology of Health and Disease," *Victorian Studies* 28, no. 3 (Spring 1985): 381–411. For a more theoretical discussion of waste and value, see Dominique Laporte, *History of Shit* (1978), trans. Nadia Benabid and Rodolphe el-Khoury (Cambridge, Mass.: MIT Press, 2000). See also *Filth: Dirt, Disgust, and Modern Life,* ed. William A. Cohen and Ryan Johnson (Minneapolis: University of Minnesota Press, 2005).

16. *Times,* July 21, 1858, 9; quoted in part in Stephen Halliday, *The Great Stink of London: Sir Joseph Bazalgette and the Cleansing of the Victorian Capital* (Stroud: Sutton, 1999), 74.

17. On this event as emblematic in English fiction, see Patrick Brantlinger, "The Well at Cawnpore: Literary Representations of the Indian Mutiny of 1857," chap. 7 in *Rule of Darkness: British Literature and Imperialism, 1830–1914* (Ithaca, N.Y.: Cornell University Press, 1988): "Victorian accounts...make Cawnpore the main setting of a melodrama, its chief villain Nana Sahib and its chief victims the women and children whose mutilated bodies were cast into 'the well of evil fame'" (204). On journalistic representations of the sepoy rebellion in relation to white womanhood, see Jenny Sharpe, *Allegories of Empire: The Figure of Woman in the Colonial Text* (Minneapolis: University of Minnesota Press, 1993); on the wider genre of narratives about the uprising, see Gautam Chakravarty, *The Indian Mutiny and the British Imagination* (Cambridge: Cambridge University Press, 2005); and for an attempt to minutely recount and in a sense to replicate the sensational stories, see Andrew Ward, *Our Bones Are Scattered: The Cawnpore Massacres and the Indian Mutiny of 1857* (New York: Henry Holt, 1996).

18. The *Illustrated London News,* in a leading article from June 26, 1858, also links the corporeal penetration of the toxic river to the colonial administration, but it does so by portraying the failure of domestic engineering in contrast to imperial triumph: "Annually — as regularly as the balmy skies of

the month of June pour down fatness and fertility upon the green fields of England — the inhabitants of the great metropolis of the British empire are scared from their property by the foul smells of the River Thames. In the cold weather the feculent corruption, the monstrous nastinesses that are poured into this great river, and kept floating up and down between Gravesend and Richmond, do not simmer and boil up fever to be inhaled by the people to the same extent as in this glowing and glorious midsummer; but, when the thermometer stands at 86 deg. or 90 deg. in the shade, the death-pot boils, and cholera morbus surges up in the airy shape of a pestilent vapour, to breathe which is destruction. . . . We can colonise the remotest ends of the earth; we can conquer India; we can pay the interest of the most enormous debt ever contracted; we can spread our name, and our fame, and our fructifying wealth to every part of the world; but we cannot clean the River Thames."

4. Senses

1. Gilles Deleuze and Claire Parnet, *Dialogues,* trans. Hugh Tomlinson and Barbara Habberjam (London: Athlone, 1987). The full passage reads: "Take as an example the case of Thomas Hardy: his characters are not people or subjects, they are collections of intensive sensations, each is such a collection, a packet, a bloc of variable sensations. There is a strange respect for the individual, an extraordinary respect: not because he would seize upon himself as a person and be recognized as a person, in the French way, but on the contrary because he saw himself and saw others as so many 'unique chances' — the unique chance from which one combination or another had been drawn. Individuation without a subject. And these packets of sensations in the raw, these collections or combinations, run along the lines of chance, or mischance, where their encounters take place — if need be, their bad encounters which lead to death, to murder. Hardy invokes a sort of Greek destiny for this empiricist experimental world. Individuals, packets of sensations, run over the heath like a line of flight or a line of deterritorialization of the earth" (39–40).

2. Peter Widdowson, *Hardy in History: A Study in Literary Sociology* (London: Routledge, 1989).

3. See John Paterson, "Lawrence's Vital Source: Nature and Character in Thomas Hardy," in *Nature and the Victorian Imagination,* ed. U. C. Knoepflmacher and G. B. Tennyson (Berkeley: University of California Press, 1977), 455–69. He writes that "Hardy dehumanizes his characters. . . . [A] feature of head or face, of lip or mouth, surprisingly changed into the nonhuman, into an aspect of Nature eerily and incongruously other than human" (465). See also Elaine Scarry, "Participial Acts: Working; Work and the Body in Hardy and Other Nineteenth-Century Novelists," in *Resisting Representation* (Oxford: Oxford University Press, 1994), 48–90. Scarry writes evocatively of "the

reciprocity of man and the object world" in Hardy, whereby "the earth [is] an extension of the human body" and, at the same time, "the human being [is] the earth's eruption into intelligence onto its own surface" (85n12). John Barrell, "Geographies of Hardy's Wessex," in *The Regional Novel in Britain and Ireland, 1800–1990,* ed. K. D. M. Snell (Cambridge: Cambridge University Press, 1998), 99–118, discusses modes of landscape perception among characters, narrators, and imagined readers in Hardy, differentiated by class and location. For an antihumanist approach based in Husserl's phenomenology, see Bruce Johnson, *True Correspondence: A Phenomenology of Thomas Hardy's Novels* (Tallahassee: University Presses of Florida, 1983). David Musselwhite's *Social Transformations in Hardy's Tragic Novels: Megamachines and Phantasms* (Basingstoke: Palgrave Macmillan, 2003) is the only full-scale attempt to bring Deleuze and Guattari into relation with Hardy. For an example of criticism emphasizing Hardy's interests as lying away from deep, subjective characterization, see Michael Irwin, *Reading Hardy's Landscapes* (New York: St. Martin's Press, 2000), which forms an extended description of Hardy as a descriptive writer of landscapes. In "Seen in a New Light: Illumination and Irradiation in Hardy," in *Thomas Hardy: Texts and Contexts,* ed. Phillip Mallett (Basingstoke: Palgrave Macmillan, 2002), 1–17, Irwin states: "Most novelists are essentially concerned with what their characters do, say and think. Hardy's emphasis tends to be on what they (and with them his readers) see and hear" (7).

4. Gilles Deleuze and Félix Guattari, *Capitalism and Schizophrenia,* vol. 2, *A Thousand Plateaus,* trans. Brian Massumi (1980; Minneapolis: University of Minnesota Press, 1987), 175. Hereafter cited in the text; all italics in original.

5. In "What Can a Face Do? On Deleuze and Faces," *Cultural Critique* 52 (Spring 2002): 219–37, Richard Rushton helpfully explicates ideas about faciality, writing that Deleuze and Guattari reserve their "harshest criticism of the face for that which reduces the face purely to its nominal register . . . as an objective expression of that which lies beneath" (223).

6. In *The Literary Notebooks of Thomas Hardy,* ed. Lennart A. Björk, 2 vols. (London: Macmillan, 1985), Björk states that "Spencer was among [Hardy's] more influential authors," citing "Spencer's undoubtedly strong general impact on Hardy . . . conveying such a mixture of contemporary thought" (1: 335n882). William R. Rutland, in *Thomas Hardy: A Study of His Writings and Their Background* (New York: Russell and Russell, 1962), calls Spencer "the speculative writer whose name is especially associated with the doctrine of the *immanence* [as opposed to transcendence] of the Primal Cause" (56).

7. On the English reception and legacy of physiognomy, see Jenny Bourne Taylor and Sally Shuttleworth, eds., *Embodied Selves: An Anthology of Psychological Texts, 1830–1890* (Oxford: Clarendon Press, 1998), 3; and Lucy Hartley, *Physiognomy and the Meaning of Expression in Nineteenth-Century Culture* (Cambridge: Cambridge University Press, 2001). On the European tradition generally, see Graeme Tytler, *Physiognomy in the European Novel: Faces*

and Fortunes (Princeton, N.J.: Princeton University Press, 1982); on the French, see Christopher Rivers, *Face Value: Physiognomical Thought and the Legible Body in Marivaux, Lavater, Balzac, Gautier, and Zola* (Madison: University of Wisconsin Press, 1994); on the German, see Richard T. Gray, *About Face: German Physiognomic Thought from Lavater to Auschwitz* (Detroit, Mich.: Wayne State University Press, 2004). These critics take "physiognomy" in its broadest sense (what Rivers in his title calls "the legible body"). They also discuss the rehabilitation of a form of physiognomy later in the century in Cesare Lombroso's criminal psychology and Francis Galton's eugenics.

8. *Literary Notebooks,* 1:92n899.

9. See Björk's introduction to Hardy's *Literary Notebooks,* 1:xiv–xxx; and J. M. Bullen, *The Expressive Eye: Fiction and Perception in the Work of Thomas Hardy* (Oxford: Clarendon, 1986), 94, 117.

10. Quoted in Michael Millgate, *Thomas Hardy: A Biography* (New York: Random House, 1982), 198. Millgate writes that in this novel, Hardy "sought to enhance the novel's claims to be regarded as a serious work of literature by manipulating his story of a primitive and isolated Wessex community so as to sustain unity of place, approximate unity of time, and parallel the foreground action with classical and biblical allusions and structural echoes of the patterns of Greek and Elizabethan tragedy" (198).

11. Bullen, *Expressive Eye,* 98.

12. Cited in Bullen, *Expressive Eye,* 103. Bullen explains that while Hardy's prose is indebted to Pater's, the *portrait* of Eustacia "bears no physical resemblance to Leonardo's masterpiece"; instead she visually recalls a pre-Raphaelite female subject. In "'The Ache of Modernism' in Hardy's Later Novels," *ELH* 34, no. 3 (September 1967): 380–99, David DeLaura calls Pater's description a "notorious excrescence" (382). By contrast, Rutland, in *Thomas Hardy,* calls "the portrait of Eustacia, in chapter seven . . . perhaps the best, the subtlest and the most significant that Hardy ever drew" (184).

13. Thomas Hardy, *The Return of the Native* (London: Penguin, 1985), 118. Except where noted, further references are to this text, which reprints the final, revised edition of 1912.

14. In "Lawrence's Vital Source," Paterson remarks that in Hardy "the human eye is not just *like* something vast or strange in Nature; it *is* something vast or strange in Nature. . . . The eye that *is* the human expression and *is* the human being is suddenly no longer human" (466).

15. In addition to being read as portraits, faces in Hardy have been taken as texts, and the two approaches do not necessarily contradict each other. Jonathan Wike, in "The World as Text in Hardy's Fiction," *Nineteenth-Century Literature* 47, no. 4 (March 1993): 455–71, proposes that "the world as text in Hardy is a matter mainly of legible faces" (455) and focuses on several striking passages, particularly about Clym Yeobright, such as the one that states: "The observer's eye was arrested, not by his face as a picture, but by his face

as a page; not by what it was but by what it recorded" (225). While I concur with Wike to the extent that the face is often presented as material text, I would emphasize its status as an inscribed surface, not a text whose meaning is transparent and abstractable.

16. His face thus resembles the process that, in *The Picture of Dorian Gray*, is transferred onto the portrait. On *Dorian Gray* as a proleptic form of moving image, see Paul Morrison, "Motion Pictures," chapter 2 in *The Explanation for Everything: Essays on Sexual Subjectivity* (New York: New York University Press, 2001).

17. *Literary Notebooks*, 1:336n885.

18. Herbert Spencer, *Principles of Biology*, 2 vols. (1867 ed.; reprint, New York: Appleton, 1897), describes the alimentary canal as an oddly inside-out structure: it "links the differentiations of the literally outer tissues with those of the truly inner tissues." Like the skin, the alimentary canal is one of the organs through which the interior of a subject encounters external objects: "The skin and the assimilating surface have this in common, that they come in direct contact with matters not belonging to the organism; and . . . along with this community of relation to alien substances, there is a certain community of structure and development. The like holds with the linings of all internal cavities and canals that have external openings" (2:307). Structures such as the sensory orifices and the alimentary canal, which form an interface between the organism and matter "alien" to itself, themselves lie at an indeterminate border between inner structure and outer surface. The interior is moist, porous, and hidden; the exterior dry, hard, and exposed. One form can become another, either in evolutionary time or through the adaptation of the individual, but the difference is essential.

19. For a discussion of perception in this novel, and in Hardy's work more generally, as illustrative of historically determined ideological arrangements, see George Wotton, *Thomas Hardy: Towards a Materialist Criticism* (Totowa, N.J.: Barnes and Noble, 1985), esp. chap. 8.

20. I am grateful to Abigail Bardi for this information and for noting *eustachian*. Writing of himself in the third person, Hardy notes: "The name 'Eustacia' which he gave to his heroine was that of the wife of the owner of the manor of Ower-Moigne in the reign of Henry IV, which parish includes part of the 'Egdon' Heath of the story." *The Life and Work of Thomas Hardy*, ed. Michael Millgate (London: Macmillan, 1984), 120.

21. See *Literary Notebooks*, 1:336n885.

22. Spencer, *Principles of Biology*, 2:305.

23. *Tess of the d'Urbervilles* (1891; Harmondsworth: Penguin, 1978) presents another picture of a blind character (Alec's mother) who sees by touch and whose face is correspondingly dynamic and fluid: "She had the mobile face frequent in those whose sight has decayed by stages, has been laboriously striven after, and reluctantly let go, rather than the stagnant mien ap-

parent in persons long sightless or born blind. . . . Her touch enabled her to recognize [each bird] in a moment, and to discover if a single feather were crippled or draggled. She handled their crops, and knew what they had eaten, and if too little or too much; her face enacting a vivid pantomime of the criticisms passing in her mind" (100).

24. "There are instances of persons who, without clear ideas of the things they criticize, have yet had clear ideas of the relations of those things. Black-lock, a poet blind from his birth, could describe visual objects with accuracy; Professor Sanderson, who was also blind, gave excellent lectures on colour, and taught others the theory of ideas which they had and he had not" (248).

25. Chapter 3 of Irwin's *Reading Hardy's Landscapes* describes Hardy's use of noise as part of his landscape portraiture, citing many of the same passages I discuss in *The Return of the Native*. In *Darwin's Plots: Evolutionary Narrative in Darwin, George Eliot and Nineteenth-Century Fiction,* 2nd ed. (Cambridge: Cambridge University Press, 2000), Gillian Beer addresses some of these passages as well, arguing that in Hardy, as in Darwin, plot moves forward in time with impersonal and often cruel inevitability, whereas "writing" evokes the pleasures of immediate sensory apprehension. She observes that "touch and hearing lie peculiarly close in [Hardy's] economy of the senses" (222).

26. Barrell, "Geographies of Hardy's Wessex," charts the source of sensory perceptions among narrator, characters, and imagined reader at various points in the novel.

27. For a classic example, see Jean Brooks, "*The Return of the Native:* A Novel of Environment," in *Thomas Hardy: The Poetic Structure* (1971), reprinted in *Thomas Hardy's "The Return of the Native,"* ed. Harold Bloom (New York: Chelsea House, 1987), 21–38. On personification of the heath, see also Avrom Fleishman, "The Buried Giant of Egdon Heath," in Bloom, *Thomas Hardy's "The Return of the Native,"* 95–109. In *Thomas Hardy,* Rutland writes: "Egdon Heath might almost be called the principal character of the book, for we are made to feel its 'vast impassivity' as a living presence" (179). In *Topographies* (Stanford, Calif.: Stanford University Press, 1995), J. Hillis Miller reads this personification as "the covert manifestation of the ubiquitous presence of the narrator's consciousness, even when he seems least there as a person" (27). After Mrs. Yeobright's death, the careless heath blots out the imagined face of Clym's cruel wife in his unseeing eyes: "The pupils of his eyes, fixed steadfastly on blankness, were vaguely lit with an icy shine. . . . Instead of there being before him the pale face of Eustacia, and masculine shape unknown, there was only the imperturbable countenance of the heath, which, having defied the cataclysmal onsets of centuries, reduced to insignificance by its seamed and antique features the wildest turmoil of a single man" (388).

28. Miller, *Topographies,* suggests that the system of mutual metaphor between character and landscape is a catachresis — "If there is no presentation

of character without terms borrowed from the landscape, so there is no presentation of landscape without personification" (27–28) — but without noting the metonymic overlap (interpenetration) between them as well.

29. On visual perception as a principal epistemological mode in Hardy, see Sheila Berger, *Thomas Hardy and Visual Structures: Framing, Disruption, Process* (New York: New York University Press, 1990). Approaching a phenomenological description of this perception, although from a psychoanalytic starting point, Perry Meisel writes of the novel's opening: "The separation between the perceiver and scene, of course, still remains; but an affinity between the perceptive sensibility and the nature of the world it beholds is clearly suggested. Hardy's early diary entry has already suggested this tendency: 'The poetry of a scene varies with the minds of the perceivers. Indeed it does not lie in the scene at all.'" Meisel, "The Return of the Repressed," in Bloom, *Thomas Hardy's "The Return of the Native,"* 53.

30. Björk, *Literary Notebooks,* notes that Hardy expresses interest in Spencer's "statement that 'it cannot be said that inanimate things present no parallels to animate ones'" (1:335n882).

31. The overlap happens at the level of psychology too: immediately preceding the eclipse, Clym is led by his distance vision to have a fully embodied experience of what he sees: "His eye travelled over the length and breadth of that distant country... till he almost felt himself to be voyaging bodily through its wild scenes" (254).

32. By contrast, when leaving the scene shortly thereafter, Wildeve perceives and embodies a visible darkness, made evident by an aural shock: "Half-way down the hill the path ran near a knot of stunted hollies, which in the general darkness of the scene stood as the pupil in a black eye. When Wildeve reached this point a report startled his ear, and a few spent gunshots fell among the leaves around him" (332).

33. For a catalog of insects in Hardy, particularly in this novel, see Irwin, *Reading Hardy's Landscapes,* chap. 2. As the *Literary Notebooks* document (1: 281–83), Hardy made extensive notes on J. G. Wood's study *Insects at Home* (1872).

34. Thomas Hardy, *The Return of the Native,* 1878 ed. (New York: Penguin, 1999), 229. In the revised edition of 1912, the passage reads: "The incongruity between the men's deeds and their environment was great. Amid the soft juicy vegetation of the hollow in which they sat, the motionless and the uninhabited solitude, intruded the chink of guineas, the rattle of dice, the exclamations of the reckless players" (293).

35. "When the farmers who had wished to buy in a new stock of reddle during the last month had inquired where Venn was to be found, people replied, 'On Egdon Heath.' Day after day the answer was the same. Now, since Egdon was populated with heath-croppers and furze-cutters rather

than with sheep and shepherds, and the downs where most of the latter were to be found lay some to the north, some to the west of Egdon, his reason for camping about there like Israel in Zin was not apparent. The position was central and occasionally desirable. But the sale of reddle was not Diggory's primary object in remaining on the heath, particularly at so late a period of the year, when most travellers of his class had gone into winter quarters" (205).

36. On the function and symbolism of the reddleman, see John Hagan, "A Note on the Significance of Diggory Venn," *Nineteenth-Century Fiction* 16, no. 2 (September 1961): 147–55.

37. See also: "His eye, which glared so strangely through his stain, was in itself attractive" (59). Diggory's face comports with Deleuze and Guattari's extended discussion of the face as a white screen with black holes; although his skin reverses these color values, the analysis is applicable.

38. For example, "a note of 19 January 1879" (shortly after the initial publication of *The Return of the Native*) "headed 'Shines' and entered into the 'Poetical Matter' notebook as potential material for a poem" (Millgate, *Thomas Hardy*): "In the study firelight a red glow is on the polished sides & arch of the grate: firebrick back red hot: the polish of fireirons shines; underside of mantel reddened: also a shine on the leg of the table, & the ashes under the grate, lit from above like a torrid clime. Faint daylight of a lilac colour almost powerless in the room. Candle behind a screen is reflected in the glass of the window, falling whitely on book, & on E's face & hand, a large shade of her head being on wall & ceiling. Light shines through the loose hair about her temples, & reaches the skin as sunlight through a brake" (204; from an unpublished manuscript). The sketch is without content but focuses intensively on acts of perception and forms of light in a human presence as they subjectively strike the viewer.

5. Soul

1. *The Journals and Papers of Gerard Manley Hopkins,* ed. Humphrey House and Graham Storey (London: Oxford University Press, 1959), 204. All further citations are to this edition. The sentence quoted here continues: "hence the true and the false instress of nature."

2. See Daniel Brown, *Hopkins's Idealism: Philosophy, Physics, Poetry* (Oxford: Clarendon, 1997). See also Tom Zaniello, *Hopkins in the Age of Darwin* (Iowa City: University of Iowa Press, 1988), on the embeddedness of Hopkins's thought in contemporary controversies over evolutionary biology and affiliated debates about materialism.

3. October 16, 1866, *Further Letters of Gerard Manley Hopkins,* ed. Claude Colleer Abbott, 2nd ed. (London: Oxford University Press, 1956), 92. He continues: "This belief once got is the life of the soul and when I doubted it I

shd. become an atheist the next day. But, as Monsignor Eyre says, it is a gross superstition unless guaranteed by infallibility. I cannot hold this doctrine confessedly except as a Tractarian or a Catholic."

4. October 22, 1879, *The Letters of Gerard Manley Hopkins to Robert Bridges,* ed. Claude Colleer Abbott (London: Oxford University Press, 1970), 95.

5. Gardner continues: "And for that energy of being by which all things are upheld, for that natural (but ultimately supernatural) stress which determines an *inscape* and keeps it in being — for that he coined the name *instress*. . . . But *instress* is not only the unifying force *in* the object; it connotes also that impulse *from* the 'inscape' which acts on the senses and, through them, actualizes the inscape in the mind of the beholder (or rather 'perceiver,' for inscape may be perceived through all the senses at once). Instress, then, is often the *sensation* of inscape — a quasi-mystical illumination, a sudden perception of that deeper pattern, order, and unity which gives meaning to external forms." W. H. Gardner, introduction to *Poems and Prose of Gerard Manley Hopkins* (1953; Baltimore: Penguin, 1966), xx–xxi. The phrase quoted is from W. A. M. Peters, S.J., *Gerard Manley Hopkins: A Critical Essay towards the Understanding of His Poetry* (Oxford: Basil Blackwell, 1948), the first chapter of which has the classic discussion of these terms.

6. Peters gives the clearest explanation of inscape; Alan Heuser, *The Shaping Vision of Gerard Manley Hopkins* (Oxford: Oxford University Press, 1958), has a helpful discussion of Hopkins's spiritualization of the senses. On sensory and bodily experience in relation to Hopkins's spiritual and poetic cosmology, see also J. Hillis Miller, *The Disappearance of God: Five Nineteenth-Century Writers* (Cambridge, Mass.: Harvard University Press, 1963); and Daniel A. Harris, *Inspirations Unbidden: The "Terrible Sonnets" of Gerard Manley Hopkins* (Berkeley: University of California Press, 1982).

7. Lesley Higgins, "'Bone-house' and 'lovescape': Writing the Body in Hopkins's Canon," in *Rereading Hopkins: Selected New Essays,* ed. Francis L. Fennell (Victoria: English Literary Studies, 1996), 11–35, applies a Foucault-inspired approach to bodily discipline in Hopkins. On sexual and gay themes, see Julia F. Saville, *A Queer Chivalry: The Homoerotic Asceticism of Gerard Manley Hopkins* (Charlottesville: University Press of Virginia, 2000); David Alderson, *Mansex Fine: Religion, Manliness, and Imperialism in Nineteenth-Century British Culture* (Manchester: Manchester University Press, 1998), chaps. 5 and 6; Joseph Bristow, "'Churlsgrace': Gerard Manley Hopkins and the Working-Class Male Body," *ELH* 59 (1992): 693–712; Wendell Stacy Johnson, "Sexuality and Inscape," *Hopkins Quarterly* 3, no. 2 (July 1976): 59–65; Renée V. Overholser, "'Looking with Terrible Temptation': Gerard Manley Hopkins and Beautiful Bodies," *Victorian Literature and Culture* 19 (1991): 25–53; Robert Bernard Martin, *Gerard Manley Hopkins: A Very Private Life* (New York: G. P. Putnam's, 1991). Also on the body in Hopkins (specifically focused on feet),

see R. J. C. Watt, "Hopkins and the Gothic Body," in *Victorian Gothic: Literary and Cultural Manifestations in the Nineteenth Century,* ed. Ruth Robbins and Julian Wolfreys (New York: Palgrave, 2000), 60–89.

8. Saville makes the most persuasive and thoroughgoing argument for sexual (and, by association, bodily) signification in Hopkins's poetry; she judiciously removes the question from issues of sexual identity and places it in the context of the poet's devotional practice of asceticism, as well as showing it to be integral to his poetic (specifically metrical) technique.

9. See, for example, the sonnet "In the Valley of the Elwy," whose layered inhabitation images — of house, land, and body — suggest an alignment of physical, sensory, and spiritual interiors.

10. All references to poems are to *The Poetical Works of Gerard Manley Hopkins,* ed. Norman H. MacKenzie (Oxford: Clarendon, 1990); poems are indicated by number in this edition.

11. Quoted in Raymond J. Ventre, "The Body Racked with Pain: Hopkins's Dark Sonnets," *ANQ* 13, no. 4 (2000): 41.

12. See Nathan Cervo, "'Sweating Selves': Hopkins' Rebuff of Gnosticism," *Hopkins Quarterly* 20, nos. 1–2 (Winter–Spring 1993): 44–51. By contrast with the caged skylark, the windhover and the kingfisher become Christlike symbols of spiritual apotheosis and fully realized inscape, largely unavailable to flesh-hindered human beings.

13. In his commentary on this poem, MacKenzie quotes F. R. Leavis's reading of the line as "lines of light (caused, I believe, by the eyelashes) that . . . converge upon the eye like so many sets of tram-rails. But 'tram' unqualified would suggest something too solid, so he adds 'tender'; and 'truckle' conveys perfectly the obsequious way in which they follow every motion of the eyes and of the eyelids." This is consistent with Hopkins's attention to the physical embodiment of the visual apparatus (of which eyelashes are sometimes the sign). The notion of tram rails converging, further conveyed by "trambeams," reinforces Hopkins's contention that perceptual reality resides in the subject, not the object, of vision.

14. "The Intertwining — the Chiasm," in *The Visible and the Invisible,* ed. Claude Lefort, trans. Alphonso Lingis (Evanston, Ill.: Northwestern University Press, 1968), 133.

15. Geoffrey H. Hartman makes this argument in a classic reading of the poem, "The Dialectic of Sense-Perception," in *Hopkins: A Collection of Critical Essays,* ed. Geoffrey H. Hartman (Englewood Cliffs, N.J.: Prentice-Hall, 1966), 117–30. Hopkins recapitulates the tour of the senses on other occasions in *Sermons and Devotional Writings of Gerard Manley Hopkins,* ed. Christopher Devlin, S.J. (London: Oxford University Press, 1959), in an abject mode, through accounts of hell (136, 241–44).

16. *Sermons and Devotional Writings,* 127; italics in original.

17. For Merleau-Ponty, even if relations between subject and object are reciprocal and reversible, they do not collapse into each other: the distinction between the two is important, for subjects can perceive themselves as objects, and can perceive the role of objects in their own constitution as subjects, only if they remain distinct.

18. Walter J. Ong, S.J., in *Hopkins, the Self, and God* (Toronto: University of Toronto Press, 1986), cites this passage, writing that it shows how "the human body is both part of the self and part of the material object world" (39).

19. In *Disappearance of God,* Miller discusses the description of nature in Hopkins's journals (279–87), including the sound and image patterns that make "miniature poems, or poems in the rough" (280). Miller's work is the most prominent among the earlier phenomenological approaches, and the one most relevant to my study. Here and in a related earlier essay, "The Creation of the Self in Gerard Manley Hopkins," *ELH* 22, no. 4 (December 1955): 293–319, Miller does not name the theoretical impetus for his study, but he writes generally about the critical effort to decipher a writer's "consciousness" and worldview, in places appearing to draw on Merleau-Ponty's phenomenology of perception. Miller focuses on the way in which self and world are coextensive to show how they emanate from (and display the generous humanity of) authorial consciousness, rather than, as I do, regarding the embodiment of subjectivity as a way of decentering a coherent consciousness, in either authorial or characterological terms.

20. Similarly, in discussing the penultimate line, "Thís Jack, jóke, poor pótsherd, | patch, matchwood, immortal diamond," from "That Nature is a Heraclitean Fire and of the comfort of the Resurrection" (174), Paul Mariani calls it an "extraordinary incremental chiming catalogue which suggests in its own protean lexical shifts the profound theological idea of death, sacrifice, and transformation." Mariani, "The Sound of Oneself Breathing," in *Critical Essays on Gerard Manley Hopkins,* ed. Alison G. Sulloway (Boston: G. K. Hall, 1990), 54. On fingernails before candles as a natural symbol, see also the poem "Moonrise June 19, 1876" (103): "The móon, dwíndled and thínned to the frínge | of a fíngernail héld to the cándle."

21. Storey notes in his preface to *Journals* that in the second volume of early diaries (in which this passage appears), "The entries are almost entirely in pencil" (xvi). In *The Pencil: A History of Design and Circumstance* (New York: Knopf, 1990), Henry Petroski documents the common use of wood for manufacturing pencils in nineteenth-century England.

22. "The ashtree growing in the corner of the garden was felled. It was lopped first: I heard the sound and looking out and seeing it maimed there came at that moment a great pang and I wished to die and not to see the inscapes of the world destroyed any more." April 8, 1873, in *Journals,* 230.

23. See William Ian Miller, *The Anatomy of Disgust* (Cambridge, Mass.:

Harvard University Press, 1997); and, in turn, Jean-Paul Sartre, Mary Douglas, and Julia Kristeva.

24. The opening scene of Luis Buñuel's classic surrealist film *Un chien andalou* draws from the same image repertoire. For related considerations of the eye, see Karen Jacobs, *The Eye's Mind: Literary Modernism and Visual Culture* (Ithaca, N.Y.: Cornell University Press, 2001).

25. This is the *b* version of the poem. MacKenzie's edition indicates that the manuscript reads "Eye" in line 8, "which [he] assume[s] is an absent-minded homophone" (484), so he emends it to "Ay"; my reading demonstrates the relevance of the authorial version.

26. Hopkins's discussion of the relation between impressions made on "the visual nerves" by perceptions and dreams is reminiscent of Henri Bergson's comparison between sense perceptions of the material world and memories (which Bergson identifies as perceptions of things past or absent): both bring worlds into consciousness — one through direct, material contact, the other through thought and imagination — and the distinction is largely spatiotemporal. See Bergson, *Matter and Memory* (1908), trans. Nancy Margaret Paul and W. Scott Palmer (New York: Zone, 1988).

27. I am grateful to Herbert Tucker for suggesting to me the double valence of "tears."

28. Although he states that "there would no doubt be something revolting in seeing the heart alone, all naked and bleeding, torn from the breast," still Hopkins dwells on it: "The Sacred Heart is that heart which swelled when Christ rejoiced in spirit and sank when he was sad, which played its dark and sacred part in all Christ's life, in all he did and suffered, which in his Agony with frightful and unnatural straining forced its blood out on him in the shape of teeming sweat, and after it had ceased to beat was pierced and spent its contents by the opening in his side." Sermon of June 26, 1881, in *Sermons and Devotional Writings*, 102–3.

29. See Brown, *Hopkins's Idealism*, 171–74, on Christ's blood in particular and, more generally, on "a pattern of imagery in Hopkins' poetry and prose that identifies the motions of life with liquidity" (171). For more on liquidity, including a contrast between Hopkins's account of viscosity and that of Sartre, see 224–32.

30. Robert Boyle, S.J., "Time and Grace in Hopkins' Imagination," *Renascence: Essays on Values in Literature* 29, no. 1 (Fall 1976): 7–24; cited in Mariani, "Sound of Oneself Breathing," 53.

31. "Juicy," particularly in reference to bluebells, has important connections to vivid embodiment for Hopkins; see the journal entry about the sense impressions these flowers make (209) and their appearance, as a metaphor for appealing bodily forms, in two unfinished poems: "The furl of fresh-leaved dogrose down" (127) and "On the Portrait of Two Beautiful Young

People" (168). On their possible homoerotic significance, see Saville, *Queer Chivalry*, 94.

32. Writing about this passage, Miller fails to recognize that, as images of covering, these are all pertinent similes specifically for the eyelid; his assessment of Hopkins's metaphorizing practice as wholly general is thus inaccurate: "If eyelids are like all these things, there seems no reason why the list could not be extended indefinitely. Anything can be metaphorically compared to anything else, and, if this is the case, then all things rhyme. . . . The possible rhymings of natural things can be extended to make all things metaphors of all things" (*Disappearance of God*, 298). As language itself — the first instance of rhyme — testifies, this is patently untrue. On rhyme as the fundamental principle of joining unlike things as the basis of Hopkins's poetry, see also 277, 284–305.

33. Here too Hopkins is close to Bataille in amassing an idiosyncratic collection of natural objects and body parts that suggests a relation to the world at once incorporative and expulsive. As Allan Stoekl writes in introducing Bataille's essays: "Filth does not 'replace' God; there is no new system of values, no new hierarchy. In the *Documents* articles, Bataille's attention wanders through a disseminated field, a labyrinth, of possibilities; flowers, excrement, toes, Gnosticism, freaks, mouth, sun, severed fingers." Stoekl, introduction to *Visions of Excess: Selected Writings, 1927–1939*, by Georges Bataille, trans. Allan Stoekl et al. (Minneapolis: University of Minnesota Press, 1985), xiv.

34. James Finn Cotter, in *Inscape: The Christology and Poetry of Gerard Manley Hopkins* (Pittsburgh, Pa.: University of Pittsburgh Press, 1972), writes: "Taking [Hopkins's] writing as a whole, one would venture to say that in his viewpoint the sun is Christ univocally and is never for him a merely natural phenomenon" (84).

35. "Spring and Fall" (144), for all the gentle melancholy of its tone, also exploits the eventually rotting status of the child's flesh in its images of decay, where "worlds of wanwood leafmeal lie." For an idiosyncratic account of Hopkins's experience and rendering of disgusting bodily pain (including the diarrhea and typhoid that killed him), see Ventre, "Body Racked with Pain," 43. On the unsanitary conditions of Dublin that probably contributed to his death, see Norman White, *Hopkins: A Literary Biography* (Oxford: Clarendon, 1992), 455, 459. Harris's discussion of debased bodily and sensory experience in Hopkins's work in *Inspirations Unbidden* is also relevant (56–71).

36. Interpreting this poem in relation to anti-Gnostic Catholic doctrines of Incarnation, Cervo suggests that the word *fell* in the poem's opening line ("I wake and feel the fell of dark, not day") "signifies a skin, hide, pelt, and a thin tough membrane covering a carcass directly under the hide," and also that it has the meaning of "a high barren field or moor" ("Sweating Selves," 45); the *OED* notes that *fell* can also mean "human skin." Hopkins uses the term in the former sense (while punning on the verb *to fall*) in his description

of a Swiss glacier: "If you took the skin of a white tiger or the deep fell of some other animal and swung it tossing high in the air and then cast it out before you it would fall and so clasp and lap round anything in its way just as this glacier does and the fleece would part in the same rifts" (*Journals*, 174). Both uses suggest the continuity between landscape and inscape. The idea of the body as container of inscape is amplified by the information that Hopkins's nickname in school was "Skin," "from the transposition of the last letters of his name" (Martin, *Gerard Manley Hopkins*, 17); Hopkins refers to himself by this name in *Journals*, 3.

37. *Sermons and Devotional Writings*, 123; partly quoted in Robert W. Hill, "A Phenomenological Approach to Hopkins and Yeats," *Hopkins Quarterly* 5, no. 2 (Summer 1978): 51–68. Hill has a useful, if limited, discussion of Hopkins as a "phenomenological" poet.

38. *Sermons and Devotional Writings*, 243. Introducing the passage on self-consciousness, Miller writes: "Hopkins's expression for self-awareness is the most immediate and inward of the senses. The proof of selfhood is a matter of tasting, not thinking. His version of the Cartesian *Cogito* is: 'I taste myself, therefore I am, and when I taste myself I find myself utterly different from everything else whatsoever.' No one has expressed more eloquently the pathos of each man's imprisonment within the bounds of his own selfhood" (*Disappearance of God*, 271). For a discussion of the background and context for the spiritual exercises, as well as a more general meditation on "selving" in Hopkins, see Ong, *Hopkins, the Self, and God*. In *Inspirations Unbidden*, Harris writes that taste in "I wake and feel the fell of dark" "generates the most radical metaphor of bodily dissociation in all of the 'terrible sonnets'" (68).

Conclusion

1. For instance, see *Posthumanism*, ed. Neil Badmington (New York: Palgrave, 2000); Kate Soper, *Humanism and Anti-humanism* (London: Hutchinson, 1986); Ann Weinstone, *Avatar Bodies: A Tantra for Posthumanism* (Minneapolis: University of Minnesota Press, 2004). In *How We Became Posthuman: Virtual Bodies in Cybernetics, Literature, and Informatics* (Chicago: University of Chicago Press, 1999), N. Katherine Hayles discusses posthumanism as a way of regarding subjectivity or cognition as separated from states of embodiment and, at the same time, as variably attachable to other bodies and machines. She articulates a distinction between, on the one hand, the disembodied subject common to Enlightenment liberal humanism and to some posthumanist perspectives, and, on the other, the emphasis on embodiment associated with identity politics: "Only because the body is not identified with the self is it possible to claim for the liberal subject its notorious universality, a claim that depends on erasing markers of bodily difference, including sex, race, and ethnicity" (4–5).

2. See, for example, Tom Wakeford, *Liaisons of Life: From Hornworts to Hippos, How the Unassuming Microbe Has Driven Evolution* (New York: John Wiley, 2001). In a related vein, Michael Pollan, in *The Omnivore's Dilemma: A Natural History of Four Meals* (New York: Penguin, 2006), has proposed that corn has genetically engineered human beings to ensure its own propagation and survival: "There is every reason to believe that corn has succeeded in domesticating us.... By evolving certain traits we happen to regard as desirable, these species got themselves noticed by the one mammal in a position not only to spread their genes around the world, but to remake vast swathes of that world in the image of the plants' preferred habitat" (23–24).

3. Teresa Brennan, *The Transmission of Affect* (Ithaca, N.Y.: Cornell University Press, 2004). Brennan views even Richard Dawkins's theory of "memes" — the materialization of cultural units that one person transmits to another — as one in which "suppositions about an individual and socially impervious mode of genetic transmission are preserved" (74). Nonetheless, Kathryn Bond Stockton has put Dawkins's theory to good use in work that resonates with Brennan's in an account of embodied selves' perviousness to one another; see *Beautiful Bottom, Beautiful Shame: Where "Black" Meets "Queer"* (Durham, N.C.: Duke University Press, 2006).

4. Gayle Salamon, "Boys of the Lex: Transgenderism and Rhetorics of Materiality," *GLQ* 12, no. 4 (2006): 594.

5. Gayle Salamon, "'The Place Where Life Hides Away': Merleau-Ponty, Fanon, and the Location of Bodily Being," *differences* 17, no. 2 (2006): 98.

6. In *No Future: Queer Theory and the Death Drive* (Durham, N.C.: Duke University Press, 2004), Edelman argues for the radical, irresolvable negativity of queerness as an agonistic principle that not only reproductive heteronormativity but humanity itself both depends on and must repudiate. For Edelman, queerness is the name for the excess, the unaccountable, the remainder beyond the social, which intolerably contests the phantasmatic coherence and regeneration of the social — which, in fact, bespeaks its death — and so must be stigmatized and cast out: "As the inarticulable surplus that dismantles the subject from within, the death drive names what the queer, in the order of the social, is called forth to figure: the negativity opposed to every form of social viability " (9). It cannot be reconciled or resolved, because to do so would only be to consign some other remainder to the category of queer.

7. It is tempting to read Butler's influential discussion of the bodily materiality of sex and gender in chapter 1 of *Bodies That Matter: On the Discursive Limits of "Sex"* (New York: Routledge, 1993) as a type of linguistic idealism: the materiality of the body is itself a discursive construction (although, as she insists, this does not mean that gender is volitional or escapable). Salamon, however, shows that, on a close reading, Butler actually presents discourse and soma, idealism and materialism, as mutually constituting each

other in an ongoing dialectic, and particularly that gender and sex are constitutive of materialization itself; see Gayle Salamon, "The Bodily Ego and the
Contested Domain of the Material," *differences* 15, no. 3 (2004): 95–122. The
form of discursive materiality that Butler synthesizes from several philosophical traditions is of a different order than the dynamic and perceptual
one associated with Merleau-Ponty and Deleuze.

8. Some theorists of disability have pointed in this direction. For instance, Lennard J. Davis, in *Bending Over Backwards: Disability, Dismodernism,
and Other Difficult Positions* (New York: New York University Press, 2002),
writes of an "ideal" that "aims to create a new category based on the partial,
incomplete subject whose realization is not autonomy and independence but
dependency and interdependence. This is a very different notion from subjectivity organized around wounded identities; rather, *all* humans are seen as
wounded. Wounds are not the result of oppression, but rather the other way
around" (30). Robert McRuer, in *Crip Theory: Cultural Signs of Queerness and
Disability* (New York: New York University Press, 2006), brings together multiple queer and disability identity formations – as well as those of race, gender, and class – to argue for a deindividualized, coalitional form of connection, in corporeal as well as political terms, that would aim to overcome the
divisions among minority groups as well as to undo any stable positing of a
norm. McRuer thus expresses admiration for work such as that of Gary
Fisher, which, through its "noncompliance" with identity formations, disin-
tegrates stable identities and is "opposed to identity politics proper" (141).

9. Rosemarie Garland Thomson, in *Extraordinary Bodies: Figuring Physical
Disability in American Culture and Literature* (New York: Columbia University
Press, 1997), provides some leverage on the term "disabled" by introducing
"normate" as its diacritical complement.

10. Oscar Wilde, *The Picture of Dorian Gray* (1891), ed. Joseph Bristow, vol.
3 of *Complete Works* (Oxford: Oxford University Press, 2005), 199.

Index

175

William A. Cohen is professor of English at the University of Maryland. He is the author of *Sex Scandal: The Private Parts of Victorian Fiction* and coeditor (with Ryan Johnson) of *Filth: Dirt, Disgust, and Modern Life* (Minnesota, 2005).